Politicising the Communist Past

Poland is a particularly interesting case of truth revelation and transitional justice in a post-communist country. This is because of the radical change of trajectory in its approach to dealing with the communist past, and the profound effect this had on Polish politics. The approach moved from 'communist-forgiving' in the early 1990s, to a mild law vetting individuals for their links with the communist-era security services at the end of the decade, through to a more radical vetting and opening up of the communist security service files in the mid-2000s. This book examines the detail of this changing approach. It explains why disagreements about transitional justice became so prominent, to the extent that they constituted one of the main causes of political divisions. It sets the Polish approach in the wider context of transitional justice and truth revelation, drawing out the lessons for newly emerging democracies, both in Eastern Europe and beyond.

Aleks Szczerbiak is Professor of Politics and Contemporary European Studies at the University of Sussex, UK.

BASEES/Routledge Series on Russian and East European Studies

For a full list of available titles please visit: www.routledge.com/BASEES-Routledge-Series-on-Russian-and-East-European-Studies/book-series/BASEES

Series editor: Richard Sakwa, Department of Politics and International Relations, University of Kent

Editorial committee

Roy Allison, *St Antony's College, Oxford*
Birgit Beumers, *Department of Theatre, Film and Television Studies, University of Aberystwyth*
Richard Connolly, *Centre for Russian and East European Studies, University of Birmingham*
Terry Cox, *Department of Central and East European Studies, University of Glasgow*
Peter Duncan, *School of Slavonic and East European Studies, University College London*
Zoe Knox, *School of History, University of Leicester*
Rosalind Marsh, *Department of European Studies and Modern Languages, University of Bath*
David Moon, *Department of History, University of York*
Hilary Pilkington, *Department of Sociology, University of Manchester*
Graham Timmins, *Department of Politics, University of Birmingham*
Stephen White, *Department of Politics, University of Glasgow*

Founding editorial committee member

George Blazyca, *Centre for Contemporary European Studies, University of Paisley*

This series is published on behalf of BASEES (the British Association for Slavonic and East European Studies). The series comprises original, high-quality, research-level work by both new and established scholars on all aspects of Russian, Soviet, post-Soviet and East European Studies in humanities and social science subjects.

120 **The South Caucasus – Security, Energy and Europeanization**
Edited by Meliha B. Altunisik and Oktay F. Tanrisever

121 **Politicising the Communist Past**
The Politics of Truth Revelation in Post-Communist Poland
Aleks Szczerbiak

Politicising the Communist Past
The Politics of Truth Revelation in
Post-Communist Poland

Aleks Szczerbiak

LONDON AND NEW YORK

First published 2018
by Routledge
2 Park Square, Milton Park, Abingdon, Oxon OX14 4RN

and by Routledge
711 Third Avenue, New York, NY 10017

Routledge is an imprint of the Taylor & Francis Group, an informa business

© 2018 Aleks Szczerbiak

The right of Aleks Szczerbiak to be identified as author of this work has been asserted by him in accordance with sections 77 and 78 of the Copyright, Designs and Patents Act 1988.

All rights reserved. No part of this book may be reprinted or reproduced or utilised in any form or by any electronic, mechanical, or other means, now known or hereafter invented, including photocopying and recording, or in any information storage or retrieval system, without permission in writing from the publishers.

Trademark notice: Product or corporate names may be trademarks or registered trademarks, and are used only for identification and explanation without intent to infringe.

British Library Cataloguing in Publication Data
A catalogue record for this book is available from the British Library

Library of Congress Cataloging in Publication Data
A catalog record for this book has been requested

ISBN: 978-1-138-82473-7 (hbk)
ISBN: 978-1-315-74047-8 (ebk)

Typeset in Times New Roman
by Wearset Ltd, Boldon, Tyne and Wear

Contents

	List of tables	vi
	Preface and acknowledgements	vii
1	Introduction: what are truth-revelation procedures and why do they matter?	1
2	Truth revelation in post-communist Poland: a case of late (and recurring) lustration and file access	11
3	What drives late truth revelation? Electoral-strategic interests or ideological-programmatic concerns (or both)	42
4	Truth revelation and post-communist democratisation: the revival of lustration and file access debates in the mid-2000s	70
5	The 'Bolek' affair: using truth-revelation procedures for political legitimation and de-legitimation	109
6	Communist-forgiving or seeking historical justice? Public attitudes towards truth revelation and dealing with the communist past	141
7	Conclusions: the unfinished business of a contested transition?	177
	Appendix: list of interviewees	192
	Index	195

Tables

6.1	Polish attitudes towards vetting key public officials, 1994–2005 (%)	142
6.2	Polish attitudes towards de-communisation, 1996–1999 (%)	147
6.3	Polish attitudes towards opening up communist security service archives (%)	148
6.4	Polish attitudes on the urgency of lustration, 1993–1996 (%)	153

Preface and acknowledgements

The original inspiration for this book came from a comparative politics undergraduate module that I taught at the University of London School of Slavonic and East European Studies in spring/summer 1998 while covering for my then PhD supervisor Kieran Williams, who was on research leave. Teaching the session that dealt with how post-communist states dealt with their communist past stimulated my original interest in the topic of lustration and security service file access. On closer examination, I realised very quickly that Poland, the country that has always been the main focus of my research interests, was a fascinating case in this respect. This led to a small project involving Kieran, Brigid Fowler and myself that resulted in a single-authored article by myself on the Polish case published in *Europe-Asia Studies* and a co-authored cross-country comparative piece covering the Czech Republic, Hungary and Poland in *Democratization*. I am extremely grateful to Kieran and Brigid for our lengthy discussions on this topic that led to this co-authored work, and for their continued interest in my ongoing research on this (and other) topic(s).

The subsequent, continued recurrence of debate on lustration and communist security service file access in post-communist Poland, which is the subject of this book, meant that what was originally supposed to be a relatively small and time-limited project grew into something much larger and has been the main focus of my research in recent years. As a topic that straddles the communist and post-communist periods, lustration and file access has also provided a source of lively and inspiring debate in my undergraduate and postgraduate East European politics seminars over the years. I have learned a great deal from these discussions, and they have informed my ongoing research on this topic, so I am also grateful to all of my students who participated in these.

An earlier version of Chapter 4 was presented at a 'Programme on Modern Poland' Conference at St Antony's College, University of Oxford in May–June 2016. Earlier versions of Chapter 5 were presented at the European Consortium on Political Research (ECPR) General Conference at Charles University in Prague and at a University of Glasgow Central and East European Studies seminar, both in September 2016. Parts of Chapter 7 were presented at conferences held at Sidney Sussex College, University of Cambridge in December 2016 and the University College London School of Slavonic and East European

Studies in May 2017. An earlier version of Chapter 4 was published in *East European Politics* (Szczerbiak 2016) and of Chapter 6 in *Europe-Asia Studies* (Szczerbiak 2017). I am grateful to Taylor and Francis (www.tandfonline.com) for their permission to reproduce material from these articles in this book.

I would like to thank my (anonymous) reviewers for these journal articles and all those who provided valuable feedback and guidance on my findings at various conferences and seminars, and on various drafts of my chapters. I would particularly like to think Sean Hanley from the University College London School of Slavonic and East European Studies for his feedback on my draft conclusions. I would also like to thank the following for agreeing to undertake interviews with me when I was conducting fieldwork in Poland in June 2016: Sławomir Cenckiewicz, Antoni Dudek, Adam Leszczyński, Arkadiusz Mularczyk, Andrzej Paczkowski, the late Janina Paradowska, Piotr Semka, Ewa Siedlecka, Bronisław Wildstein and Andrzej Zybertowicz (their biographical details are set out in the Appendix). The intellectual stimulation from these various discussions and debates played an invaluable role in helping to shape my thinking on this topic and when writing this book. I do, of course, take full responsibility for the interpretation and analysis of the data, and the arguments and conclusions presented here (including – indeed, especially – any factual or analytical errors!). I would also like to thank the University of Sussex for providing me with research leave in spring 2014 and 2017, which allowed me time to research and complete the book, and to my wonderful colleagues in the Department of Politics for their ongoing encouragement and support.

Finally, and above all, I would like to thank my family for all their support and encouragement, especially my wife Jackie, daughter Anna, and parents Krystyna and Stanisław. I would like to dedicate this book to all of my family – especially those who currently live in, or originally came from, Poland, and particularly my late (and much missed) grandparents Ignacy and Jadwiga Maćkowiak. All of them have done so much over the years to nurture my emotional attachment to and ongoing intellectual interest in this wonderful and fascinating country.

Bibliography

Szczerbiak, A., 2016. Deepening Democratisation? Exploring the Declared Motives for 'Late' Lustration in Poland. *East European Politics*, 32 (4), 426–445.
Szczerbiak, A., 2017. Communist-Forgiving or Communist-Purging? Public Attitudes towards Transitional Justice and Truth Revelation in Post-1989 Poland. *Europe-Asia Studies*, 69 (2), 325–347.

1 Introduction

What are truth-revelation procedures and why do they matter?

This chapter sets out the conspectus for the book. It defines lustration as vetting or screening individuals, generally public officials and other prominent individuals, for their past associations and links with the communist regime that were kept secret from the public. It explains why I have adopted the distinctive and relatively novel approach of examining lustration broadly as a 'truth-revelation procedure' in conjunction with the issue of communist security service file access.

Having previously been one of the most under-researched and scantily understood areas of transitional justice, the former Soviet Union and Eastern bloc has become a growing area of research and academic discussion in recent years. Although it started as a subject for historians and lawyers primarily, there is now an expanding political science literature that looks at the measures taken by the former communist states to deal with past atrocities and overcome the legacy of communist dictatorship.[1] However, despite the existence of a large and expanding comparative literature on this topic, the late implementation of lustration and access to communist-era security service files – together with the intense, ongoing and recurring politicisation of the issue – in countries like Poland remains something of a puzzle. Poland moved from a communist-forgiving approach that avoided radical transitional justice measures in the early 1990s, to passing a mild lustration law and legislation to open up communist secret service file access at the end of the decade, and then to a more radical lustration and file access law passed in the mid-2000s, while the issue of communist security service collaboration retained the capacity to constantly surface and re-surface in Polish political debates even decades after the collapse of the communist regime. It is this puzzle, of 'late' and recurring lustration and communist security service file access, that this book seeks to address.

This introductory chapter begins by reflecting upon the various definitional debates in the comparative literature that have sought to answer the questions of (a) what are lustration and truth-revelation procedures and (b) how do they fit with other transitional justice measures? It examines why it is important to focus on truth revelation in general, and lustration in particular, as a (if not the) key transitional justice mechanism for (and certainly among the most controversial means) of dealing with the non-democratic past in the post-communist states of

Central and Eastern Europe. It also makes the case for examining lustration laws in conjunction with the question of the regulation of access to the archives and files compiled by the communist-era security service more generally. The chapter concludes by setting out the conspectus for, and structure of, the rest of the book.

So, what are lustration and file access? How do they fit in with other transitional justice measures? And why are they important to examine, particularly in relation to the way that post-communist states have pursued transitional justice? Stan (2009b) defines transitional justice as 'the measures and policies adopted by governments and civil society actors to address, and possibly redress, legacies of widespread and systematic human rights abuse, mass atrocity, genocide or civil war'. Similarly, drawing upon Kritz, Horne (2014, p. 496) defines it as 'a broad set of measures by which society confronts the wrongdoings in its past with the goal of obtaining some combination of truth, justice, rule of law and durable peace for the future'. According to Nalepa (2010a, p. 165), the transitional justice literature is 'an inter-disciplinary field concerned with how democracies deal with collaborators of the past regime'. It has, she argues, both a *normative* component, originating in the literature on legal and constitutional theory that examines possible reasons for (and problems created by) retroactivity, and a *positive* component trying to explain empirically occurring phenomena such as why democracies try and right wrongs, who are the actors responsible for implementing transitional justice measures, and whether or not these institutions have led to reconciliation.

The repertoire of transitional justice procedures is vast and diverse, but, as Nalepa (2010a, p. 5) points out, can be divided into four broad sets of measures. The first is using *court trials and criminal proceedings* to bring to justice prominent or representative members of the former dictatorial regime, particularly those who are accused of being perpetrators of human rights violations. This can include both high-ranking dignitaries and low-ranking officials such as secret service officers and agents. Second are *compensation packages* for victims and/or their surviving relatives, such as official apologies; monetary compensation; and restitution of rights to, and the return of, property expropriated by the former regime. Third are *legal or symbolic acts* directed against the former regime, such as legislation condemning it and expropriating the former rulers of their assets; programmes to re-write history textbooks in order to better reflect the plight of the victims of the regimes; changing the names of streets and localities; opening new museums and exhibitions; and removing statues associated with the regime. Fourth are what might be termed *truth-revelation procedures* (Kaminski and Nalepa 2006; Nalepa 2008). In the post-communist context, these have included vetting public officials and other prominent individuals for their links with the former regime's security services as either secret police officers or informers, and possibly banning them (together with other prominent or representative members of the former regime) from public office and positions of influence in society. They have also involved de-classifying and providing access to the extant secret archives and files of the former communist security services for public inspection. In other contexts, truth-revelation procedures have also involved establishing historical or 'truth' commissions, temporary bodies of formal inquiry appointed to re-examine the past and document the repressive activities of the previous regime, sometimes with the objective of achieving societal reconciliation.

Why is it worth focusing particularly on lustration and other truth-revelation procedures as transitional justice mechanisms in the post-communist context? Lustration was one of, if not the, most important and controversial transitional justice methods used in post-communist Central and Eastern Europe. The region was the first to embrace it so comprehensively, and it has remained an important means of dealing with the communist past; so much so that, as Stan (2009c, p. 12) put it, '[many] observers have employed it as a yardstick for measuring the progress of transitional justice in Eastern Europe and the former Soviet Union'. This could be attributed in large part to the level of societal surveillance by the communist authorities, as such infiltration by informants became the prevalent means by which communist regimes harassed their opponents. This was particularly the case towards the end of communist rule, as the random terror and enforced societal mobilisation of the Stalinist totalitarianism gave way to the atomisation and pervasive mass surveillance that characterised the so-called 'post-totalitarian' period (Linz and Stepan 1996, pp. 42–51). For example, according to Stan (2009d, pp. 76–77), the total number of full-time communist security service agents in Poland increased from 10,000 in 1957 to 25,600 in 1985, while the number of secret informers reached 98,000 in 1988. As a consequence, across the communist bloc, hundreds of thousands of citizens were functionaries of, or collaborators with, the internal security services, leaving these countries to have to deal with what Linz and Stepan (1996, p. 251) dubbed an 'informer legacy'.[2]

The term 'lustration' had long been used by Slavophone archivists simply to refer to the compilation of an inventory or register. To lustrate someone was to check whether their name appeared in a database. The term was more widely adopted not because, as is commonly alleged, of its etymological association with ancient Roman rites of purification, but because politicians and the public heard it used by bureaucrats during battles for control of Czechoslovak files in the early 1990s. Definitional debates over the term have focused on whether it should encompass the exclusion from, or limiting of access to, certain offices or simply vetting individuals to identify those who worked for and collaborated with the communist secret services without any such consequences flowing automatically; and whether this vetting and exclusion should also include communist party officials above a certain level and those who held senior positions within the party-state bureaucracy more generally. David (2003, p. 388), for example, defines lustration as 'the examination of certain groups of people, especially politicians, public officials, and judges, to determine whether they had been members or collaborators of the secret police, *or held any other positions in the repressive apparatus of the totalitarian regime*' (emphasis added). Similarly, Stan (2009c, p. 11) defines it as 'the *banning* of communist officials and secret police officers and informers from post-communist politics and positions of influence in society' (emphasis added). Horne (2014, p. 500) conceptualises lustration as

> a legislatively mandated and legally constrained process by which the backgrounds of certain public and some quasipublic/private officials are examined to determine whether they were members of, or collaborators with, the secret police, or whether they *held certain positions in the former communist regime*
>
> (emphasis added)

although she leaves open the question of whether it entails removal from office or position.

My own preference is to adopt the Polish convention, which defines lustration as being aimed at revealing whether an individual (generally an occupant of, or candidate for, a particular post) had links with the communist regime that were kept secret from the public, such as working, or collaborating as an informer, for the communist security services. Leadership (or even membership) of the communist party or employment in other branches of the party-state bureaucracy was more openly known. In terms of whether consequences follow automatically, reflecting the broader vernacular usage of the term across the region,[3] I would argue that lustration includes all forms of vetting and file access and not simply those which carry the consequence of (automatic) exclusion. Consequently, here, as in earlier papers that I have written or co-written (with Williams and Fowler) on this topic, I define it as 'measures directed against former officers of and collaborators with the state security apparatus' (Williams *et al*. 2005, p. 23). As I pointed out in a single-authored paper, this could include

> simply vetting or screening individuals for past associations with the communist security services without any sanction necessarily following (other than the damage to their reputation that the disclosure of this information could cause) ... [rather than necessarily also] then attempting to automatically exclude them from public life on the basis of such links.
>
> (Szczerbiak 2002, p. 553)[4]

Moreover, although the terms 'lustration' and 'de-communisation' are often used interchangeably, I would argue that it is important to distinguish the two processes, with the latter referring to the wider removal from public life of the former functionaries of the communist party or related institutions (generally above a certain rank).[5] In other words, here I understand and have defined lustration as vetting or screening individuals – generally occupants of, or candidates for, particular posts, such as public officials and other prominent individuals – for their past associations and links with the communist regime that were kept secret from the public, such as functionaries of or collaborators with the communist-era state security services, without any sanctions (such as banning them from public office or positions of influence in society) necessarily following.

Moreover, lustration, in the sense of truth revelation, depends a great deal upon access to the extant secret archives compiled by the communist-era security services. So, one can only get to grips with the issue properly by studying it both as a 'personnel system' (David 2011) or (regionally specialised) 'employment vetting policies' (albeit with moral cleansing features) (Horne 2014) and also – or perhaps, more accurately, even more so – more broadly as a 'truth-revelation procedure' in conjunction with the issue of de-classifying and opening up these archives and files for public inspection. Indeed, as we shall see, in Poland after the passage of the 1998 law that granted access to security service files to journalists, historians, researchers and some individuals – and in other countries that granted such access – there was also a great deal of 'informal' screening of individuals and groups not covered by the procedures set down in the lustration law, and public identification of former agents, conducted by state and non-state actors. Consequently, it is only by examining *both* lustration as a personnel and employment policy *and* the question of access to the communist-era security service files that one can get to grips properly with this issue in post-communist states. That is the distinctive and relatively novel approach that I have taken in this book.

This book aims to tackle three key questions: (a) Why do truth-revelation debates recur in post-communist Poland? (b) To what extent was such recurrence explained by instrumental-strategic or programmatic-ideological factors? and (c) Was recurrence popular demand- or political elite supply-driven? In order to get to grips with these questions, the book is structured as follows.

Chapter 2 surveys the progress of, and debates surrounding, the various attempts to introduce lustration and file access laws in post-1989 Poland. It reflects on why Poland is interesting as a case of late (and recurring) lustration and file access and debates about truth-revelation procedures. The chapter shows how this significant delay in introducing legislation, and the recurrence of these issues in political debate, was one of the most striking features of transitional justice in post-communist Poland – indeed, one of the leitmotifs of post-1989 Polish politics more generally – and identifies it as a phenomenon that requires further analysis and explanation. In doing so, it locates the Polish case within the various comparative and theoretical analytical frameworks and typologies that have been developed to categorise lustration laws and so-called 'lustration systems', together with cases of truth revelation and transitional justice that have occurred, in other post-communist states. As an archetypal case of late and recurring lustration and communist security service file access, the Polish case provides us with an excellent basis for developing frameworks to explain the phenomenon of 'late' and recurring lustration laws and file access debates. Examining the politics of truth revelation in post-communist Poland can both allow us to draw broader conclusions about lustration and transitional justice in Central and Eastern Europe, particularly with regard to the phenomenon of so-called late and/or recurring lustration, and provide valuable insights into patterns of post-communist politics more generally.

Chapter 3 examines the existing comparative and theoretical academic literature that has developed in recent years, including my own analytical frameworks, to understand and explain patterns of transitional justice and truth revelation in the post-communist states of Central and Eastern Europe, and specifically to tackle the extent and recurrence of 'late' lustration and file access in countries such as Poland. It shows that these approaches often divide into two broad schools of thought. First, there are authors who focus on parties' political and electoral-strategic motives, what might be broadly termed the 'politics of the present' approach (which I, among others, developed in my earlier collaborative work). Second, there are those who argue that the motives for pursuing transitional justice may be more ideologically, programmatically – and, thus, more normatively – driven. On the basis of this analysis, it explains the shortcomings in existing approaches to explaining the phenomenon of late truth revelation in post-communist democracies. It considers whether 'politics of the present'-type approaches need to be modified to reflect the fact that they underestimate the extent to which the motives of those pushing for transitional justice and truth revelation may also have been driven (in part, or even primarily) by genuine ideological and programmatic concerns rather than simply being instrumentalised as a power tool by political actors attempting to gain an electoral-strategic advantage over their competitors. It argues that further theoretical and empirical analysis, including case studies such as that undertaken on Poland in this book, are needed in order to further develop our understanding of the phenomenon of late and recurring lustration and truth revelation.

Chapter 4 examines in detail the re-emergence of the lustration and file access debate in the mid-2000s, which led to the passage of an amended law in 2006 that was eventually gutted by the constitutional tribunal. It shows how the creation of the Institute of National Remembrance – and concomitant access to communist security service archives afforded to historians, journalists and victims of communist repression – created momentum around the issue of, and a demand for further, truth revelation. The normative literature on post-communist transitional justice has posited arguments both for and against radical approaches towards lustration and communist security service file access from a liberal democratic perspective. This chapter examines how transitional justice and truth-revelation debates in Poland at this time often overlapped and became entwined with broader concerns about the perceived failures of democratisation and projects designed to implement post-communist renewal. It considers how these debates often focused on freedom of information and the public's 'right to know' the backgrounds of its public representatives. It also examines how calls for more radical lustration and file access were driven by concerns about the need to tackle corruption as an endemic feature of post-communist Poland and the extent to which these were felt to stem from the perceived ability of elites linked to the former regime to take advantage of their communist-era networks, including those rooted in the former security services, to turn their old political power into new economic power. The chapter considers the relationship between calls for more radical truth-revelation procedures and the so-called 'Fourth Republic' project, which was part of a broader, radical critique of post-1989 Poland as corrupt and requiring far-reaching moral and political renewal and reform. It also examines the arguments used by opponents of radical lustration and how, as well as defending the existing court-based Polish lustration model, they accused its proponents of supporting an instrumentally motivated and politically destructive project aimed primarily at achieving elite turnover.

Chapter 5 moves on to examine another example of how the lustration and file access issue had the capacity to recur as a topic of political debate. This was the divisions within the political elites that emerged from the Solidarity independent trade union and mass anti-communist opposition movement over whether or not its one-time legendary leader, and the first democratically elected President in post-1989 Poland, Lech Wałęsa, had collaborated with the communist secret services in the early 1970s as an informer codenamed 'Bolek'. This provoked a stormy, indeed often ferocious, national political debate over the nature and significance of Mr Wałęsa's apparent collaboration. After examining the arguments used by Mr Wałęsa's supporters and opponents, it discusses how the 'Bolek' affair shows that the lustration and file issue recurred because it was an instance, probably the most controversial and high profile, of debates about how to deal with the communist security service archives becoming entwined with the process of legitimation and de-legitimation. This legitimation and de-legitimation occurred at a number of levels: of the post-communist state's genesis and foundational myths, of particular political actors and formations, and of the transitional justice and truth-revelation process itself.

Chapter 6 examines polling data on public attitudes towards transitional justice and dealing with the communist past in post-communist Poland, including Mr Wałęsa's alleged communist security service collaboration. Specifically, it considers the notion that the issue of lustration and secret service file access may have recurred in Polish politics due to public demand for more radical transitional justice. Based on an analysis of publicly available opinion polls covering the whole of the period examined, the chapter examines why, although Poles have generally supported a radical approach towards transitional justice and truth revelation, dealing with the communist past has not, on its own, been an especially salient issue in determining voting patterns and election outcomes. However, it also considers whether polling data pointing to the low salience of the truth-revelation issue may be misleading, because attitudes towards lustration and communist security access were linked to political identities and party alignments more generally. They were also, in the public mind, often entwined with other, more salient, issues and concerns about the shortcomings of post-communist democratisation in Poland, such as freedom of information, the need to tackle corruption and the importance of renewing the political system.

The concluding Chapter 7 summarises and synthesises the main findings from the book and attempts to draw some broader theoretical conclusions that go beyond the Polish case. It returns to the three key questions that were posed in this chapter and have been tackled in the book. In doing so, it considers whether existing comparative literature and theoretical frameworks that attempt to

8 Introduction

explain the trajectories of lustration and transitional justice in post-communist states help us to understand the Polish case of late implementation of truth-revelation laws. It also reflects on the wider lessons and broader theoretical conclusions that can be drawn about the politics of lustration and transitional justice in post-communist Central Europe beyond the Polish case. It thereby examines the implications of, and insights from, the Polish case of late truth revelation for understanding politics in Poland, the region and other democratising states more generally.

The main primary data source for Chapter 4 was a qualitative analysis of contributions to the parliamentary debates on the revised lustration and file access law held on 9 March and 20 July 2006, together with the justificatory statement from the draft bill on which the law was based. I draw upon both statements from the main party spokesmen and other representative contributions from second-ranked speakers. In Chapters 4 and 5, I also draw on news articles, opinion-editorial pieces and analyses of parliamentary debates, primarily those published in the (at various points centre-right or centrist) *Rzeczpospolita* daily newspaper, the main Polish newspaper of record; the key opinion-forming liberal-left *Gazeta Wyborcza* daily newspaper and *Polityka* weekly journal; and the influential right-wing *wSieci* and *Do Rzeczy* weekly journals and the *wPolityce* news and commentary web portal. Chapter 6 is based on an analysis of publicly available polling data and opinion surveys, particularly those published by the Centre for Public Opinion Research (Centrum Badania Opinii Społecznej: CBOS) agency, as well as those contained in various news reports. To triangulate the findings from these written primary and secondary sources, I also undertook a series of elite interviews in June 2006 with individuals who played a key role as observers of, or participants in, the lustration and file access debates and processes. These included parliamentary deputy and party spokesman Arkadiusz Mularczyk; historians Sławomir Cenckiewicz, Antoni Dudek and Andrzej Paczkowski; and sociologist Andrzej Zybertowicz and commentators Adam Leszczyński, (the late) Janina Paradowska, Piotr Semka, Ewa Siedlecka and Bronisław Wildstein. Full relevant biographical details of these individuals and the timing of the interviews are set out in the Appendix.

Notes

1 See, for example, Stan (2009a), Nalepa (2010a), David (2011), Pettai and Pettai (2015), Stan and Nedelsky (2015) and Horne (2017).
2 For example, in a journalistic account of transitional justice in the Czech Republic, German Democratic Republic (GDR) and Poland, Rosenberg draws attention to the fact that in authoritarian Latin America repression was 'deep', while in post-totalitarian Eastern Europe it was 'wide', to explain why so few court proceedings were launched against communist leaders and secret agents (Stan 2009b).
3 Although in some countries, such as Hungary and the former GDR, the term is not actually used at all to describe truth-revelation procedures.
4 Interestingly, having initially defined lustration as a set of 'laws *limiting the access to public office* of politicians with an authoritarian past' (Nalepa 2008, p. 222) or 'a truth-revelation procedure in which public officials who collaborated with the former

authoritarian regime are *disqualified* from holding high-level public positions in the public sector' (Nalepa 2010b, pp. 735–736) (emphasis added), Nalepa (2012, p. 333) also went on to adopt a broader definition of the process as simply 'revealing links to the former communist secret police of persons holding public office'.
5 Bertschi (1995, p. 437) also makes this distinction when he defines de-communisation (along with de-Stalinisation, de-partyization and de-idolization) as '[a] transformational process[es] that pertains more to institutions and social structures than people'. Similarly, Kaminski and Nalepa (2006, p. 384) argue that de-communisation was analogous to de-Nazification in post-war Germany in the sense that it denoted 'purging the state's administration and bureaucracy of high-ranking communist (or Nazi) officials', and, unlike in lustration, the identity of a high-ranking communist (or Nazi) official was common knowledge, so they were not vulnerable to blackmail in the same way as the former undercover agent.

Bibliography

Bertschi, C.C., 1995. Lustration and the Transition to Democracy: The Cases of Poland and Bulgaria. *East European Quarterly*, 28 (4), 435–451.

David, R., 2003. Lustration Laws in Action: The Motives and Evaluation of Lustration Policy in the Czech Republic and Poland (1989–2001). *Law and Social Inquiry*, 28 (2), 387–439.

David, R., 2011. *Lustration and Transitional Justice: Personnel Systems in the Czech Republic, Hungary and Poland*. Philadelphia: University of Pennsylvania Press.

Horne, C.M., 2014. The Impact of Lustration on Democratization in Postcommunist Countries. *The International Journal of Transitional Justice*, 8 (3), 496–521.

Horne, C.M., 2017. *Building Trust and Democracy: Transitional Justice in Post-Communist Countries*. Oxford: Oxford University Press.

Kaminski, M.N. and Nalepa, M., 2006. Judging Transitional Justice: A New Criterion for Evaluating Truth Revelation Procedures. *The Journal of Conflict Resolution*, 50 (3), 383–408.

Linz, J. and Stepan, A., 1996. *Problems of Democratic Transition and Consolidation: Southern Europe, South American and Post-Communist Europe*. Baltimore: Johns Hopkins University Press.

Nalepa, M., 2008. To Punish the Guilty and Protect the Innocent: Comparing Truth Revelation Procedures. *Journal of Theoretical Politics*, 2 (2), 221–245.

Nalepa, M., 2010a. *Skeletons in Closet: Transitional Justice in Post-Communist Europe*. New York: Cambridge University Press.

Nalepa, M., 2010b. Lustration. In M.C. Bassiouni, ed., *The Pursuit of International Criminal Justice: A World Survey on Conflicts, Victimization, and Post-Conflict Justice. Volume 1*. Mortsel: Intersentia, 735–778.

Nalepa, M., 2012. Lustration as a Trust-Building Mechanism? Transitional Justice in Poland. In M. Serrano and V. Popovski, eds, *After Oppression: Transitional Justice in Latin America and Eastern Europe*. Washington DC: Brookings Institute Press, 333–362.

Pettai, E.-C. and Pettai, V., 2015. *Transitional and Retrospective Justice in the Baltic States*. Cambridge: Cambridge University Press.

Stan, L. ed., 2009a. *Transitional Justice in Eastern Europe and the Former Soviet Union*. London and New York: Routledge.

Stan, L., 2009b. *Transitional Justice*, SciTopics [online], 6 February. Available from: www.scitopics.com/Transitional_Justice.html (accessed 6 February 2014).

Stan, L., 2009c. Introduction: Post-Communist Transition, Justice, and Transitional Justice. In L. Stan, ed., *Transitional Justice in Eastern Europe and the Former Soviet Union*, London and New York: Routledge, 1–14.

Stan, L., 2009d. Poland. In L. Stan, ed., *Transitional Justice in Eastern Europe and the Former Soviet Union*. London and New York: Routledge, 76–101.

Stan, L. and Nedelsky, N., eds., 2015. *Post-Communist Transitional Justice: Lessons from Twenty-Five Years of Experience*. Cambridge: Cambridge University Press.

Szczerbiak, A., 2002. Dealing with the Communist Past or the Politics of the Present? Lustration in Post-Communist Poland. *Europe-Asia Studies*, 54 (4), 553–572.

Williams, K., Fowler, B. and Szczerbiak, A., 2005. Explaining Lustration in Central Europe: A 'Post-Communist Politics' Approach. *Democratization*, 12 (1), 22–43.

2 Truth revelation in post-communist Poland

A case of late (and recurring) lustration and file access

This chapter surveys the progress of, and debates surrounding, the various attempts to introduce lustration and file access laws in post-1989 Poland. It reflects on why Poland is an interesting case of 'late' (and recurring) lustration and file access and debates about truth-revelation procedures. The chapter shows how this significant delay in introducing legislation, and the recurrence of these issues in political debate, was one of the most striking features of transitional justice in post-communist Poland – indeed, one of the leitmotifs of post-1989 Polish politics more generally – and identifies it as a phenomenon that requires further analysis and explanation. In doing so, it locates the Polish case within the various comparative and theoretical analytical frameworks and typologies that have been developed to categorise lustration laws and so-called 'lustration systems', together with cases of truth revelation and transitional justice that have occurred, in other post-communist states. As an archetypal case of late and recurring lustration and communist security service file access, the Polish case provides us with an excellent basis for developing frameworks to explain the phenomenon of 'late' and recurring lustration laws and file access debates. Examining the politics of truth revelation in post-communist Poland can allow us to draw broader conclusions about lustration and transitional justice in Central and Eastern Europe, as well as providing valuable insights into patterns of post-communist politics more generally.

In Stan's (2009a, pp. 261–262) general typology of post-communist states' approaches to transitional justice – based on whether they instituted court proceedings against former communist regime functionaries, as well as their enactment of lustration laws and access to communist security service archives – Poland was (along with Hungary) classified as a 'mild' case. In such countries, transitional justice was both delayed in time and less radical in scope than in those that, to a greater or lesser extent, pursued all three of these processes strongly and vigorously through citizenship and electoral as well as screening laws (such as the former GDR, the Czech Republic and the Baltic states) but more advanced than those that adopted weak approaches to transitional justice with only one or two of the methods outlined (such as Bulgaria and Romania) or that resisted attempts to re-evaluate the past and seemingly followed a 'forgive and forget' approach (such as Slovakia, Slovenia, Albania and all of the Soviet successor republics except for the Baltic states).

Similarly, in her rather more narrowly focused lustration typology, Horne (2014, pp. 10–16) categorises Poland (alongside Hungary and Lithuania) as a case of 'narrow and voluntary' institutional bureaucratic change and public disclosure. These countries were characterised by the passage of lustration or lustration-type laws covering a limited scope of positions, with voluntary resignation from office rather than a compulsory penalty (except, in some cases, for lying about collaboration) and an emphasis on truth telling coupled with formal proceedings to catalyse voluntary bureaucratic change. This was in contrast to cases of wide and compulsory institutional bureaucratic change and public disclosure (the Czech Republic, Latvia and Estonia); limited and/or informal vetting through public disclosure and symbolic change (Bulgaria, Romania and Slovakia); and no symbolic or institutional change (Albania, Russia and Ukraine).

In Poland, the revelation of links between persons holding public office and the former communist secret police by lustration and file access was by far the most extensively used transitional justice mechanism, much more so than trials or compensation of victims of communist rule. While Poland was the first country in the region to overthrow communism, as a result of peaceful negotiations between the outgoing regime and the former opposition, it was more than eight years after the transition to democracy began that the country finally approved a lustration law. However, although it began with an initial avoidance of the issue, lustration and file access retained a remarkable capacity to endure and remain on the political agenda when one might have expected them to fade from public memory. Indeed, one of the most striking things about the Polish case was the ongoing politicisation of the lustration issue, with communist security service secret archives generating a number of public scandals, which, as we shall see, contributed to the collapse of two governments in the 1990s. David (2003, p. 418) argues that it was precisely due to the length of the pre-lustration period that Polish discourses on this issue developed such a 'poisonous' character.

Mr Mazowiecki's 'thick line' policy

In August 1989, Tadeusz Mazowiecki, a Catholic intellectual adviser to the Solidarity opposition movement and the first non-communist prime minister in Poland since the country was incorporated into the Soviet bloc at the end of the 1940s, announced in his inaugural policy speech that a 'thick line' ('gruba linia') would be drawn between the communist past and the present.[1] The precise meaning of the 'thick line' speech has been contested. Mazowiecki and his supporters claimed that he simply intended to symbolically divide the old and new Poland and separate his government's responsibility from that of the previous regime, especially the damage done to the national economy. In terms of transitional justice, rather than applying collective guilt for former party or security service activity, the new government pledged itself to de-communise through dismantling the communist power monopoly and assessing supporters of the previous regime on the basis of their actual performance and loyalty towards the new government.

In fact, Mazowiecki's defenders argue that it is wrong to suggest that he consciously did not seek to come to terms with the communist past in any way and that, given the political context, his government actually introduced a number of important transitional justice measures and initiatives in areas such as rehabilitation, restitution and trials of former regime functionaries. They also claim that – although they were not publicised and, in a deliberate attempt to avoid sensationalism, were often carried out without necessarily being officially presented as verification procedures – Mazowiecki's government did undertake some considerable and quite extensive institutional reforms and personnel changes in a number of spheres of public life. For example, the interior ministry was re-organised, and in May 1990 the communist-era secret Security Service (Służba Bezpieczeństwa: SB) was dissolved and replaced by the State Security Office (Urząd Ochrony Państwa: UOP), whose intelligence and counter-intelligence remit did not include monitoring the political opposition. Of the 24,000 Security Service functionaries, 14,000 were reviewed by central and local verification commissions, which determined whether they had fulfilled the moral qualifications for service or were disqualified by virtue of having violated the law, infringed human rights or used their position for private gain. Following appeals, 10,439 functionaries were verified positively and 3,595 negatively. Around 5,000 of the former were re-hired by the State Security Office, with the remainder finding further employment with the police and private security firms (Piotrowski 2008, pp. 18, 22).

However, Mr Mazowiecki's speech was widely interpreted as excluding the former communist establishment from punishment for its mistakes, and the 'thick line' was often cited as a metaphor epitomising the lenient approach to the previous regime and abdication of responsibility for a reckoning with the past adopted by his administration. The Security Service verification process was heavily criticised for its unevenness among districts, prompting charges of gross unfairness and even 'procedural nihilism' (Calhoun 2004, p. 105), as well as for being excessively lenient and leaving in place many figures linked to the previous regime, some of whom later became the subject of political controversy. Moreover, despite the many complaints, the procedure was not revised substantially following the initial vetting, with politicians fearing that further screening of the secret services could deprive the country of skilled intelligence professionals and thereby weaken national security (Stan 2009b, p. 78). At the same time, although verification commissions were set up at all levels of the legal system to examine individual service records, only 359 of the 3,278 public prosecutors (including one-third of the staff of the General Prosecutor's Office) were dismissed, with 48 restored on appeal (Podemski 1997; Calhoun 2004, p. 106). The areas where the least progress was made were in de-communisation – in the sense of weeding out and banning from public office former communist officials, security service informers and other collaborators with the communist system of power – and truth revelation. The Mazowiecki government explicitly rejected any systematic lustration, verification of persons holding or running for public office for collaboration with the communist security services, or file access programmes.

Mr Mazowiecki's motives for pursuing this kind of policy were mixed. Partly, they were rooted in a principled justification based on classical liberal arguments against applying collective guilt to former regime functionaries: the need to spare a defeated enemy, respect for the rule of law and the fact that secret police files were felt to be an untrustworthy basis for pursuing historical justice. However, it was also partly for practical reasons, and there were pragmatic elements underpinning the policy as well; namely, that the new government had to deal with an economy in ongoing severe crisis, and lustration and de-communisation were felt to be politically destabilising. Moreover, as will be discussed in greater detail in Chapter 3, Mr Mazowiecki was also constrained by the fact that, as part of the elite bargain securing the transfer of power, the communists retained considerable influence over the political process during the transition period, and, until July 1990, he headed up a coalition government in which they controlled the so-called 'power' defence and interior ministries. Initially at least, the geo-political situation was uncertain, as Mr Mazowiecki's government was relatively isolated within the Soviet bloc until the other East European communist regimes began collapsing at the end of 1989. In one sense, although it had many defects, the continuation of the 'round table' elite compromise was seen as the best possible solution: an unavoidable and necessary cost of the peaceful extraction from communism and a way of stabilising the new regime during a period of uncertainty. In fact, although the precise terms of the elite bargain agreed at the 'round table' were quickly overtaken by events and the changing geo-political situation as communism collapsed in the rest of the Soviet bloc, there were also normative justifications for the 'thick line' policy. The Mazowiecki government clearly believed that the new, post-communist state needed to promote societal reconciliation and avoid retribution. So, the logic of the political process and the broad, underlying philosophy (or 'spirit') of the compromise embodied by the 'round table' agreement – that the new elites could not attack those with whom they had negotiated – needed to be honoured.

However, in spite of the apparently 'communist-forgiving' policies pursued by both the Mazowiecki government and the subsequent post-Solidarity government led by Jan Krzysztof Bielecki from the small Liberal Democratic Congress (Kongres Liberalno-Demokratyczny: KLD) party – who took over when Mr Mazowiecki resigned as prime minister following the latter's defeat in the November–December 1990 presidential election – the issue of dealing with the communist past did not go away. By 1990, with the collapse of communism in neighbouring countries creating a radically different geo-political environment and growing dissatisfaction with the social consequences of finance minister Leszek Balcerowicz's radical economic reform programme of rapid transition from a centrally planned to a market economy, criticism of the 'thick line' policy and Mr Mazowiecki's strictly legalistic approach intensified. While Mr

Mazowiecki's supporters defended the policy as a good way of avoiding destructiveness during the transition phase, it also produced something of a backlash, with the issues of lustration and de-communisation continuing to re-surface as a recurring theme in Polish politics. Indeed, the issue of secret police files gained notoriety in the years prior to the initiation of a formal lustration programme, and public identifications of former agents conducted by state and non-state actors and 'informal' screening of individuals and groups not covered by procedures set down in lustration laws occurred on many occasions to discredit political opponents.

Calls for a more radical approach began to gather pace in 1990–1991, and the issue was used as a lever by those political elites on the right of the Solidarity movement who felt excluded from the Mazowiecki government and appeared to find a natural champion in the union's legendary leader Lech Wałęsa, who led it from its formation at the beginning of the 1980s through the democratic transition. Indeed, a more radical approach to 'dealing with the past' was to emerge as a major (if somewhat unspecified) theme in Wałęsa's 1990 presidential election campaign, based on the slogan of 'acceleration', against Mr Mazowiecki. However, Mr Wałęsa soon abandoned these themes once elected, appointing Mr Bielecki as prime minister, who, as noted above, essentially continued with Mr Mazowiecki's 'thick line' policy.[2] Indeed, Mr Wałęsa's attitude towards the de-communisation issue at that time generally involved a combination of often sharp anti-communist rhetoric with a much more communist-forgiving approach in practice (Walicki 1997, p. 195). Nonetheless, de-communisation and lustration remained major elements in the discourse of 'post-Solidarity' right-wing parties such as the Centre Agreement (Porozumienie Centrum: PC) – which had provided the organisational backbone for Mr Wałęsa's presidential campaign, and whose leader Jarosław Kaczyński was once his key aide and became (for a brief period) chief of staff in his presidential chancellery before resigning, breaking with and denouncing him in 1991 – and the clerical-nationalist Christian-National Union (Zjednoczenie Chrześcijańsko-Narodowe: ZChN). These parties went on to enjoy relative success in the first fully free parliamentary election held in October 1991.

The 'Macierewicz list'

Following this election, lustration was to move to the top of the political agenda with the advent in December 1991 of a right-wing administration led by the Solidarity-linked lawyer Jan Olszewski, which came to office as a self-proclaimed government of 'breakthrough'. The Olszewski government comprised a coalition of post-Solidarity parties, including the Centre Agreement and the Christian-National Union, that had made criticism of the 'thick line' policy a major theme in their election campaigns. Although it was always a weak, unstable and ultimately short-lived minority coalition – enjoying the support of only 114 out of 460 members of the Sejm, the more powerful lower house of the Polish parliament – Mr Olszewski's government had huge political ambitions and offered a radical break with both the communist past and the communist-forgiving policy of the two previous cabinets, promising radical lustration and de-communisation and immediately signalling its determination to expose former communist security service agents. It set about this task by creating a special department in the interior ministry to sift through secret police archives from the communist period and identify former security service functionaries and collaborators.

However, events took an unexpected twist when, on 28 May 1992, the Sejm voted by 186 votes to 15 (with 32 abstentions) to adopt a controversial resolution proposed by Janusz Korwin-Mikke from the small liberal-conservative Union of Real Politics (Unia Polityki Realnej: UPR) party. This required the then interior minister, Antoni Macierewicz, to publicly disclose within 21 days the names of and information about all current leading members of the Polish political elite and senior public officials in the government, parliament and other state bodies occupying the rank of provincial governor upwards who, according to the archives, had collaborated with the communist security services as secret informers. However, because the motion had been neither channelled through the relevant parliamentary committees nor debated in a plenary session, Mr Macierewicz was not provided with any guidelines on how this objective should be achieved (Nalepa 2010, p. 15). Consequently, a special investigation bureau was established within the interior ministry to compile a list of collaborators based on the secret archives, and, on 4 June, Mr Macierewicz duly presented the then President Lech Wałęsa and parliamentary party leaders with secret lists of 66 leading public officials who had allegedly figured in the communist security service archives as informers (Y-Elita Pl undated, Stankiewicz and Zychal 2017).

Both the contents of the so-called 'Macierewicz list' and the timing of its release were to prove extremely controversial, creating a political storm that precipitated one of the most serious political crises in post-communist Poland and resulted in the ousting of the Olszewski government. The revelation that it included Mr Wałęsa, the foreign minister and many other senior officials and parliamentarians, including other prominent anti-communist dissidents and anti-communist opposition activists, some of whom had previously advocated lustration – such as Wiesław Chrzanowski, the speaker of the Sejm and leader of the Christian-National Union, and Leszek Moczulski, the leader of the radical anti-communist Confederation for an Independent Poland (Konfederacja Polski Niepodległej: KPN) – created doubts about its accuracy. These were reinforced by the fact that Mr Macierewicz had prefaced it with a proviso that the names included were part of the archival record but did not conclusively demonstrate collaboration (Vinton 1992). However, the fact that the 'Macierewicz list' was leaked immediately to the press on the day before a no-confidence vote that the government was likely to lose fuelled the suspicion that it was simply part of a desperate attempt to save the crumbling minority administration by discrediting its political opponents. On the other hand, supporters of the Olszewski government – which was, indeed, dismissed on 5 June by 273 votes to 119 (with 33 abstentions) – argued that the prime minister and Mr Macierewicz had fallen victim to a dark conspiracy by political forces linked to the previous communist regime.[3]

To its critics, the Olszewski government's apparently incompetent and politically motivated attempt to unmask secret services functionaries, which came across as a battle for power among various factions within the Solidarity movement, appeared to discredit the whole lustration process by demonstrating how it could be manipulated to advance short-term political objectives. On 19 June, the constitutional tribunal also ruled the Korwin-Mikke resolution incompatible with articles in the Polish Constitution on democratic principles and human rights and laws governing state secrecy and the protection of individual reputations, and stipulated that only a law, not a parliamentary resolution, could authorise a minister to enact lustration in this way. In July, a special Sejm investigative commission report also accused Mr Macierewicz and Mr Olszewski of acts aimed at compromising and paralysing the Polish state. Mr Macierewicz's supporters, on the other hand, argued that the premature Korwin-Mikke resolution had undermined the interior minister's careful plan for a thorough investigation of security service archives and rigorous legislation governing its findings.[4]

Nonetheless, while some felt that the controversy that ensued from this failed attempt to introduce lustration had discredited and delayed the entire process, the issue did not go away. In September 1992, the Sejm debated and referred to a parliamentary committee six draft lustration laws submitted by the Centre Agreement, Christian-National Union, Confederation for an Independent Poland, Congress of Liberal Democrats, Solidarity trade union and the human rights commission of the Senate, the less powerful second chamber of the Polish parliament. However, the new government, led by Hanna Suchocka, a member of Mr Mazowiecki's liberal-centrist Democratic Union (Unia Demokratyczna: UD) party, clearly had other priorities, and the issue quickly slipped down the Sejm's agenda. The lustration bills had failed to make any progress by the time that the Suchocka government fell and parliament was dissolved following the passage of a May 1993 no-confidence vote that precipitated an early parliamentary election in September of that year.

The 'Oleksy affair'

Indeed, the communist successor Democratic Left Alliance (Sojusz Lewicy Demokratycznej: SLD) grouping[5] and the Polish Peasant Party (Polskie Stronnictwo Ludowe: PSL),[6] another regime successor grouping, won a sweeping victory in the snap September 1993 parliamentary election, obtaining nearly two-thirds of the seats in the Sejm between them. Together with the virtual exclusion from parliament of the Polish right, particularly those parties, such as the Centre Agreement and Mr Olszewski's Movement for the Republic (Ruch dla Rzeczypospolitej: RdR), that had pursued lustration and de-communisation most vigorously, the Democratic Left Alliance's victory was widely interpreted as a clear signal that Polish society did not support this kind of approach to dealing with the communist past or, at least, did not view these kinds of issues as a priority. Consequently, it was predicted that lustration would be suppressed and fade from the political agenda,[7] with some commentators interpreting the Democratic Left Alliance's victory as part of a broader trend in post-communist Eastern Europe and declaring the 'end of de-communisation' (Holmes 1994).

Certainly, in July 1994 the new parliament debated eight lustration-related bills. Two were from the Confederation for an Independent Poland, and one each from the Democratic Left Alliance; the liberal-centrist Freedom Union (Unia Wolności: UW), which was formed from a merger of the Democratic Union and Congress of Liberal Democrats and comprised many of the former members of the Mazowiecki government that had introduced the 'thick line' policy and helped to bring down the Olszewski government (and was, at one point, actually led by Mazowiecki); the Labour Union (Unia Pracy: UP), a social democratic party that comprised both ex-Solidarity members and former communists; the Peasant Party; the interior ministry; and a private member's bill proposed by a Freedom Union deputy (Grzelak 2005, pp. 96–105). However, the only bills to progress to the committee stage for further deliberation were those proposed by the Democratic Left Alliance and the government. These had little to do with lustration and simply involved running background checks on officials for criminal offences. Zolkos described the Democratic Left Alliance bill as a 'de facto anti-lustration measure' (Zolkos 2006, p. 232), which meant that the issue continued to languish on the legislative back-burner.

However, for a number of reasons, in the mid-1990s Polish politics actually became polarised on the basis of attitudes towards the communist past (Grabowska 2004), which helped to move debates about lustration and de-communisation up the political agenda. The formation of a Democratic Left Alliance-led government fostered a growing perception that members of the pre-1989 communist elite were returning to key positions of power and influence at both national and local level. This exacerbated the resentment that many Poles already felt towards the phenomena of 'nomenklatura capitalism', the way that former members of the communist political elite had successfully re-invented themselves as private businessmen.[8] Moreover, although Mr Wałęsa had helped to scupper the Olszewski government's attempt to introduce lustration, and many of his former allies, such as Mr Kaczyński, accused him of betraying Solidarity's ideals in order to cover up his involvement as a communist security service collaborator, in the run-up to the bitter and closely fought November 1995 presidential election, the incumbent actually deployed very sharp and aggressive anti-communist rhetoric in order to re-rebuild his support (Millard 1996). Although it appeared to vindicate Democratic Left Alliance leader Aleksander Kwaśniewski's communist-forgiving slogan 'Let us choose the future' ('Wybierzmy przyszłość'), his narrow victory over Mr Wałęsa actually served to re-inforce the perception that former communists now controlled all the main state institutions.

Perhaps most significantly, however, the lustration issue re-surfaced and came to a head dramatically in December 1995 when outgoing President Wałęsa and his interior minister Andrzej Milczanowski warned that Poland's security was endangered by the Democratic Left Alliance prime minister Józef Oleksy, who they claimed had been a Soviet spy, and still was a Russian one, who passed secret documents on to a KGB agent (*Rzeczpospolita* 1995). Although Mr Oleksy declared his innocence, and military prosecutors later dismissed the charges, he was subsequently forced to resign as prime minister in January 1996. The so-called 'Oleksy affair' moved the issue of politicians' links with the security services, and lustration more specifically, back to the top of the political agenda. For a brief period, the call to tackle the legacy of the former communist security services dominated political debate, and this was echoed in parliament, setting off a chain of events that culminated in the passage of a lustration law in April 1997 (Szczerbiak 2002). As Misztal (1999, p. 42) put it, 'the growing societal suspicion about the connection between the Polish communists and the Russian security services was the cost the SLD had to pay for its rejection of lustration'.

In the middle of the political scandal surrounding the 'Oleksy affair', the newly elected President Kwaśniewksi tried to take the political initiative by unexpectedly introducing his own lustration bill. His proposal was a fairly modest one that involved the vetting of candidates and high-ranking state officials for their communist security service links by a new Commission of Public Trust (Komisja Zaufania Publicznego: KZP), which included giving individuals access to their own files. The commission, which would oversee the communist security service archives, would comprise senior judges nominated by the representative bodies of the Polish judiciary but appointed by the President himself (*Rzeczpospolita* 1996). Critics interpreted Mr Kwaśniewski's volte face as merely an attempt to protect his tainted Democratic Left allies by directing public attention away from the 'Oleksy affair' while personally controlling the vetting process and defining collaboration in a way that was most likely to encompass post-Solidarity politicians rather than ex-communists.[9] Nonetheless, Calhoun argues that Mr Kwaśniewski's proposal marked a fundamental shift in the political dynamics of lustration because it meant that, ironically, it was the left that brought new energy to the issue as its opposition subsided, at least temporarily. The 'Oleksy affair', she says, changed the left's perception of the lustration issue by bringing down a left-wing government and thereby demonstrating that 'the lack of lustration imposed costs on parties from both sides of the political spectrum' and convincing Democratic Left Alliance leaders that 'some form of lustration was necessary and inevitable, even though some still expressed regret at this necessity' (Calhoun 2002, p. 512).

The 1997 'civilised' lustration law

Mr Kwaśniewski's initiative encouraged others to submit lustration proposals, and, in addition to the President's, four more were tabled from the Freedom Union, Labour Union, Peasant Party, and a joint draft backed by these three parties. In July 1996, the Sejm set up an extraordinary parliamentary commission to consider the lustration bill, which began meeting in August. By then, with the atmosphere of crisis stemming from the 'Oleksy affair' having subsided, the Democratic Left Alliance began to cool on the idea of lustration and did not support Mr Kwaśniewski's bill in the commission. However, the party could not abandon the issue entirely; it remained ostensibly in favour of lustration but changed its strategy to one of proposing amendments and raising procedural issues and concerns designed to delay the law or make it unworkable (Paradowska 1997, 1998; Grzelak 2005, pp. 126–136). For example, it argued that intelligence and counter-intelligence agents should be excluded from its provisions, claiming that to include these agencies within the scope of lustration could lead to the total collapse of the security services and would therefore compromise national security. The party's critics counter-argued that most of the work undertaken by these agencies during the communist era was actually directed against the democratic opposition, primarily the Polish emigré communities, and therefore equally contemptible. They also said that this was the kind of spying activity that communist party members were most likely to be engaged in and that arguments for excluding these agents from lustration were simply a ploy to help Democratic Left Alliance members and supporters slip through the net. The Alliance also wanted 'collaboration' with the security services to be defined quite precisely as 'conscious participation in actions against the Church, the independent trade unions, the nation or creating a threat to civil liberties and property of others' (Misztal 1999, p. 44). Valid proof of such 'conscious collaboration' would be an original, hand-written, signed statement setting out unambiguously the individual's commitment to act as a secret collaborator. Critics responded that that it would be extremely difficult to prove that someone had met all of these very specific criteria, thereby rendering the whole process a sham.

However, in spite of their apparently firm grip on all of the main state institutions, Mr Kwaśniewski and his Democratic Left Alliance allies then proceeded to lose control of the lustration debate, and a parliament that they appeared to dominate ended up passing a lustration law against their wishes. The key factor accounting for this was the emergence of a coalition of three 'centrist' parties supporting a proposal for a 'moderate' or 'civilised' lustration law.[10] Two of these were post-Solidarity opposition parties, the Freedom Union and the Labour Union, but the third, crucial element of this 'lustration coalition' was the governing Peasant Party. Although the Peasant Party was the Democratic Left Alliance's junior coalition partner in government, it started to adopt a different approach to the lustration issue. As noted above, the politicians who comprised the Freedom Union were drawn from a milieu most of whom had strongly supported Mr Mazowiecki's 'thick line' and had equally strongly opposed the Olszewski government's lustration efforts. However, the groundswell over the issue was becoming so great, and it was starting to harm them politically as the party faced constant accusations that they were opposed to lustration because they had something to hide and feared the truth, that many of its leaders came to the conclusion that it could no longer be avoided. As a consequence, a number of their key leaders decided that they had to take a risk and ended up changing their approach and switching sides in the debate: supporting the 1997 law, which they saw as a civilised, court-based project based on a judicial process that gave those accused the right to appeal, with the alternative being the continuation of informal 'wild lustration'. Indeed, my own analysis of the parliamentary debates during the passage of the 1997 lustration bill found that the main arguments advanced by deputies from the 'lustration coalition' were a desire for openness in public life and the notion that citizens had a right to know the backgrounds of their public representatives; the idea that lustration was necessary for national security, because it would ensure that individuals in prominent public positions were not vulnerable to blackmail on account of their past associations with the communist security services; and to de-politicise the issue of secret service collaboration and avoid informal, 'wild' lustration by subjecting it to a judicial process. In so far as the bill's sponsors used this line of argument at all, a desire to secure historical justice and settle scores with the past was very much a secondary justification (Szczerbiak 2002, pp. 563–565, 2003, pp. 41–45). The three parties quickly agreed a joint draft law, which was to become the basis for debate in the special parliamentary commission, and were able to reject all of the Democratic Left Alliance's amendments and ensure that the Sejm passed their version of the lustration law in April 1997, with 214 votes in favour, 162 against (virtually all Alliance deputies) and 16 abstentions.

The 1997 lustration law contained a number of provisions (Sejm RP 1997). First, all elected state officials and other senior functionaries from the rank of deputy provincial governor up to ministers, the prime minister and the President, parliamentary candidates, judges, and leading figures in the public mass media were required to submit written declarations stating whether or not they had consciously worked for or collaborated with the communist security services at any point from 1944 to 1990. The law was thus directed only at former communist spies, not party officials, and was, therefore, an example of lustration without de-communisation. Second, all statements denying collaboration were transferred to a state prosecutor, the so-called Public Interest Spokesman (Rzecznik Interesu Publicznego: RIP), who used the communist security service secret archives to assess their accuracy. Third, if the prosecutor found evidence that the lustration declaration was false, the public official was to be tried before a special lustration court, which would determine the veracity of the statement. It was originally envisaged that this would be drawn from a panel of 21 judges recommended by their professional association (and who would themselves first be subject to lustration). The lustration court would have access to the archives of the defence ministry, the internal affairs ministry and the State Security Office. Fourth, office holders or candidates for office who made false statements were banned from public office for ten years. Fifth, verdicts could be appealed, but the appeal court's rulings were legally binding, and anyone found guilty of being a 'lustration liar' had to resign immediately upon the court making judgement (although the lustration process could be re-opened subsequently if the Supreme Court overturned the decision of the appeal court through the so-called 'cassation' process).

The lustration law could still have been blocked if Mr Kwaśniewski had chosen to exercise his veto power, given that the lustration coalition lacked the two-thirds parliamentary majority required at that time to overturn it. The President was dissatisfied with the law because it did not define collaboration narrowly enough for him; he still wanted it to exclude military intelligence and counter-intelligence. Nor did it offer all citizens access to their communist security service files, which critics argued that Mr Kwaśniewski wanted so that former security service operatives would have the opportunity to view what had been retained about their activities in their files before submitting a lustration declaration and, more generally, because it would make the law unworkable. Nevertheless, in spite of pressure from his Democratic Left Alliance allies, Mr Kwaśniewki signed it into law in June 1997, ahead of the parliamentary election scheduled for September of that year.

Why did Mr Kwaśniewski decide not to veto the lustration bill? It may have been for a purely Machiavellian reason: that he foresaw the difficulties there would be in finding sufficient judges to serve in the special lustration court (see below) and did not, therefore, believe that it would ever actually come into force. However, just (if not more) important was the fact that, following his narrow 1995 election victory, Mr Kwaśniewski had been vigorously pursuing a strategy of trying to present himself as the 'President of all Poles', thereby attempting to broaden his base of political support. Signing the lustration bill into law was thus a very dramatic and visible way of demonstrating his independence from his Democratic Left Alliance base. At the same time, Mr Kwaśniewski deprived his political enemies of the opportunity to portray him as simply exploiting his veto power to protect his political allies from having their (alleged) close links with the communist security services exposed.

The lustration law becomes operational

However, due to organisational difficulties in establishing the lustration court, the process did not actually take effect until 1999. The 1997 law initially proved unworkable because it was impossible to find 21 judges willing to conduct lustration trials and be involved in passing such sensitive moral and political judgements (Podemski 1997; Pietkiewicz 1998; Misztal 1999, p. 51). There were a number of possible explanations for this. First, some commentators saw judges as very much part of the old system and therefore intrinsically hostile to the idea of exposing secret service collaborators. Second, lustration was a very controversial piece of legislation, and most judges may simply not have wanted to become involved in making what could be viewed as highly 'political' judgements. Third, many of the victims of lustration would be members of the legal profession, and judges may have been motivated by a sense of professional solidarity. Fourth, they were not consulted about the shape of the law but simply instructed to implement it. Their refusal to co-operate with the legislation can thus be seen, in part at least, as a desire to protect their prestige and social standing. Whatever their motives, only 11 of the required 21 judges agreed to serve on the new lustration court.

The problem was solved, and the lustration law made workable, following the election in September 1997 of the right-wing Solidarity Electoral Action (Akcja Wyborcza Solidarność: AWS) grouping, which formed a coalition government with the Freedom Union as its junior partner. Solidarity Electoral Action was a broad and somewhat amorphous electoral conglomerate of 30 centre-right and right-wing parties and political groupings led by the Solidarity trade union. It had made the need to secure a more comprehensive break with the communist past an important part of its election programme and included many of the parties and individuals that had attempted to introduce more radical lustration and de-communisation measures in previous parliaments. Consequently, in June 1998 the Sejm amended the law so that the Warsaw District Appeal Court simply assumed the role of the lustration court.

The 1998 amendments also introduced three other significant changes that strengthened the law. First, its scope was widened quite substantially to include all barristers, bringing the total number of officials subject to lustration to approximately 20,000 (Kroner 1998a). Second, a new procedure was introduced allowing Polish members of parliament to initiate lustration procedures directly themselves through what became known as the 'parliamentary denunciation' (donos parlamentarny), whereby they could demand the investigation of particular individuals. Third, and most significantly, the role and powers of the Public Interest Spokesman were clarified and strengthened. The original version of the lustration law envisaged the Spokesman as a kind of 'postman' who simply delivered the relevant documents to the court and indicated where he had certain doubts but then essentially left the rest of the process in its hands. As a result of the 1998 amendments, the Spokesman became the key figure in charge of the entire lustration process, determining who would appear before the lustration court and when. In other words, the Spokesman was transformed into a kind of lustration prosecutor: analysing the statements, collecting documents, interrogating witnesses and initiating trials. The Spokesman was to be a senior judge (or retired judge) appointed for a six-year period (the 1998 amendments extended this from four) by the Chairman of the Supreme Court.

Mr Kwaśniewski made one further attempt to challenge the lustration law by referring some of its provisions to the constitutional tribunal, but in an October 1998 ruling it declared these to be in line with the Polish Constitution. However, in a separate November 1998 verdict in response to a series of motions from Democratic Left Alliance parliamentary deputies, the tribunal also clarified what represented 'collaboration' with the communist security services in a way that shifted the burden of proof significantly to the advantage of the accused and made it much more difficult for the Public Interest Spokesman to prove that someone was a lustration liar. Specifically, it stipulated a number of conditions that had to be fulfilled for collaboration to have occurred: namely, that there had to be proof that it was secret, conscious and active, and was not limited to a declaration of intent but involved the undertaking of specific activities, including maintaining regular contacts with, and gathering operational materials in the form of information reports for, the communist security services (Kroner 1998b;

Grzelak 2005, pp. 157–158). Similarly, the Supreme Court's October 2000 verdict in the case of Marian Jurczyk[11] introduced an additional hurdle: that the information submitted by a secret collaborator had to be 'useful' to the relevant state organs (Gadrocki 2001).

Nalepa (2008), who distinguishes between two types of lustration system, categorised the Polish law as an example of a so-called 'confession-based truth revelation procedure' (CTR) that gives the target of lustration a chance to self-report before any charges are presented by a prosecutor. Confession-based lustration thus targets only collaboration with the communist regime by an informer or agent that was kept secret from the public, not open membership or leadership of the communist party. Other examples of these kinds of systems were Estonia, Lithuania and Romania. Nalepa distinguishes these from 'accusation-based truth revelation procedures' (ATRs) that make specific accusations relying on evidence of collaboration with the former regime from archival and other sources. Examples of these kinds of systems included Bulgaria, the Czech Republic and Hungary.

According to his typology of what he terms 'lustration systems', David (2006a and 2011), on the other hand, classified the Polish model as an example of a *reconciliatory* system, which institutionalises forgiveness and gives those in public employment a second chance; or, rather, *semi-reconciliatory*, because, while it resembled the South African Truth and Reconciliation process (which exchanged amnesty of perpetrators for truth), in so far as the Polish law facilitated the access of collaborators to leading public offices in exchange for disclosure, it did not provide a wider forum for the country to come to terms with the past, thus also performing a reconciliatory function (David 2006a, p. 360).[12] However, in contrast to simple *inclusive* systems, whereby a public official could, under certain circumstances (generally a bargain to exchange the retention of public office for the revelation of truth about their past) or their own election, remain in their position despite past collaborations,[13] in the Polish semi-reconciliatory system, a person could only remain in office on condition of *demonstrating a change in their behaviour* by making inclusion conditional upon the individual's *own* public revelation of past collaboration.[14] The only sanction applied was for submission of a false statement, and the lustration did not impose any automatic sanctions for having worked for or collaborated with the security services unless the individual attempted to conceal this information. In the case of elected officials, it was then up to voters to decide whether they still wanted to support an individual who had admitted to such links. The system thereby sought to avoid the charge that it was applying collective guilt retrospectively.[15]

The first Public Interest Spokesman, retired judge Bogusław Nizieński, was appointed in October 1998 (Kroner 1998c). During his six-year term between 1998 and 2004, nearly 26,686 candidates or occupants of public offices were required to file lustration declarations (Sejm RP 2005, p. 8), and Mr Nizieński and his two deputies investigated 18,714 (70 per cent) of these (Sejm RP 2005, p. 15). Two hundred individuals admitted to having been communist security service agents or collaborators (Sejm RP 2005, p. 16), while court cases were initiated against a further 153 whom the Public Interest Spokesman suspected of having submitted false lustration declarations (Sejm RP 2005, p. 28). Of these, the lustration court issued 100 final judgements: in 63 cases the accused were found to have been lustration liars, 24 were cleared and 13 were discontinued (Sejm RP 2005, p. 35). There were ten cases of so-called 'self-lustration', whereby individuals who felt that they had been wrongly accused of collaboration could initiate court cases themselves in order to clear their names, which included five parliamentary deputies and three Senators (Sejm RP 2005, pp. 30–32). In April 1999, Mr Nizieński was also asked by deputies from the Confederation for an Independent Poland-Patriotic Camp (Konfederacja Polski Niepodległej-Obóz Patriotyczny: KPN-OP) faction (a breakaway from Mr Moczulski's party), who had defected from Solidarity Electoral Action the previous year, to investigate the veracity of the lustration statements of several parliamentary deputies, including the then Solidarity Electoral Action prime minister Jerzy Buzek, under the parliamentary denunciation procedure; but, due to the lack of specific and credible evidence of a false declaration, he declined to pursue these cases.

The individuals against whom the Public Interest Spokesman initiated court cases also included some high-profile figures. The first such case was Solidarity Electoral Action deputy prime minister and interior minister Janusz Tomaszewski, who was forced to resign by his political grouping when the Public Interest Spokesman questioned the veracity of his statement and initiated a lustration trial against him in September 1999. Mr Tomaszewski's case was eventually discontinued, but two other members of the Buzek government were found by the courts to be lustration liars: Solidarity Electoral Action-nominated deputy transport minister Krzysztof Luks and Freedom Union-nominated deputy defence minister Robert Mrozewicz. Other high-profile lustration cases included two former Democratic Left Alliance prime ministers, Mr Oleksy and Włodzimierz Cimoszewicz; Democratic Left Alliance justice minister Jerzy Jaskierna; Marek Wagner, head of the chancellery of Democratic Left Alliance prime minister Leszek Miller (who succeeded Mr Buzek in 2001); and, discussed above, former legendary Solidarity activist and independent Senator Marian Jurczyk. High-profile figures who took advantage of the law's provision for 'self-lustration' in order to clear their names included several individuals who appeared on the infamous 'Macierewicz list', such as Mr Chrzanowski, Mr Moczulski and Peasant Party justice minister Aleksander Bentkowski. In all of these cases (except for Mr Moczulski's, which, at the time of writing, is still to be resolved), either the individuals concerned were cleared of lying in the lustration declarations or their cases were discontinued, often after extremely lengthy legal processes involving (sometimes several) appeals.

The 18 candidates who contested the October 2000 presidential election were lustrated in accordance with a separate, special procedure, and, due to the short space of time between the registration of candidates and polling day, the whole lustration process was telescoped into a much shorter timetable. There was no 'clarification phase', which normally lasted for several months while the Public

Interest Spokesman gathered documents, interrogated witnesses and, on the basis of this, decided whether or not to introduce a motion for trial. Rather, the lustration court was supplied directly with the relevant documentation by the various ministries involved and the State Security Office, with both the Spokesman and the candidate's lawyers only having access to the files at the last moment.

One of the main candidates, former finance and foreign minister Andrzej Olechowski, admitted to having been a secret communist security service informer while working in international economic institutions, something of which he had never made a secret. In the event, Mr Olechowski finished second, with 17.3 per cent of the vote, which he used as a springboard to launch the Civic Platform (Platforma Obywatelska: PO) grouping in January 2001 together with Solidarity Electoral Action and Freedom Union defectors. Lustration trials were also initiated against both Mr Kwaśniewski and Mr Wałęsa. The Public Interest Spokesman accused Mr Kwaśniewski of having lied in his statement when, in August 2000, the State Security Office forwarded documents to the lustration court suggesting that the incumbent President might have been a secret service collaborator codenamed 'Alek'. Both Mr Kwaśniewski and Mr Wałęsa, who faced ongoing accusations that he had been a communist security service collaborator (examined in greater detail in Chapter 5) because he featured on the 'Macierewicz list', were cleared of having submitted false declarations, although the court did not completely rule out the possibility that the incumbent President was agent 'Alek', while (as we shall see) historians later questioned the reliability of the former Solidarity leader's verdict.

The 1998 file access law

As discussed above, the issue of how to establish and manage a publicly accessible archive of the communist security services ran alongside, was often intertwined with, and was eventually addressed at the same time as that of lustration during the 1990s. At the end of 1998, the Solidarity Election Action-dominated parliament voted to establish the Institute for National Remembrance (Instytut Pamięci Narodowej: IPN), which, apart from investigating Nazi and communist crimes and informing and educating the Polish public about the country's recent past, was set up as the custodian of the communist security service files (Sejm RP 1998). All the relevant documents were transferred to the Institute from the interior ministry, the State Security Office and the Military Information Service (Wojskowe Służby Informacyjne: WSI), although only a fraction of the extant secret archives (which, themselves, were only a small proportion of the original communist security service records, many of which were destroyed during the transition) were opened up to the public.

The 1998 law granted researchers, journalists and historians access to the secret archives, and citizens who had been victims of secret police invigilation ('pokrzywdzony' – literally 'persecuted', 'harmed' or 'wronged') access to their own files. Those who were not felt to be victims of communist persecution – or who were, but had also worked as informers for, or collaborators with, the communist security services – could not have access to their files (even if they had themselves been spied upon by the regime). However, those whose files could not be found, or where there was evidence indicating their collaboration, received the same letter, saying that, according to the Institute's records, they were not victims. While the intention of this provision was to prevent former security services collaborators from checking the contents of the archives before submitting their lustration declarations it also, as Dudek (2011, p. 43) put it, 'locat[ed] the IPN in the role of a quasi-court which, by granting (or denying) someone the status of persecuted, basically passed a judgement on their past, issuing a kind of certificate of morality'.

Mr Kwaśniewski attempted to veto the 1998 law on the grounds that file access should be available to everyone, not just those whom the Institute deemed victims of communist persecution: a move that critics argued would allow public office holders or candidates for office to access their files to find out what information was stored on them before completing lustration declarations. However, the government was able to overturn his veto in December 1998 with the support of the opposition Peasant Party. Nonetheless, as in the case of the 1997 lustration law, the implementation of this file access legislation was delayed following difficulties in agreeing a procedure to elect, and then identifying a suitable candidate to act as, its chairman. Amending the law to stipulate that the Institute's chairman should be elected by a qualified three-fifths, rather than simple, parliamentary majority was one of the Peasant Party's conditions for voting to overturn the presidential veto. In fact, the Institute did not actually become operational until June 2000, when parliament elected independent centre-right Senator Leon Kieres as its first chairman for a five-year term. Nonetheless, by 2005 some 14,000 individuals had been able to access their files (Stan 2009b, p. 88).

Attempts to weaken the lustration law

Following the 2001 parliamentary election – which returned the Democratic Left Alliance to office, until 2003 once again in coalition with the Peasant Party – there were various ongoing attempts to weaken and restrict the scope of the lustration law and modify its procedure, which partly involved reviving the amendments that the party and Mr Kwaśniewski (who was re-elected as President in 2000) had promoted during the 1997 debates (Grzelak 2005, pp. 179–197). Some of the amendments introduced by Mr Kwaśniewski in October 2001 proved to be relatively uncontroversial, such as scrapping the parliamentary denunciation provisions; obliging the lustration prosecutor to inform suspects about any doubts that he had about declarations in advance of their trial; and requiring the lustration court to pass a clear guilty or not guilty verdict, and not to set aside a case for lack of evidence. However, they also included proposals to limit the scope of the law by, for example, once again attempting to exclude those who worked for military and counter-intelligence from its provisions. Moreover, inspired by the October 2000 Supreme Court judgement in the Jurczyk case – which, as noted above, shifted the emphasis considerably towards a more substantive understanding of collaboration – Mr Kwaśniewski's bill also tried to narrow the definition of the latter so that it had to be 'genuine, harmful and conscious' and not faked ('pozorny') to protect those individuals who only 'pretended' to collaborate, despite fulfilling all of the formal requirements expected from the security services. During the bill's committee stage, another very imprecise clause was introduced, which many feared would make the lustration unworkable by defining the scope of collaboration even more narrowly, so that it only encompassed conscious actions with the intention of providing information damaging to the Church, independent trade unions, the underground opposition or the Polish nation, or which threatened the personal and civil liberties, freedoms or property of others.

However, when in January 2002 the bill returned to the Sejm, where the Democratic Left Alliance did not have an outright majority, it rejected these amendments when the Peasant Party refused to support its coalition partner and voted to preserve the original definition of collaboration. Nonetheless, the amendments were re-instated by the Alliance-dominated Senate and then finally accepted in February when the ruling party persuaded deputies from the radical agrarian Self-Defence (Samoobrona) party to support the amended version of the law when it returned to the Sejm for final approval. In the event, in June 2002 the constitutional tribunal struck down the Senate amendments on procedural-legislative rather than substantive grounds, arguing that in voting for them the second chamber had exceeded its jurisdiction.

Unbowed, the Democratic Left Alliance immediately re-introduced its amendments in the Senate: once again excluding military intelligence and counter-intelligence from the definition of collaboration, and restoring the proviso that that it had to be genuine and not faked, but the party dropped the proposal that the information provided had to be damaging to certain groups and endanger civil liberties and freedoms. The amendments were approved by the Sejm in September 2002 when enough deputies from the Self-Defence parliamentary caucus (which was divided almost equally on the issue) voted with the Alliance and gave them a majority. However, in May 2003 the constitutional tribunal once again struck down the amendments exempting collaboration with military intelligence and counter-intelligence from the scope of the lustration law. Following tensions within the coalition that led to its break-up in March 2003, internal divisions within the ruling party, and relentless corruption allegations that led to the resignation of Democratic Left Alliance prime minister Leszek Miller in May 2004, the party did not make any further attempts to amend the lustration law.

However, at the same time, a number of other developments during the early to mid-2000s, examined in more detail in Chapter 4, once again brought the issues of lustration and communist security service file access to the fore and led to calls for strengthening rather than weakening existing laws and truth-revelation procedures or introducing more radical ones. Indeed, the very act of opening up the communist security service files by the Institute of National

Remembrance led to pressure for further truth revelation. The process started to gather momentum in December 2004 when it was revealed that the Institute's archives suggested that the Mazowiecki government's media spokesman Małgorzata Niezabitowski had collaborated with the communist security services as a secret informer (Niezabitowska 2004). Then, in February 2005, the allegedly slow pace at which the Institute's files were being made available, and its apparent failure to fulfil its mandate and publicly name secret agents, prompted journalist Bronisław Wildstein to disclose a 'working' list of 240,000 persons on whom secret files existed (including former agents, military intelligence, secret informers, prospective candidates for informers, and victims) and to post it on the Internet. The list contained no information on whether those named were victims or informers and no details regarding their date of birth or place of residence that would identify them. As well as leading to heavy criticisms of the Institute for allowing such a security breach, the publication of the 'Wildstein list' also increased pressure on the Polish authorities to open up the communist security service secret archives more widely (Kublik and Czuchnowski 2005; *Rzeczpospolita* 2005).[16]

Although they were not covered by the lustration law, calls for further lustration and file access were also spurred on by the emergence of links between prominent Catholic clergymen and the communist security services. These began with the revelation by the Institute of National Remembrance in April 2005 that Father Konrad Hejmo, an acquaintance of Pope John Paul II who for 20 years was the main link between the Polish-born pontiff and Polish pilgrims visiting Rome, had been a communist spy. At a press conference, the Institute's director Leon Kieres said that it had proof that Father Hejmo, a Dominican monk, had collaborated with the Polish communist secret police in the 1980s under the codenames 'Hejnal' and 'Dominik' (Kaczyński *et al.* 2005). News of the allegations broke at a time when Poles were still mourning Pope John Paul II, who had died three weeks earlier, and Father Hejmo had played a central role in organising the pilgrimage of up to one million Poles who flocked to Rome for the former pontiff's funeral. A series of further revelations about links between Catholic clergymen and the communist security services followed, and in October 2006 the Catholic Church convened an Episcopal Historical Commission to examine the invigilation of clergymen by the communist security services, following the earlier decision to form these in a number of local Dioceses. The issue of lustration of the Catholic Church peaked in January 2007 when the new Archbishop of Warsaw, Stanisław Wielgus, resigned a few days after his consecration (but immediately prior to his public investiture) following revelations in the Institute's files about his collaboration with the communist security services, which he had initially denied (Terlikowski 2007).[17]

The (more radical) 2006 lustration and file access law

The September 2005 parliamentary election saw the election of the right-wing Law and Justice (Prawo i Sprawiedliwość: PiS) party, which was formed in 2001 and led by Jarosław Kaczyński to capitalise on the popularity of his twin brother Lech, who had served briefly as justice minister in the Solidarity Electoral Action-led government in 2000–2001 and was also elected Polish President in October 2005 (Jarosław also became prime minister in May 2006). Both Law and Justice and Mr Kaczyński promised a radical reconstruction of the post-1989 Polish Third Republic state, which they considered to be inherently weak and controlled by corrupt cliques, and its replacement with a strong and moral 'Fourth Republic'. (The Fourth Republic project is discussed in greater detail in Chapter 4.) Broadening the scope of lustration was seen by many as a key element of this project of moral and political renewal. Following an uneasy period of minority government, in May 2006 Law and Justice agreed a coalition with two smaller radical parties: Self-Defence and the clerical-nationalist League of Polish Families (Liga Polskich Rodzin: LPR). The League was an enthusiastic advocate of expanding the scope of lustration and file access, while Self-Defence, which was more agnostic about the issue (as noted above, the party was divided in its attitudes towards the Democratic Left Alliance's attempts to water down the lustration law in the previous parliament) but willing to go along with Law and Justice's plans.

Consequently, the Polish parliament passed a series of amendments – first at the end of 2006 and then, in a revised version after President Kaczyński refused to approve the original, at the beginning of 2007 – which led to a radical expansion of the scope of the lustration law. The debates on this law are examined in greater detail in Chapter 4, but, as we shall see, although the legislation was based largely on the Law and Justice draft, it was passed with cross-party support that encompassed all of the main parliamentary groupings except for the Democratic Left Alliance. This included Civic Platform, by now the main opposition grouping, which narrowly lost the 2005 parliamentary election and whose leader Donald Tusk was defeated by Lech Kaczyński in the presidential poll second round run-off, having finished ahead of him in the first round of voting. Indeed, although Civic Platform was evolving in an increasingly liberal-centrist direction, it had, if anything, adopted a more radical approach towards lustration and file access in the run-up to the 2005 elections, when more right-wing conservative elements were in the ascendant within the party. However, although there was an authentic and ideologically committed radical pro-lustration wing within Civic Platform, notably its parliamentary caucus leader and prime ministerial candidate Jan Rokita, the party's stance was arguably driven mainly by a strategic concern not to be outbid in a context where the political climate in the country was radicalised by a backlash against (and fear of being associated with) corrupt post-communist political and business elites (discussed in greater detail in Chapter 4).

The original revised law that was finally approved by parliament in October 2006 in many ways marked a radical departure from the provisions of previous Polish lustration and file access legislation. First, in order to streamline the verification process, the Public Interest Spokesman's office was abolished and replaced by a special lustration department within the Institute of National Remembrance that determined which declarations raised suspicion and warranted investigation. It was felt that the provisions of the previous law, whereby during lustration proceedings the Spokesman conducted the initial screening and then directed questions to the Institute, had slowed the lustration process down too much.

Second, lustration declarations and the process of determining whether or not someone was a 'lustration liar' were to disappear. Instead, the Institute would issue every person with a certificate ('zaświadczenie') about what kind of documents were held on them in the communist security service archival records. Specifically, these certificates would state whether the security services had regarded the person undergoing lustration as a so-called 'personal information source' (osobowe źródło informacji: OZI), not just as a secret collaborator (Tajny Współpracownik: TW) but also as an operational contact (Kontakt Operacyjny: KO), functionary, official contact or consultant. In other words, these categories included people from whom communist security functionaries had obtained information but who might not have consented, or even been aware that they were qualified as a 'personal information source' (Kaczyński 2006). Those persons in certain positions, or fulfilling functions, requiring public trust, or aspiring to hold them, would be issued with such a certificate ex officio – which could then be used as a basis for evaluating their moral qualifications – and private individuals could request them as well. As lustration declarations would no longer exist, there would be no sanctions for individuals who failed to reveal involvement in the communist security services. Rather, the body appointing or employing the person in question – or the voters, in the case of elected officials – would decide whether someone who was described in their certificate as a communist security service agent or informer should occupy the public function in question. For those occupying these positions, such certificates, together with any documents that related to them, would be held in a publicly available register, which every citizen would have the right to see, and be published on the Internet.

Third, although there would no longer be a special lustration court, there were still two possible sources of legal redress available to those who wanted to appeal against what was written about them in the certificates. If someone felt that the Institute had acted improperly from a procedural point of view, they could appeal to its governing bodies and then to the administrative court. On the other hand, if someone disagreed with the contents of the archival files, then they could appeal to the civil court. In the case of a successful appeal, the court judgement would be added to the certificates, but the contents of the communist security service files and the certificates themselves would not be amended.

Fourth, it significantly broadened the scope of existing rules on disclosing collaboration and expanded the categories of persons covered by the lustration law to encompass all 'persons filling a public function', an estimated 400,000–700,000 individuals (the exact number was not clear). This included, for the first time, teachers and the heads of educational institutions; University lecturers and senior administrators; journalists, editors and publishers of both public and private media; diplomats; legal counsellors, notaries, tax advisers and certified accountants; local councillors; the heads of state-owned companies and those in which the state treasury held a share; members of the management and supervisory boards of companies listed on the stock exchange; senior national state administration and local government officials; and employees of, among others, para-state bodies such as the Supreme Audit Chamber (Naczelna Izba Kontroli: NIK), the National Insurance Fund (Zakład Ubezpieczeń Społecznych: ZUS) and the Agricultural Social Insurance Fund (Kasa Rolniczego Ubezpieczenia Społecznego: KRUS), as well as the Institute for National Remembrance itself (Cienski 2007; Gardyniuk 2007a, 2007b).[18]

Fifth, the Institute would publish lists of persons registered as communist security service functionaries and their 'personal information sources' with an explanation of why the latter appeared in the archives. The first list was to be published within three months of the new law coming into effect and then updated at least once every six months.

Sixth, following an October 2005 constitutional tribunal ruling that former communist security service personnel had a right to see the contents of their own files (but not of those whom they invigilated), the law removed the status of 'persecuted' as the only category of persons able to view their own communist security service files, although the new law also contained a clause aimed at preventing former collaborators from accessing such documents.

In November 2006, President Lech Kaczyński signed the new draft into law, but, reflecting concerns among some Law and Justice and Solidarity-linked figures that the new certification system did not give those individuals who were found to be 'personal information sources' sufficient opportunity to appeal against these decisions, he agreed to do so only on condition that a series of significant amendments were passed. First, in place of the Institute of National Remembrance certificates outlining the contents of the archives on candidates for public office, lustration statements – in which such candidates or office holders declared whether or not they had secretly collaborated with the communist security services – would be brought back, although these would still be checked by a special lustration prosecutor's department within the Institute rather than the Public Interest Spokesman. Second, penalties for submitting false lustration declarations would return, as would the use of the criminal procedure if there was a discrepancy between the contents of the files and the individual's lustration declaration or if an individual wanted to appeal against their inclusion in the list of communist secret service collaborators. Third, while the Institute would still be required to publish lists of 'personal information sources', to ensure that 'real' agents were not lost in the mass of names, these would be divided into four registers, covering secret collaborators, security service functionaries, communist party functionaries, and those who had been invigilated. These amendments were approved, together with two others, which extended the scope of lustration into several additional categories, including bailiffs, other academics, members of the supervisory boards of companies with specific importance to public order and state security, members of local and national examination commissions, and National Bank of Poland managers, and introduced penalties for failing to submit a lustration declaration in the required time, leading to automatic loss of public function.

However, the new lustration law, which came into force in March 2007, was met with vigorous protests from the 'Third Republic' political and cultural elites. A number of prominent liberal politicians – notably MEP, former foreign minister and one-time leader of the Freedom Union Bronisław Geremek, at the time representing its successor, the Democrats (Demokraci), in the European Parliament – joined journalists and academics in refusing to comply with the new law and submit the required revised lustration declarations.

Then, in May 2007, the constitutional tribunal gutted the provisions of the new law when it ruled that large sections of it violated the Constitution (Czuchnowski and Wroński 2007; Olczyk and Sopińska 2007). First, it ruled that the definition of who held public offices was too broad, and significantly limited the number of categories undergoing lustration. It ruled that the provisions of the law should not include any academics employed by private universities (and only senior academic managers in public higher education institutions should be included); heads of state primary and middle schools, and private schools; the heads of private companies; journalists; private TV and radio producers; the publishers and editors of private journals; bailiffs; statutory auditors; tax advisers; and members of sports governing bodies. Second, it struck down provisions that, it argued, defined the state security organs too broadly: deleting the state censor's office and office for religions from the list of communist-era institutions defined as being part of the security services; removing references to 'personal information sources' from the law's preamble; and tightening up the definition of collaboration in line with its earlier judgements, which stipulated that this had to have 'materialised'. Third, it ruled that removing elected officials and lawyers from public office for failing to submit a lustration declaration was unconstitutional. Fourth, it also banned as unconstitutional the proposed publication by the Institute for National Remembrance of a catalogue of so-called 'secret collaborators' and 'operational contacts'[19] on the Internet. Fifth, it struck down the clause that limited former security service informers' access to their files.[20] However, the tribunal did not question the provisions for lustrating candidates for senior offices, or those that required the loss of office for anyone found to be submitting a false lustration declaration. As Nalepa (2013, p. 202) put it, 'even with the provisions struck down by the Tribunal, the Institute still expanded its powers compared to what they were under the 1997 law'.

Lustration and file access become less salient

After 2007, the issue of lustration and file access appeared to become less salient in Polish politics. To some extent, this was due to the constitutional tribunal's gutting of the new legislation, which created some confusion as to what the new law's precise provisions were, in the short term at least. The lustration process continued: by the end of 2015, 371,579 declarations had been submitted to the Institute of National Remembrance's lustration department, of which 56,000 had been verified (IPN 2017, p. 207). It continued to refer cases to the lustration court, but these involved fewer well-known figures and did not generate the same publicity, focusing mainly on local councillors, public officials (especially in the foreign office) and lawyers. The last really high-profile lustration trial was that of Law and Justice finance minister (and, at one time, deputy leader of Civic Platform) Zyta Gilowska in 2006; she stood down from her post temporarily until she was cleared by the lustration court of having submitted a false declaration. However, by extending lustration to such a large number of categories but without creating mechanisms by which it could deal with them effectively, the new law simply meant that the Lustration Bureau was overwhelmed, which also contributed to killing off lustration as an issue in public debate. Meanwhile, the Catholic Church's Historical Commission ended its work in 2008, having earlier concluded that although some 16 members of the Episcopate were found to be registered on the communist security service files, no current senior clergymen had actually been collaborators (Dudek 2016).

This decline in salience was partly an inevitable by-product of generational change, given the passage of time since the collapse of communism. However, it was also because an early parliamentary election in October 2007 saw Civic Platform oust Law and Justice from government, with Mr Tusk becoming prime minister; in 2011 he also became the first incumbent premier in post-1989 Poland to secure re-election. As noted above, Civic Platform had supported the 2006 lustration and file access law, but after 2007 downplayed the issue as part of a conscious effort to come to terms and reach an accommodation with the liberal-left cultural and media establishment, which, as we saw, had always been extremely wary of – and, in some cases, openly hostile to – these processes, especially the more radical versions. The constitutional tribunal's May 2007 ruling and the controversy leading up it to was, in many ways, a turning point for Civic Platform in its relationship with the Third Republic establishment. With so many individuals from the post-1989 cultural and opinion-forming elites protesting against the requirement to submit lustration declarations, a very deep caesura emerged between Law and Justice and the opponents of lustration, with Civic Platform coming under enormous pressure to weaken and distance itself from the pro-lustration stance, even though it had co-authored the 2006 law which generated these protests. Partly, it was no longer profitable, either ideologically or pragmatically, for Civic Platform to pursue the issue. Whereas, in the mid-2000s, the party still had two opponents on its right and left flanks, with Law and Justice becoming a monopolist on issues such as lustration and anti-communism more generally, Civic Platform needed to extend its appeal to the ex-communist left and took over the Democratic Left Alliance's role as the representative of these anti-lustration social constituencies. At the same time, the group of ideological conservative supporters of radical lustration within Civic Platform who had worked with Law and Justice on the 2006 law lost importance and became increasingly marginalised within the party by the more pragmatic, liberal-managerial elements led by Mr Tusk, especially after Mr Rokita left its governing bodies and did not even stand as a Civic Platform candidate in the

2007 election. In fact, with the Gilowska trial showing how risky lustration could be for the party too, after 2007 Law and Justice also tended to avoid the issue.

The main controversy and legislative initiatives concerned the governance of the Institute of Public Remembrance. In 2010 the Civic Platform government amended the law regulating the Institute's work, which it hoped would 'de-politicise' it by making it easier to replace its then chairman, Janusz Kurtyka (Gmyz 2010), who was heavily criticised by the party and anti-lustration liberal-left media for allegedly being too closely politically aligned with Law and Justice.[21] The Institute's governing College was replaced by a new Council, whose members had to be professionally qualified and who would nominate a new chairman from a shortlist comprising nominees from University history departments. The latter were criticised by proponents of lustration for failing to properly engage with the issue of the communist past, particularly the role of the former security services.[22] In fact, Mr Kurtyka, together with Lech Kaczyński and 94 others, including many leading Polish officials, died tragically in the April 2010 plane crash in Smolensk in western Russia before the law took effect. (Civic Platform candidate Bronisław Komorowski was elected to replace Mr Kaczyński as President in the snap June/July 2010 presidential election.) The Institute's new chairman Łukasz Kamiński, elected for a five-year term in 2011, was felt to be less closely aligned with Law and Justice, although criticised by some on the political right for further downgrading lustration as one of the Institute's work priorities.

In the October 2015 elections, Law and Justice was returned to office as the first party in post-1989 Poland to secure an outright parliamentary majority (although he was still party leader, Jarosław Kaczyński did not occupy any formal state offices), while earlier that year, in May, its candidate Andrzej Duda defeated incumbent and odds-favourite Mr Komorowski. However, the Law and Justice government did not return to the issues of lustration and file access, other than a pledge to open the restricted access files, which were meant to contain documents with national security implications (but, some commentators speculated, were used as a pretext to ensure that certain files were not made publicly available), and a fairly modest proposal to extend the scope of lustration to sports associations. The main changes once again concerned amendments to the law governing the Institute's work, with the Council replaced by a new College, which elected Jarosław Szarek, whose vision of how the organisation should function was closer to Law and Justice's, as its new chairman.

Nonetheless, lustration and communist security service file access continued to retain their capacity to flare up as major political issues. For example, a group of journalists linked to the right-wing, pro-lustration *Gazeta Polska* newspaper used the communist security service archives as the basis for a series of books on the media, politicians and the security services, which, they argued, revealed the phenomena of the so-called 'departmental children' ('resortowe dzieci'). These were the new post-1989 elites that had an opportunity to rise to prominent positions in Poland's post-communist media, business, political and academic elites (undeservedly in the authors' view) due to their family links with the previous communist regime, particularly its security services (Kania et al. 2013, 2015, 2016).

However, the capacity of the lustration and file access issue to continue to recur in political debate was perhaps best seen in the case of the continuing allegations of Lech Wałęsa's collaboration with the communist security services. The issue re-surfaced dramatically in June 2008 when two historians working for the Institute of National Remembrance, Sławomir Cenckiewicz and Piotr Gontarczyk (2008), published (with Mr Kurtyka's blessing) an academic monograph which Mr Wałęsa's opponents said provided compelling new circumstantial evidence suggesting that the former Solidarity leader and President had been recruited as a communist security service informer codenamed 'Bolek' while under arrest during the December 1970 shipyard workers' strike and collaborated with them in the early 1970s. Similarly, in March 2009 Paweł Zyzak (2009), who had worked as an intern archivist at the Institute, published a biography of Lech Wałęsa based on his Master's thesis at the Jagiellonian University, echoing these allegations and citing anonymous sources who claimed that the former Solidarity leader had collaborated with the communist security in the 1970s.[23] The 2010 amendment to the law regulating the Institute's work was one of the side-effects of the political debates surrounding the publication of these books, especially the one by Cenckiewicz and Gontarczyk (Gmyz 2010). Then, in February 2016, the Institute released copies of original agent 'Bolek' files hidden illegally in the home of General Czesław Kiszczak, a one-time high-ranking security services officer and former communist interior minister who died in November 2015. These appeared to fill in the missing pages from the incomplete 'Bolek' files and confirmed unequivocally that Mr Wałęsa had collaborated with the communist security services in the 1970s as a paid secret collaborator. The significance of the recurrence of debates surrounding Mr Wałęsa's communist security service collaboration is discussed in more detail in Chapter 5.

Conclusions

Poland is, therefore, an archetypal case of the phenomenon of late and recurring lustration. It began with an initial communist-forgiving approach and avoidance of the lustration and file issue in the early 1990s, exemplified by the so-called 'thick line' policy that avoided radical transitional justice measures. However, the issue did not fade from public memory, retaining a remarkable ability to endure and remain on the political agenda, with the following years punctuated by various attempts to renew efforts aimed at securing lustration and file access. Despite various attempts to pass lustration laws in the early to mid-1990s, a formalised, functioning lustration programme came late to Poland and was only finally adopted and became operational at the end of the decade. A mild lustration law was passed in 1997 and legislation to open up communist secret service file access approved in 1998, with the two finally taking effect in 1999 and 2000, respectively, following further amendments. Attempts were then made to extend these truth-revelation processes in the mid-2000s, culminating in the passage of a more radical lustration and file access law in 2006, which significantly expanded their scope, although many of its provisions were not fully enacted and were subsequently struck down by the constitutional tribunal in 2007. Although the issue of communist security service collaboration declined in political salience after 2007, it retained the capacity to constantly surface and re-surface in Polish political debates even decades after the collapse of the communist regime. It is this significant delay and, more broadly, the recurrence of the issue in political debates that is one of the most striking features of the development of lustration in Poland, and one that needs explanation and analysis. The Polish case thus provides us with an excellent basis for examining and developing frameworks to explain the phenomenon of 'late' lustration.

Notes

1 'We mark off the past with a thick line. We will be responsible only for what we have done to rescue Poland from the current state of collapse' (Mazowiecki 1989; Domarańczyk 1990, p. 108; Calhoun 2002, p. 499).
2 For attempts to introduce lustration and file access during the Mazowiecki and Bielecki governments, see Grzelak (2005, pp. 17–41).
3 See, for example, Kurski and Semka (1993).
4 For a favourable overview of Mr Olszewski's tenure, see Droszewska (1992).
5 The Democratic Left Alliance emerged at the beginning of the 1990s as an electoral coalition comprising various parties and groupings clustered around Social Democracy of the Polish Republic (Socjaldemokracja Rzeczypospolitej Polskiej: SdRP), formed in 1990 as the direct organisational successor to the former ruling Polish United Workers' Party (Polska Zjednoczona Partia Robotnicza: PZPR), and became a single, unitary party in 1999.
6 The direct organisational successor to the communists' erstwhile agrarian satellite, the United Peasant Party (Zjednoczone Stronnictwo Ludowe: ZSL).
7 See, for example, Osiatynski (1994).
8 See, for example, Tittenbrun (1993, pp. 176–198).
9 See, for example, Król (1996).
10 The term 'centrist' is used here to denote someone adopting a political stance somewhere between a communist-purging (right-wing) and communist-forgiving (left-wing) policy.
11 A former legendary Solidarity activist and leader of the 1989 Szczecin strike that led to the union's formation, and in post-1989 Poland an independent Senator.
12 However, in later work he argues that the Polish system should be described as simply 'reconciliatory'. See David (2011, pp. xi–xii). For more on the similarities and differences between the Polish and South African models, see David (2006b).
13 The model that was, according to David (2006a, pp. 357–359), adopted in Hungary (1994), Romania (1999) and partly in Serbia (2003).
14 According to David (2006a, pp. 361–363), the two other kinds of lustration systems were exclusive systems, where a public official associated with particular departments or activities in the former regime was excluded automatically from certain state positions in the new administration (adopted in Czechoslovakia in 1991, and subsequently the Czech Republic, Bulgaria in 1992, Albania in 1993 and, for some high-ranking public officials, in Serbia in 2003); and mixed systems that gave an opportunity to adopt any or all of the other three strategies, deciding on a case-by-case basis whether

that person would receive tenure or not (adopted in the former GDR following German re-unification).
15 In spite of this, at the beginning of 1999, when the law came into force, the then justice minister Hanna Suchocka began to dismiss regional procurators who had acknowledged their links with the communist security services in their lustration statements and issued an appeal to court chairmen to remove judges who had done so and for the head of the appeal procuracy to do the same. See *Rzeczpospolita* (1999a, 1999b), Krasnowska (1999). In his later classification of 'personnel systems' (of which 'lustration systems' were an East European regional variant), David (2011, pp. 31–32) also adds the category of 'systems of continuation', in which he locates Slovenia and (pre-lustration) Poland.
16 Mr Wildstein (2016) argues that he released the list in order to counter a campaign being run by the anti-lustration media, notably the *Gazeta Wyborcza* daily, to deny journalists access to the security service archives on the grounds that, with a few obsessive exceptions, they were not interested in the contents of these files. Arguing that he always made it clear that it was not a list of security service functionaries and collaborators, he was thus trying (successfully, he claims) to generate interest among journalists in some of the names included on it.
17 In fact, the new lustration law that was passed in 2006 did not encompass clergymen, and the Church was left to deal with the issue through its own internal procedures. Law and Justice deputy Zbigniew Girzyński argued that the reason for this was that

> [w]e knew that we were writing a revolutionary law, anyone who does not understand that will quickly be convinced. It was a question of political caution, why do we need to open up another front? ... our revolution cannot eat us – its children. Anyway, I have the impression that the Church is now [itself] dealing with lustration.
>
> Smoleński (2006)

18 It was estimated that the Institute would be able to process around 40,000–50,000 of these certificates per year. See *Nasz Dziennik* (2006).
19 'Secret collaborator' was the operational name for those individuals who collaborated consciously with the communist security services from 1957 to 1990. 'Operational link' was a special category of collaborators with simplified recruitment procedures created in the 1970s when the security services stepped up their goal of infiltrating the dissident movement. Most of these were conscious collaborators, but, due to simplified recruitment procedures, some of them (those drawn from the communist party and its satellites) may not have known about their secret collaboration (Nalepa 2013, p. 202).
20 Although the Institute continued to reject such applications, citing a different provision in the law which had similar content but which the tribunal did not evaluate.
21 See, for example, Paradowska (2008) and Friszke (2009).
22 See, for example, Zybertowicz (undated, p. 4).
23 The book contained other controversial claims, including one that Mr Wałęsa had allegedly fathered an illegitimate child in the 1960s, which later died by drowning, and escaped his home village and went to work in Gdańsk because of his girlfriend's pregnancy.

Bibliography

Calhoun, N., 2002. The Ideological Dilemma of Lustration in Poland. *East European Politics and Societies*, 16 (2), 494–520.

Calhoun, N. 2004. *Dilemmas of Justice in Eastern Europe's Democratic Transition*. London: Palgrave Macmillan.

Cenckiewicz, S. and Gontarczyk, P., 2008. *SB a Lech Wałęsa. Przyczynek do biografii.* Warsaw: IPN.
Cienski, J., 2007. Polish witch-hunt 'risks business chaos'. *Financial Times*, 14 March.
Czuchnowski, W. and Wroński, P., 2007. Lustracja to nie zemsta. *Gazeta Wyborcza*, 12–13 May.
David, R., 2003. Lustration Laws in Action: The Motives and Evaluation of Lustration Policy in the Czech Republic and Poland (1989–2001). *Law and Social Inquiry*, 28 (2), 387–439.
David, R., 2006a. From Prague to Baghdad: Lustration Systems and Their Political Effects. *Government and Opposition*, 41 (3), 347–372.
David, R., 2006b. In Exchange for Truth: The Polish Lustrations and the South African Amnesty Process. *Polittikon*, 31 (1), 81–99.
David, R., 2011. *Lustration and Transitional Justice: Personnel Systems in the Czech Republic, Hungary and Poland.* Philadelphia: University of Pennsylvania Press.
Domarańczyk, Z., 1990. *100 dni Mazowieckiego.* Warsaw: Wydawnictwo Andrzej Bonarski.
Droszewska, U. 1992. Why Olszewski's Government Was Doomed? *Uncaptive Minds*, 5(2), 93–102.
Dudek, A., 2011. *Instytut: Osobista historia IPN.* Warsaw: Wydawnictwo Czerwona i Czarna.
Dudek, A., 2016. Author interview, 7 June.
Friszke, A. 2009. Jak hartował się radykalizm Kurtyki. *Gazeta Wyborcza*, 8 April.
Gadrocki, L., 2001. Orzecznictwo dla lustracji i lustrowanych. *Rzeczpospolita*, 22 January.
Gardyniuk, A., 2007a. 400 tysięcy osób do sprawdzenia. *Rzeczpospolita*, 27–28 January.
Gardyniuk, A., 2007b. Trudne wyzwanie dla Instytutu Pamięci. *Rzeczpospolita*, 15 February.
Gmyz, G., 2010. IPN według Platformy. *Rzeczposolita*, 19 March.
Grabowska, M., 2004. *Podział postkomunistyczny: Społeczne podstawy polityki w Polsce po 1989 roku.* Warsaw: Wydawnictwo Naukowe Scholar.
Grzelak, P., 2005. *Wojna o lustrację.* Warsaw: Trio.
Holmes, S., 1994. The End of Decommunization. *East European Constitutional Review*, Summer/Fall, 33–36.
Horne, C.M., 2014. The Impact of Lustration on Democratization in Postcommunist Countries. *The International Journal of Transitional Justice*, 8 (3), 496–521.
IPN, 2017. *Informacja o działalności 1 stycznia 2015r-31 grudnia 2016r.* Warsaw: IPN.
Kaczyński, A., 2006. Agenci będą eliminowani. *Rzeczpospolita*, 22–23 July.
Kaczyński, A., Czaczkowska, E.K. and Siennecki, P. 2005. Donosił z Wiecznego Miasta. *Rzeczpospolita*, 28 April.
Kania, D., Targalski, J. and Marosz, M., 2013. *Resortowe dzieci. Media.* Warsaw: Wydawnictwo Fronda.
Kania, D., Targalski, J. and Marosz, M., 2015. *Resortowe dzieci. Służby.* Warsaw: Wydawnictwo Fronda.
Kania, D., Targalski, J. and Marosz, M., 2016. *Resortowe dzieci. Politycy.* Warsaw: Wydawnictwo Fronda.
Krasnowska, V., 1999. Lista Nizieńskiego. *Wprost*, 14 March.
Kroner, J., 1998a. Lustrowane będzie tylko kłamstwo. *Rzeczpospolita*, 29 October.
Kroner, J., 1998b. Trybunał przeciwko permanentnej niepewności. *Rzeczpospolita*, 12 November.
Kroner, J., 1998c. Sędzia Niezeński [sic] rzecznikiem interesu publicznego. *Rzeczpospolita*, 17–18 October.

Król, M., 1996. Lustracja czy szantaż. *Gazeta Wyborcza*, 1 February.
Kublik, A. and Czuchnowski, W., 2005. *Wildstein wyniósł listę 240,000 nazwisk z IPN* [online], gazeta.pl, 31 January. Available from: http://serwisy.gazeta.pl/kraj/2029020,34317,2520547.html (accessed 31 January 2005).
Kurski, J. and Semka, P., 1993. *Lewy Czerwcowy*. Warsaw: Editions Spotkania.
Mazowiecki, T., 1989. Przeszłość odkreślamy grubą linią: Przemówienie Tadeusza Mazowieckiego w Sejmie. *Gazeta Wyborcza*, 25 August.
Millard, F., 1996. The 1995 Polish Presidential Election. *Journal of Communist Studies and Transition Politics*, 12 (1), 101–107.
Misztal, B.A., 1999. How Not to Deal with the Past: Lustration in Poland. *European Journal of Sociology*, 40 (1), 31–55.
Nalepa, M., 2008. To Punish the Guilty and Protect the Innocent: Comparing Truth Revelation Procedures. *Journal of Theoretical Politics*, 2 (2), 221–245.
Nalepa, M., 2010. *Skeletons in the Closet: Transitional Justice in Post-Communist Europe*, New York: Cambridge University Press.
Nalepa, M., 2013. Institute of National Remembrance – Commission for the Prosecution of Crimes against the Polish Nation/Instytut Pamięci Narodowej – Komisja Scigania Zbrodni przeciwko Narodowi Polskiemu. In L. Stan and N. Nedelsky, eds, *Encyclopaedia of Transitional Justice: Volume 3*, New York: Cambridge University Press, 200–205.
Nasz Dziennik, 2006. Ujawnimy wszystkich funkcjonariuszy bezpiekim. Z prof. Januszem Kurtyką, prezesem Instytutu Pamięci Narodowej, rozmawia Wojciech Wybranowski'. *Nasz Dziennik*, 24 August.
Niezabitowska, M. 2004. Prawdy jak chleba. *Rzeczpospolita*, 18–19 December.
Olczyk, E. and Sopińska, A., 2007. Trybunał Konstytucyjny obalił cześć spornych przepisów. *Rzeczpospolita*, 12–13 May.
Osiatynski, W., 1994. Decommunization and Recommunization in Poland. *East European Constitutional Review*, Summer/Fall, 36–41.
Paradowska, J., 1997. Agent dla każdego. *Polityka*, 22 February.
Paradowska, J., 1998. Kto ma teczki, ten ma władze. *Polityka*, 21 November.
Paradowska, J., 2008. Twierdza IPN. *Polityka*, 5 July.
Pietkiewicz, B., 1998. Sąd nad sędziami. *Polityka*. 17 January 1998.
Piotrowski, P. ed., 2008. *Aparat bezpieczeństwa w Polsce: kadra kierownicza, Tom 3: 1975–1990*, Warsaw: Instytut Pamięci Narodowej-Komisja Ściągania Zbrodni przeciwko Narodowi Polskiemu.
Podemski, S., 1997. Lustracja zlustrowana. *Polityka*, 13 September.
Rzeczpospolita, 1995. Milczanowski oskarza Oleksego o szpiegostwo. *Rzeczpospolita*, 22 December.
Rzeczpospolita, 1996. Projekt ustaway o Komisji Zaufania Publicznego. *Rzeczpospolita*, 2 February.
Rzeczpospolita, 1999a. Odwołania prokuratorów. *Rzeczpospolita*, 4 March.
Rzeczpospolita, 1999b. Następna lista prawdopodnie we wtorek. *Rzeczpospolita*, 5 March.
Rzeczpospolita, 2005. To nie jest lista agentów. *Rzeczpospolita*, 31 January.
Sejm RP, 1997. *Ustawa z dnia 11 kwietnia 1997 r. o ujawnieniu pracy lub służby w organach bezpieczenstwa państwa lub współpracy z nimi w latach 1944–1990 osób pełniących funkcje publiczne* [online], Dziennik Ustaw, nr 70 poz. 443. Available from: http://isap.sejm.gov.pl/Download;jsessionid=E3D8BFA1046DCE6E02F87BD035C0DEB8?id=WDU19970700443&type=2 (accessed 13 February 2015).

Sejm RP, 1998. *Ustawa z dnia 18 grudnia 1998 r. o Instytucie Pamięci Narodowej – Komisji Ścigania Zbrodni przeciwko Narodowi Polskiemu* [online], Dziennik Ustaw, 1998 nr 155 poz. 1016. Available from http://isap.sejm.gov.pl/Download;jsessionid=CA1405B658D079ABB3B206BFD076EBF0?id=WDU19981551016&type=2 (accessed 20 February 2014).

Sejm RP, 2005. *Informacja Rzecznika Interesu Publicznego o dzialalnosc w latach 1999–2004*. Warsaw: Sejm RP.

Smoleński, P., 2006. *Młodzi lustrują* [online], wyborcza.pl, 5 August, Available from: http://wyborcza.pl/1,76842,3529550.html (accessed 7 August 2006).

Stan, L., 2009a. Conclusion: Explaining Country Differences. In L. Stan, ed., *Transitional Justice in Eastern Europe and the Former Soviet Union*. London and New York: Routledge, 247–270.

Stan, L., 2009b. Poland. In L. Stan, ed., *Transitional Justice in Eastern Europe and the Former Soviet Union*. London and New York: Routledge, 76–101.

Stankiewicz, A. and Zychal, R., 2017. Lista agentów – ćwierć wieku później. Onet, 4 June [online]. Available from: http://wiadomosci.onet.pl/tylko-w-onecie/lista-macierewicza-cwierc-wieku-pozniej/w9b3yw7 (accessed 4 June 2017).

Szczerbiak, A., 2002. Dealing with the Communist Past or the Politics of the Present? Lustration in Post-Communist Poland. *Europe-Asia Studies*, 54 (4), 553–572.

Szczerbiak, A., 2003. Civilized Lustration? Evaluating the Polish Model. *Studia Polityczne*, 14, 35–72.

Terlikowski, T.P., 2007. Arcybiskup Stanisław Wielgus był agentem wywiadu PRL. *Rzeczpospolita*, 4 January.

Tittenbrun, J., 1993. *The Collapse of 'Real Socialism' in Poland*. London: Janus.

Vinton, L., 1992. Olszewski's Ouster Leaves Poland Polarized. *RFE/RL Research Report*, 1 (25), 1–10.

Walicki, A.S., 1997. Transitional Justice and the Political Struggles in Post-Communist Poland. In A.J. McAdams, ed., *Transitional Justice and the Rule of Law in New Democracies*. Notre Dame and London: University of Notre Dame Press, 185–237.

Wildstein, B., 2016. Author interview, 9 June.

Y-Elita Pl, undated. *Lista Macierericza* [online]. Available from: http://yelita.pl/artykuly/art/lista-macierewicza (accessed 16 December 2013).

Zolkos, M., 2006. The Conceptual Nexus of Human Rights and Democracy in Polish Lustration Debates, 1989–97. *Journal of Communist Studies and Transition Politics*, 22 (2), 228–248.

Zybertowicz, A., undated. *Polish Anti-Lustration Stories: Conflicts of Interest and Truth Nullification*.

Zyzak, P., 2009. *Lech Wałęsa. Idea i Historia*. Kraków: Arcana.

3 What drives late truth revelation?
Electoral-strategic interests or ideological-programmatic concerns (or both)

This chapter examines the way in which the large and growing comparative and theoretical academic literature that has developed in recent years to explain the patterns and extent of transitional justice and truth revelation in the post-communist states of Central and Eastern Europe (including my own analytical frameworks) has attempted to explain the recurrence of the lustration and file access issue. It begins by looking at attempts to explain such variance using structural factors such as the nature of the previous regime and the transition to democracy in that country. It examines the shortcomings of these approaches, particularly their inability to explain changes of trajectory and the phenomenon of 'late' and recurring lustration and file access in countries such as Poland. It moves on to consider what might be termed 'politics of the present' approaches (which I, among others, developed in my earlier collaborative work), which stress the role of post-communist party competition as a key explanatory variable, and those that have tried to refine historical-structural and transition-type approaches, sometimes by supplementing them with 'politics of the present'-type explanations.

It then considers one particular variant of the 'politics of the present' approach, what might be termed the 'political elite strategy explanation', which is based on the notion that political actors changed their trajectory in terms of strategic positioning because they responded rationally to impulses such as (actual or anticipated) popular and societal demand to further their own partisan interests. It also examines attempts to account for different patterns of lustration and transitional justice, including the recurrence of the issue and changes of trajectory, through examining ideological-programmatic factors, based on the idea that political elites believed, or came to believe, that the phenomenon was entwined with the ongoing post-communist democratisation process and that a more radical approach to such issues was both necessary and desirable from a normative perspective.

On the basis of this analysis, this chapter explains the shortcomings of existing approaches to explaining the phenomenon of late truth revelation in post-communist democracies. Specifically, it considers whether 'politics of the present'-type approaches need to be modified to reflect the fact that they underestimate the extent to which those pushing for transitional justice and truth revelation may also have been driven (in part, or even primarily) by genuine ideological and programmatic concerns rather than simply being instrumentalised as a power tool in post-communist politics by actors attempting to gain an electoral-strategic advantage over their competitors. It thereby lays the groundwork for the further theoretical and empirical analyses, including carefully selected case studies as developed in this book, that are needed to further develop our understanding of the phenomenon of late and recurring lustration and truth revelation.

Explaining the Polish case using prior communist regime and transition frameworks

A large and growing number of scholars have attempted to develop comparative explanatory frameworks to analyse why and how the newly emerging democracies of Central and Eastern Europe have chosen to come to terms with their communist past and whether or not they attempted to secure some kind of historical justice. Many of these have tried to explain why some countries have dealt with the issue more promptly and decisively than others; why truth-revelation procedures such as lustration and file access were pursued; and, where they were, why more or less radical methods of transitional justice were adopted. All of them have attempted to explain variations in country differences through examining factors such as the nature of their dictatorial past and the injustices that their peoples suffered, the legitimacy of the dictatorial and post-communist democratic regimes, the type of exit from dictatorship to democracy, and the balance of power between – and different strategic and ideological motives driving – old and new elites, particularly during the first stages of democratisation. How can the Polish case be located within the current literature, and to what extent do these explanatory frameworks help us to understand it?

In the broader transitional justice literature, authors such as Elster (1998, 2004) and Nino (1996) have argued that the demand for prosecutions of functionaries linked to the previous regime would be greater where citizens faced gross, widespread human rights abuses, and these crimes had been committed recently, than where they cost fewer lives and were committed long ago. In line with these arguments, some authors argue that the scope of the transitional justice programmes in post-communist states depends on structural factors such as the nature of the previous communist regime and the injustices that it inflicted. Moran (1994), for example, argues that the intensity of transitional justice depended upon the nature of the former communist regime: how liberal it was, and how much scope there was for expressing dissent and tolerating emigration; what he conceptualised as 'the psychological variables of "exit" and "voice"'. If a regime did not allow citizens the opportunity to voice discontent, there would be more pressure for the settling of scores, and former regime functionaries faced an 'explosive situation' as the anger produced by repression was channelled into vengeance. However, if a country allowed its citizens some scope for self-organisation and protest, or permitted emigration as an alternative 'pressure release', there would, he argued, be little desire for retribution.

Moran's empirical case studies were Bulgaria, Czechoslovakia and the GDR, and he did not examine the Polish case in any detail. The communist regime in Poland was a relatively liberal one that allowed its citizens some scope for dissent and protest.[1] In their comparative typology of communist regimes, for example, Kitschelt *et al.* (1999, pp. 39–40) categorise Poland alongside Hungary in the more liberal 'national-accommodative' type.[2] Indeed, in their typology of all non-democratic regimes (not just communist ones), Linz and Stepan (1996, p. 255) argue that Poland was the only former communist state that never actually experienced a period of totalitarian rule, and, therefore, they place it in the milder 'authoritarian' rather than the 'post-totalitarian' category. Consequently, Moran (1994, p. 101) argues that in a country like Poland (and Hungary), 'where exit and/or voice were allowed by the former regime', there would be a 'tendency to forgive and forget'. On the basis of his model, therefore, one would have expected Poland not to pursue a policy of radical lustration, whereas, of course, although it did indeed initially adopt a relatively 'communist-forgiving' approach, the issue re-surfaced until lustration and file access laws were passed and then strengthened and their scope widened.

Other authors, notably Huntington (1991, p. 228), argue that 'justice was a function of political power' and attempt to find a predictive link between the new regime's policy towards dealing with previous non-democratic leaders and the type of transition that a society underwent in its efforts to democratise, particularly the role of elite bargains in the 'mode of exit' from authoritarianism to democracy. Writing in a seminal book on the so-called 'third wave' of democratisation at the beginning of the 1990s as the Central and East European revolutions were just beginning (and, therefore, at something of a disadvantage compared with other analysts, given the short time span that he was able to investigate) and focusing on the actions taken against communist leaders in a small number of cases, Huntington extrapolates from other regions' experiences to try to explain and predict the outcome of what he terms 'the torturer problem'. According to Huntington, if the last leaders of the non-democratic regime did not go willingly or had to be overthrown by revolutionary forces, a mode of exit that he termed transition by 'replacement', there would be a desire for retribution, and officials in these regimes would be in no position to demand any kind of amnesty. If such leaders participated willingly in the democratisation process and gave up peacefully following revolts, so-called 'transplacements' (a process which often involved amnesty as part of the negotiated transition), or initiated reform themselves and stepped down once those reforms went beyond their initial intentions, so-called 'transformations', they were able to declare amnesties to protect their positions. Thus, the more broadly society was implicated alongside the regime in its injustices, the less likely it was that former regime officials would be held accountable for their previous actions in the new democracy. On the other hand, the weaker an authoritarian regime was at the time of the transfer of power to democratic forces, the more likely it was that officials and collaborators would be held accountable for their acts of oppression. According to Huntington's predictions based on transition type, therefore, the only East European countries where the intransigent communist officials were replaced by new elites (transition by replacement), such as Romania and the GDR, would be likely to confront the past and enact transitional justice legislation, prosecuting and punishing former communist regime officials and secret agents. Looking around Central and Eastern Europe, therefore, Huntington saw an 'initial overall tendency' to forgive and forget.

Nonetheless, in spite of the criticisms that Huntington encountered fairly soon after his book was published, his approach of trying to explain patterns of variation by the nature of the democratic transition was adopted by several authors working on this broad topic, either implicitly or explicitly. For example, without acknowledging Huntington explicitly, Bertschi (1995, p. 449) argues that '[t]he method of transition of power in many ways conditioned the course of future lustration attempts'. Thus, 'genuinely revolutionary transfers' of power led to 'more retribution and a stronger will to pursue elements of the old regime', while cases of brokered or negotiated transitions, such as Poland, were less likely to lead to a wholesale purge. Similarly, but drawing more explicitly on Huntington's framework, David (2006, pp. 81, 84–85) argues that transition type was the main causal driver of 'the substance and shape' of transitional justice measures in a particular country – and, subsequently, the origin of the four 'lustration systems' that he went on to develop. David sets out in detail a model that links a country's mechanisms for dealing with the past with Huntington's modes of exit of the authoritarian regime, such that if old elites were defeated, new leaders would be able to determine transitional justice unimpeded, but if the transition was negotiated, as in Poland, the new leaders would face 'political and structural constraints that undermined or obstructed any serious attempt to deal with the past'.[3] Making a similar argument, Appel (2005, p. 403) cites the speed with which communism was dismantled as a possible explanatory factor for the intensity of what she terms 'anti-communist programmes'. The greater rigidity of the orthodox communist regimes, she argues, meant that they collapsed suddenly compared with those countries, such as Poland, where political and economic change emerged gradually in the 1980s with the aid or acquiescence of former communists, so that communist leaders in these countries gained legitimacy as they embraced democratic and capitalist change.

As with approaches based on the nature of the previous regime, the transition-type model, therefore, also suggests that Poland should have been a relatively 'communist-forgiving' state and not pursued a policy of radical lustration and de-communisation. In Poland, as in most of the rest of the Soviet bloc, the transition to democracy was a negotiated one, exemplified by the so-called 'round table' negotiations between representatives of the communist regime and Solidarity democratic opposition, and the peaceful surrender of power by the latter.[4] This was an example of what Huntington terms a 'transplacement', with the last communist leaders initiating reform themselves and then stepping down once those reforms went beyond their initial intentions. As a result of the 'round table' negotiations held in February–April 1989 the regime agreed to allow 35 per cent of the seats in the Sejm to be contested. They also agreed to the formation of a less powerful but freely elected second chamber, the Senate. In fact, the communists were trounced in the 'semi-free' elections that were held in May–June 1989, with Solidarity winning all of the 161 contested Sejm seats and 99 out of 100 of the Senate seats (Lewis 1990). On their own, the communists only held 38 per cent of the seats in the new Sejm, and the subsequent defection of their erstwhile allies in the so-called 'satellite' parties deprived them of a parliamentary majority and the ability to form a government. In August 1989, therefore, Tadeusz Mazowiecki was, as discussed in Chapter 2, confirmed as the first non-communist premier in post-war Poland, heading up a government in which the communists were in a minority.

Calhoun (2002, p. 500) argues that the 'round table' negotiations 'created a climate where the opposition acknowledged the communists as legitimate partners in building a democratic state' and that by surrendering power peacefully, the latter 'earned the moral right to participate in the country's democratic politics'. Indeed, much of the comparative democratisation literature posited 'pacting' processes, such as the elite-level bargain that occurred during the Polish 'round table' negotiations, as the most normatively desirable model of how such processes of regime change should proceed. This was because it was a process of peaceful, non-violent consensual extraction from a non-democratic regime that was felt to offer something for everyone, specifically a 'soft landing' for the old outgoing elites and representatives of the previous regime, thereby giving them a strong 'stake' in – and, therefore, an incentive not to undermine – the new democratic system.[5] In fact, for many Poles, the elite bargain that led to the collapse of the previous regime and facilitated a peaceful transfer of power, and the spirit of compromise that it was felt to embody, which was carried forward into the 'thick line' policy adopted by the first non-communist government, was the 'foundational myth' of the new, democratic post-communist Polish state (Wildstein 2014), highlighted by the fact that a series of similar 'round table' negotiation processes followed and accompanied the process of regime change in most of the other states of communist Eastern Europe throughout the rest of 1989 (Elster 1996). In so far as it was ever on the political agenda, the transitional justice issue should, therefore, have faded away fairly quickly.

Transition theories such as Huntington's were, therefore, quite helpful in predicting that Poland's new Solidarity-led democratic government would put the past behind it and focus on building the future, explaining why it chose not to pursue lustration in the months after the 1989 semi-free election. However, the key problem with these accounts, as with all those frameworks that try to explain such phenomena through historical and structural factors, is that, although they may account successfully for the lack of an *early* interest in lustration and pursuit of transitional justice in countries such as Poland, they are too static and have problems in accounting for and explaining what might have made the issue arise *subsequently* and the often quite radical changes of trajectory in the way that the countries dealt with it. This recurrence or 'meandering path' that lustration and transition justice sometimes take (Nedelsky 2004, p. 104) flatly contradicts Huntington's prediction that the politics of transitional justice could only be pursued during a limited window immediately following the transition to democracy (Stan 2009a, p. 267). As Nalepa (2010a, p. 22) points out, theories such as Huntington's were derived from explanatory approaches based on politicians responding to electoral demand and echoed other, broader accounts of transitional justice in other contexts. As noted above, these argued that public support for dealing with past oppressors was strongest immediately after the transition and that the other pressing issues confronting post-transition governments would dampen further demands for post-authoritarian retribution. However, by predicting that former autocrats would be held to account in the immediate aftermath of the transition or not at all, such theories failed to account for the specific timing of lustration in much of Central and Eastern Europe, including its late emergence in Poland.

Explaining recurrence through the 'politics of the present'

So, what are the possible explanations for the recurrence of lustration and file access as issues in post-communist Poland? And how can examining the Polish case tell us more about lustration, transitional justice and post-communist politics in general, both in Poland and in other Central and East European states? It may, of course, simply have been the case that if a country did not tackle this issue of how to deal with the communist past, it came back to haunt them, regardless of whether or not they tried to be forward-looking and adopted a 'forgive and forget' approach. However, there have been a number of attempts to try to explain the recurrence of lustration and file access as issues in countries such as Poland in a more systematic way.

One of these is what might be termed the 'politics of the present' approach, which stresses the role of post-communist party competition as a key explanatory variable. For example, Welsh (1996) was one of the first analysts to make a crucial distinction between those factors that accounted for an *early* pursuit of transitional justice and lustration and those that may make it arise as an issue *subsequently*. Welsh argues that, instead of disappearing as time passed, as Huntington and others predicted, the issue could become even more salient if used by various post-communist politicians against their opponents in party competition. Like Moran and Huntington, Welsh recognises that the nature of the previous communist regime – whether or not it remained consistently severe until its demise – and whether it was willing to negotiate and bargain the transition to democracy or resisted change until it was forced out were both critical explanatory factors. However, she posits a more intricate multi-casual model that recognises the potential importance of a range of different explanatory factors in various combinations at different times.

Moreover, Welsh also factors in what she terms the 'politics of the present', which, she argues, was as important for determining a country's willingness to push ahead with transitional justice as the 'politics of the past'. Central to this was early elite turnover, particularly the balance of power between the new political elites, drawn from former dissident anti-communist circles, who were willing to enact transitional justice measures, and the old elites, who blocked efforts to deal with the communist past. Welsh focuses particularly on the question of whether or not the communists or their successor parties not only retained power during the transition but then also performed well in (or rigged) – and, therefore, remained in power after – the first free (or 'founding') elections, which, for Welsh, was a proxy for the degree of elite turnover in the early post-communist period. Thus, 'the weaker the electoral strength of the former communists, the easier it has been to move ahead with de-communisation efforts' (Welsh 1996, p. 422).[6] According to Welsh, therefore, the necessary and sufficient pre-conditions for an *early* interest in lustration and a radical approach to dealing with the communist past were the refusal of an orthodox communist regime to relax repression and bargain with the opposition until faced with mass protest, and the communists' loss of influence on the policy agenda after failing in 'founding' competitive elections.

Precisely because the Polish transition was (as noted above) based on a high-level elite bargain, and the May–June 1989 'founding' election was only partially free, there was low elite turnover, and the communists were able to retain both a number of key positions and a considerable influence in the new parliament. In addition to the sizeable bloc of communist deputies in the so-called 'Contract Sejm' (which lasted until the first fully free elections of October 1991), as discussed in the previous chapter, communist appointees retained control of defence and internal affairs, the so-called 'power' ministries (and, therefore, of the army and the security services) until July 1990, and former communist leader General Wojciech Jaruzelski held the post of President until December 1990. In other words, none of the conditions that were assumed to be necessary for an early interest in lustration and transitional justice were present during the first period of non-communist rule in Poland, so, as predicted, the country did not initially pursue lustration, de-communisation or other radical forms of transitional justice.

However, citing Bertschi's (1995, p. 447) argument that '[w]hen political power is threatened the weapon of lustration can be wielded to gain sympathy and to quiet opposition', Welsh goes on to argue that, as time passed, dealing with the communist past could become a tool in the struggle for political power and be exploited by some politicians to undermine their opponents, especially if former communists were able to re-invent themselves in the eyes of the public, as they were in Poland and much of Central Europe. Drawing parallels with post-war France, Germany and Italy, Welsh argues that 'the past does not simply disappear with the passage of time and ... troubling questions do resurface', also citing the case of post-authoritarian Argentina to show that it can become 'a central political commodity'. In the case of post-communist Central and Eastern Europe, where former communists were able to re-habilitate themselves with the public, the issues of dealing with the past, she argues, 'never cease to be instrumental in the struggle for political power', and questions of how to deal with former communists and communist security service functionaries would 'probably continue to resurface as a pawn in the struggle for political power' (Welsh 1996, p. 425). Here, Welsh builds on Bertschi's argument, based on his analysis of the Polish (and Bulgarian) case, that power politics was the primary motivation for lustration. Bertschi (1995, p. 447) argues that while the aims and motives of those who pursued lustration may have been to preclude the corrupt from continuing in power in the democratic era, the practice and methods used to implement it suggested that it had been 'conjured to mask more common and base political goals'. Thus, for Bertschi, the 'primary cause of the failure of lustration in Poland' was that it 'was wielded clumsily as a political weapon by Olszewski and Macierewicz'.

Given that it posits the possibility that the issue would not simply fade away with time, Welsh's multi-causal model is certainly extremely useful in helping to explain how lustration evolved as a political issue in Poland and why the country belatedly adopted, and then strengthened, lustration and file access laws. However, Welsh does not go on to elaborate and discuss *why and under what precise circumstances* the lustration and file access issue was likely to recur and attitudes towards the communist past to become instrumentalised as part of the political game, and why this was likely to happen in some countries rather than others. Welsh's framework clearly requires some further elaboration here.

In my own analysis of the how the 1997 Polish lustration law in Poland was passed (and amended in 1998) (Szczerbiak 2002), and in later co-authored, cross-country comparative papers (covering the Czech Republic and Hungary as well as Poland) with Williams and Fowler (Williams *et al.* 2003, 2005), I build and elaborate upon Welsh's 'politics of the present' approach by trying to identify the circumstances in which the lustration issue became instrumentalised in this way and by specifying the motives animating advocates of screening procedures. With my collaborators, I argue that, because of the pervasive networks of secret informers and the continuous political prominence of unrepentant communist leaders, many of the political divisions in the newly democratising East European states were based upon attitudes towards the communist past, which developed into an issue on which parties co-operated and competed. Our conclusion is that the breakthrough that ensured the passage of lustration laws in Poland and elsewhere was achieved 'through rhetorical devices that removed lustration from the context of transitional justice, and thus relieved it of the expectations that accompany and often paralyse conventional judicial approaches to the past' (Williams *et al.* 2005, p. 39). The discourse of lustration was convincing because it responded to major events of the transition, such as the discovery of chaos in the archives, the extent and possible survival of surveillance networks, the hardship and confusion caused by profound economic change, and the return of former communists to power.

Lustration, we argue, resulted from public scandals involving the security services, disillusionment with post-communist outcomes among elites, the political needs of the post-communist right, the impact of earlier lustration efforts, or a public demand for information. Whereas Huntington and Moran believed that the past decided the timing and strength of transitional justice, we noted that none of the five sources of the demand for lustration had much to do with the nature of the preceding regime or the exit from it. The passage of each lustration bill, and the sanctions contained therein, similarly reflected not so much the country's political history as the parliamentary arithmetic of fluid party systems, trial and error, and learning from neighbours' recent experiences. Building on Welsh's argument that a key factor explaining the progress of transitional justice was the electoral strength of the former communists, we, therefore, say that the variables determining lustration legislation in Central Europe were the differing access of former opposition groups to power and their ability to put together a coalition supportive of lustration. We also argue that the story of lustration was one of post-communist political competition and legislative coalition-building and should be told with emphasis on the rhetoric, moves and compromises that competition and coalitions required. The adoption of a lustration bill depended on the ability of its advocates among former anti-communist opposition politicians to put together a heterogeneous coalition supportive of lustration; if necessary, by modification to secure a parliamentary majority.

Explaining recurrence through blending structural and post-communist factors

Another approach to explaining the extent and recurrence of the lustration and transitional justice issue in countries like Poland involves trying to return to and refine historical-structural and transition-type approaches, sometimes by supplementing and blending them with 'politics of the present'-type explanations. For example, in a sophisticated account, Nedelsky (2004) attempts to draw a link between the nature of the previous regime and later developments and, in doing so, argues against the claim by Williams, Fowler and myself that the dynamics of competition between the new party elites over the lustration issue had 'little to do with the nature of the preceding communist regime' (Nedelsky 2004, p. 81).[7] She argues that the continuities in the various elites' views of the previous regime from the communist to post-communist periods indicated that lustration debates and struggles over transitional justice issues should not be considered exclusively, or even primarily, as 'the politics of the present' or 'the politics of the past', but, rather, that they were influenced by the legacy of communist regime–society relations.[8]

For Nedelsky (2004, p. 65), thus, the strongest determinant of the nature and level of transitional justice in a country was 'the level of the preceding regime's legitimacy as indicated during the communist period by levels of societal co-optation, opposition or internal exile and, during the post-communist period by levels of elite re-legitimation and public interest in "de-communization"'.[9] The orientation of societal groups towards the previous communist regime was shaped by their experiences of it, and this set the context for their response in both the communist and post-communist periods. Thus, Nedelsky (2004, pp. 107–108) claims, the 'politics of the past and the politics of the present are linked' in the sense that 'the previous regime's legitimacy is directly relevant to societal support for transitional justice because it addresses a central question: did the people find it unjust?' Nedelsky's (2004, p. 88) core theoretical assumption is, therefore, that 'the extent and progress [of transitional justice] is at least partially shaped by the levels of the previous regime's legitimacy'. Thus, the higher the society's view of the previous regime's legitimacy, the less likely it is that the new elites will want to pursue transitional justice, and the more likely it is that old elites will return quickly to political influence, which, in turn, further reduces the likelihood of vigorous transitional justice. On the other hand, a lower view of the former regime's legitimacy was likely to produce an anti-communist counter-culture and electorally popular opposition counter-elites – who would, in turn, probably pursue a vigorous approach to dealing with the past.

Nedelsky develops her framework by examining two cases, the Czech Republic and Slovakia, which, despite sharing a communist regime as part of Czechoslovakia, adopted different approaches to transitional justice once they became independent states (at least initially), as the Czechs continued with the radical Czechoslovak lustration law while the Slovaks left it to expire. She argues that the explanation for this lay in the fact that 'the lower levels of regime repression in Slovakia both reflected and produced a higher level of [communist] regime legitimacy than existed in the Czech lands', which 'contributed to a lesser interest in transitional justice' (Nedelsky 2004, p. 81) and dissatisfaction with early post-communist rule, while the Czechs' attitude towards the previous regime meant that they viewed the post-communist government as more legitimate.

Nedelsky goes on to test her theory in countries with different kinds of communist regimes and applies her framework explicitly to Poland (as well as Hungary and Romania) to try to explain the extent of transitional justice that was applied. She argues that the Polish case displayed conflicting impulses as far as the legitimacy of the communist regime was concerned, but that it nonetheless tended to support her theory that this factor played a role in the post-communist lustration policy, so that 'while various factors may have shaped the outcome of power struggles, controversies over lustration reflect[ed] the legacy of regime-society conflicts of the communist past' (Nedelsky 2004, pp. 101–102).[10] On the one hand, Polish communist leaders' 'flexibility and willingness to reform during certain periods' meant that the regime 'may not have engendered the depth of antipathy that more rigid and repressive ones' (Nedelsky 2004, p. 101) (such as the Czech regime) did, and the communist successor party, the Democratic Left Alliance, was, as discussed above, able to re-establish its legitimacy fairly quickly and win elections. On the other hand, the breadth and depth of organised societal opposition to communism in Poland went far beyond anything experienced in the rest of the Soviet bloc, so that not only was the regime 'not highly legitimate' but 'a very substantial anti-communist counter-elite existed in the country and, after the transition, it dominated positions of political influence for the first years in the post-communist period' and subsequently, in the form of Solidarity Electoral Action, defeated the communist successors electorally four years after they returned to office. This, she argued, produced a '"bi-polar tendency" with regard to "Communist-purging" and "Communist-forgiving" orientations', which, she implied, was what led to the issue being contested and moving up and down the political agenda during the post-communist period.

Another attempt to try to blend historical-structural factors with 'post-communist politics'-type approaches came in a piece by Moran co-authored with Eva Jaskovska, where, with his collaborator, he develops a further iteration of his 'psychological' model, what they term the 'pressure cooker approach' (Jaskovska and Moran 2006). Although the empirical foci of their piece are the Baltic states, in developing the revised model Moran and Jaskovska acknowledge the shortcomings of his earlier explanatory framework by accepting that it did not conform to the empirical outcome in Poland. Moran and Jaskovska point out that Poland was, as discussed above, a 'transplacement' country in terms of Huntington's transition type, in which the exercise of 'voice' was allowed during the communist period, so it should have adopted a forgiving orientation according to both psychological and transition-type explanations. However, Moran and Jaskovska acknowledge that the 'perennially paradoxical' Polish case represented a 'significant anomaly' for both of these explanatory models, given that, as discussed above, the country enacted lustration laws in which former communist security service agents were subject to screening procedures.[11]

In the revised iteration of the psychological model, Moran and Jaskovska argue that his original pressure cooker analogy still provided the best point of departure for identifying the determinants of post-communist transitional justice and return to the 'exit' and 'voice' themes in his earlier approach. However, in addition, they also posit three possible additional 'release valves' from the post-communist period, namely the high political legitimacy of the previous communist regime (acknowledging Nedelsky); the replacement of communism by nationalism as the dominant form of political legitimacy in the post-communist period (as was seen in, for example, the former Yugoslavia); and the disappearance of the compromised members of the previous regime through death or exile. Unless one of these valves operated to relieve the pressure, the country would, they argue, arrive at a point at which some form of criminal, civil or political transitional justice measures would be realised. Continuing the analogy, Moran and Jaskovska (2006, p. 500) argue that the 'fuel' that heats up the political pressure cooker had to be derived from an untainted non-communist political elite who were not simply converted communists, so that '[o]nce this "fuel" has been found, and finds itself in power, the pressure cooker will heat up, exerting greater and greater pressure to prosecute and punish the former communist torturers'.

To put it another way, they argue that a 'double transition' had to occur in many countries, and, unless one of the release valves operated to relieve the pressure, the country would then arrive at the point at which prosecutions would be realised. In order for this analogy to operate in Poland (and Hungary), they also take into account my 'politics of the present' explanation, arguing that if a post-communist state had, as in the Polish case, a large reformed communist successor party that could legitimately contend for power and re-emerged successfully as the ruling party, the temptation for non-communist opposition forces to use calls for lustration as a political weapon greatly increased the likelihood of transitional justice being pursued. This, they argue, was precisely what happened in Poland after the Democratic Left Alliance and Peasant Party won the 1993 Polish parliamentary election, so that non-communist politicians had an incentive to use the issue of lustration for political purposes, unlike in the cases where communist successors did not pose a threat.

Another notable attempt to synthesise and bring together 'historical', 'transition type' and 'politics of the present'-type explanatory approaches to explain the scope and pace of transitional justice efforts, and why some countries re-examined and condemned their past sooner and more comprehensively than others, is developed by Stan (2009a). Stan's empirical base is a very broad survey of all post-communist states from 1989 to 2007 examining the adoption of transitional justice legislation in the areas of lustration, court proceedings and secret service file access. In a similar approach to Nedelsky's, Stan argues that three factors – the relationship between the regime and opposition during the communist and pre-communist periods, the legitimacy of the communist (and post-communist) elites, and the relative political power of communist successor parties and their former opposition – were, in combination, the strongest predictors in explaining the comprehensiveness and stringency of transitional justice efforts. This is measured by the groups targeted by lustration and file access laws and the implications for those encompassed by them, together with the number of trials against former communist officials and security service functionaries. Stan argues that, in a clear pattern across the region, former communists voted against lustration and file access laws, while parties emerging from the anti-communist opposition provided the impetus for them. The outcome of this struggle was strongly influenced by three interrelated factors: the country's pre-communist level of experience with pluralism; the composition, orientation and strength of the opposition, both before and after 1989; and the communist regime's dominant methods of ensuring societal compliance with its rule through repression and/or co-option. Critiquing other theories, she argues that they draw too sharp temporal distinctions between different time periods – namely, the (pre-communist and communist) past, the transition to democracy and the post-communist present – suggesting that one particular period was of greater importance, and, therefore, neglect the integral relationships between them. Rather, she claims that the past and the present were closely linked, so that '[t]he national specificity of the communist past led to a particular type of transition which, in turn led to a specific post-communist political constellation that facilitated or prevented transitional justice' (Stan 2009a, p. 269).

Thus, in countries like Poland (but also the Czech Republic, Hungary and the Baltic states) that had a pre-communist history of strong multi-party politics, and where the opposition to the communist regime comprised a combination of dissidents, mass movement members and internally exiled technocrats, a well-organised, well-educated, potentially powerful alternative elite emerged in the post-communist period.[12] These counter-elites were able to gain sufficient electoral strength to adopt transitional justice legislation such as lustration. However, their orientation towards communism's legitimacy was, according to Stan, grounded in their experience under that regime, so that transitional justice in countries like Poland (and, even more so, Hungary), where the communist regime relied more on co-optation and allowed some level of reform, was less stringent than in those countries (such as the Czech Republic, East Germany and the Baltic states) where communist rule was enforced primarily through repression and ideological rigidity.

Explanatory models such as these that try to blend and synthesise communist and post-communist (and, in Stan's case, pre-communist) factors to explain variations in transitional justice – and specifically why, in cases such as Poland, progressively more radical lustration and file access legislation was introduced – are ambitious and often produce complex explanatory frameworks. However, they are vague in explaining the precise mechanisms involved in exactly how and why particular historical legacies in a country like Poland produced *particular lustration outcomes* at *particular times*; in other words, why the issue recurred *in the way that it did* and *at the point in time that it did.* Here, much more contingent 'agency' factors still come into play, and not all of these can be traced back to historical-structural causes. In particular, these models do not take into account that the ebb and flow of lustration in cases such as post-communist Poland may have been due to the fact that political elites actually changed their stance on the issue. Interestingly, although Stan (2009a, p. 269) argues that 'it [history] matters a lot', at the end of her account, she also acknowledges that it 'is not destiny' and that the 'individual personalities of politicians assuming leading roles in speeding up or slowing down the transitional justice process, and awareness of developments and problems in neighbours make an imprint on how national elites approach the politics of memory'; in other words, an acknowledgement that 'agency matters' too.

Explaining recurrence through party elite strategies

One of the key issues that arise when trying to identify and explain with more precision why transitional justice and truth revelation recur at particular times and in particular forms is the extent to which political strategy and calculation or ideological and programmatic motives are the key drivers of (late) lustration and truth revelation. One particular variant of the 'politics of the present' approach that has been developed to try to explain the recurrence of the lustration issue is what might be termed the *political elite strategy explanation.* This is based on the notion that political actors responded rationally to impulses such as (actual or anticipated) popular and societal demand to further their own partisan interests. Although this angle was not developed explicitly in my own collaborative work with Williams and Fowler, and our analysis left open the possibility that lustration may have been motivated by ideological conviction, the clear implication as it built on Welsh's framework was that the issue was, to some extent at least, instrumentalised as an element of inter-party competition. One attempt to explain (late) lustration trajectories with reference to elite strategic positioning developed by Nalepa (2010a) is rooted in a much more explicitly rational-choice framework and based on the idea that, when determining their strategic choices, supporters of lustration used the issue in a calculating way for party advantage.[13] Based on a combination of elite interviews, archival evidence and statistical analysis of survey experiments conducted in the Czech Republic and Hungary as well as Poland, Nalepa tries to tackle two key puzzles regarding the specific timing of transitional justice in post-communist states, particularly in cases such as the Polish one where pacted, peaceful transitions to democracy were followed by delayed lustrations. First, why did the anti-communist opposition not pursue retributive justice immediately after the transition, in spite of the prevailing incentives to do so, but later, when popular support for its adoption had (apparently) dampened? Second, why was transitional justice adopted in some countries when communist successor parties, who had initially insisted that they should be immune from such measures as part of the (implicit) price for their negotiating liberalisation and democratisation, were in office; again, such as (Nalepa argues was the case in) Poland?

Nalepa's explanatory framework, and answers to both of these questions, is based on what she terms a 'skeletons in the closet' argument, which models the incentives of former dissidents from the anti-communist opposition and regime functionaries. Given that former dissidents, who comprised a considerable part of the new democratic elite, were uncertain about the extent to which the opposition groups of which they had previously been members were infiltrated by communist security service informants, they exercised restraint in introducing lustration and transitional justice procedures, fearful that this would have exposed the 'skeletons' in their own 'closet'. This uncertainty, she argues, acted as the former regime elites' insurance against possible transitional justice policies, because it meant that, at the beginning of the 'round table' negotiations, they had a distinctive 'informational advantage' over the opposition (Nalepa 2010a, p. 228) and thus made the anti-communist opposition's commitments to amnesty credible. The former regime elites knew, she argues, the extent to which members of the various dissident groups had been engaged in collaboration and could successfully use this information to their advantage. On the other hand, the risk-averse opposition preferred to keep these 'skeletons in the closet' even if there were fewer of them than the communists led them to believe.

In terms of tackling the second puzzle – why did former communists apparently behave in a seemingly irrational way and 'self-lustrate'? – Nalepa develops an agenda-setting model in which the critical parameters are electoral turnover and restrictions of procedures for parliamentary decision-making. She argues that communist successor parties such as the Democratic Left Alliance passed mild lustration bills because they anticipated that they would lose power to anti-communist forces; as, indeed, they did in Poland 1997. She also argues that because 'accepted lustration proposals in one legislative term form the status quo of the succeeding term' the ex-communists thus tried to appease a pivotal median political party in order to 'set the future status quo strategically' in a way that prevented harsher legislation in the future by reducing 'the future win-set of the future median party' and thus 'the room for the new proposing party – the anti-communists – to shift policy in the extreme (harsher) direction' (Nalepa 2010a, pp. 227–228). In other words, the reformed communists' seemingly irrational behaviour was rational, because initiating (less punitive versions of) transitional justice was 'part of a pre-emptive strategy to avoid brutally harsh transitional justice policies' (Nalepa 2010a, p. 29). So, while the timing of the lustration law may have been influenced heavily by the timing of a future election, which they anticipated losing, it was not introduced to respond to electoral demands but, rather, to eliminate electoral competition. For Nalepa, thus, the former communists' support for lustration was not the result of a desire for an honest re-examination of the communist past, but a pre-emptive strategy designed to protect their political careers from more radical policies.

In terms of the Polish case, one of the things that Nalepa also attempts to explain is why the issue of truth revelation re-surfaced again in the mid-2000s, so many years after the transition to democracy, and, specifically, why the lustration law was amended and strengthened after Law and Justice came to office in 2005 (a puzzle that is examined in greater detail in Chapter 4). She argues that this was due to the rise of political elites that emerged from anti-communist opposition groupings that had not been infiltrated by communist security services and, therefore, had fewer collaborators in their ranks and were untainted by collaboration with the previous regime. Lustration, Nalepa (2010a, p. 85) says, had distributive effects, and Law and Justice had all the pre-requisites of a party that would have benefited from it. She maintains that, earlier in their political careers, Law and Justice leader Jarosław Kaczyński and his twin brother Lech – who, as noted above, was elected as the party's candidate for President of Poland at the same time as it came to office in 2005 – knew that their party's leadership was free from security service informers. She claims that they had this knowledge as a result of Lech Kaczyński holding the posts of head of the Supreme Audit Office between 1992 and 1995 and justice minister in the Solidarity Electoral Action-led government between 2000 and 2001, which allowed him to survey the files of party members and locate hidden 'skeletons' (Nalepa 2010a, p. 18). Armed with this knowledge of who would probably be the most affected by lustration, and having a parliamentary caucus comprising new political elites, very young members and those with a background in opposition groups that had maintained low profiles before the transition – and which, therefore, had not been infiltrated by the communist security services and contained fewer collaborators – Law and Justice was, therefore, not afraid that lustration would uncover skeletons in its own closet. Moreover, she goes on to claim that the fact that the Kaczyński brothers changed their party organisation four times provided them with 'an opportunity to purge party ranks of known collaborators', which, she argues, they 'took liberal advantage of'. In other words, by belonging to low-profile underground groups prior to the transition, enjoying access to secret information about which parties were infiltrated with former secret police agents, and purging known collaborators from party ranks when reinventing party labels, the Kaczyński brothers reached a point at which they were certain they would benefit from lustration

(Nalepa 2010a, p. 19)

when they took office.

There are, however, problems with both Nalepa's explanation of the Polish case specifically and her explanatory framework more generally. First, her assertion that 'the opposition's preferences over transitional justice were shaped by its beliefs about its degree of infiltration' (Nalepa 2010a, p. 53) is based mainly on conjecture and assumption and is suggestive rather than conclusive. Her only firm supporting evidence for her claim that opposition politicians undertook this 'skeletons in the closet'-type calculus are 13 anonymised interviews with no direct quotes from any of the individuals concerned (Nalepa 2010a, p. 141). Nalepa (2010a, p. 150) herself admits that she cannot 'test directly the hypothesis about how the type of dissident groups in which ECE [East-Central European] parties originated explains attitudes towards lustration', as this 'require[d] data on [the] pre-transition activities of politicians', but this does not prevent her making bold claims that 'skeletons' were distributed among the post-opposition parties in the way that she suggests. As contemporary political historian and specialist in the communist security service archives Antoni Dudek (2016) put it, 'I am sceptical of the theory that there are some people who were exceptionally well-informed [about the contents of the files].' While '[t]here are specific people who have knowledge of a certain range of these materials, because either they had links with these services or because they got to know it through certain circumstances', this was 'particular knowledge, within various (specific) boundaries (such as General Kiszczak on Lech Wałęsa)'. This was because

> [t]he essence of the (communist security service) archive is its enormity and no individual can embrace it, particularly because it was compiled in an era ... (when it would have comprised) hundreds of thousands of paper files which (given their scale) are not possible to comprehend.

Nalepa's argument also ignores the fact that many, if not most, members of anti-communist democratic opposition groups were not, in fact, secret service infiltrators; indeed, it is contradicted somewhat by her quotation from one of her interviewees from the communist successor elites that the opposition representatives in the 'round table' agreements were those who could not be broken by the secret police (Nalepa 2010a, p. 134).

In terms of her explanation of why former communists chose to 'self-lustrate', there are a number of empirical problems with this in the Polish case, the most serious of which is the fact that, as discussed above, although the Democratic

Left Alliance and President Kwaśniewski proposed lustration measures in parliament, they did so in 1996: well before the next parliamentary election was due, and at a time when the Polish pro-lustration right was actually weak, divided and at a low ebb politically. At the time when they might have acted in anticipation of a possible election defeat, in April 1997, the communist successor party actually voted *against* the lustration law in parliament, although, for various reasons (also discussed above), Mr Kwaśniewski chose not to veto the legislation and signed the law in July. Moreover, while there may have been an element of pre-emption in both the Democratic Left Alliance and Mr Kwaśniewski's behaviour – proposing lustration bills in 1996 and, in the President's case, signing the new legislation in July 1997 to head off more radical proposals – that was not the reason why they were passed in parliament in April 1997. This was, as noted above, due to the emergence of a 'lustration coalition' comprising two opposition parties and the communist successor's junior coalition partner, the Peasant Party (admittedly a regime successor grouping, but not the communist successor party). Mr Kwaśniewski may well have acted strategically in approving the 1997 lustration bill to pass into law, but, as discussed in Chapter 2, this was probably as much about *political positioning* as *pre-emption* to prevent the subsequent emergence of more radical proposals. Specifically, the President's actions may, as previously discussed, have been part of a broader political calculation that involved trading off passing a law that he was uncomfortable with and trying to distance himself from his political base as part of a longer-term political strategy of attempting to portray himself as a non-partisan 'President of all Poles'. Moreover, as Calhoun (2002, p. 515) speculates, it may well have been that 'with parliamentary elections quickly approaching, he [Mr Kwaśniewski] did not want his party to appear to be concealing or justifying the errors of the past'. In fact, the degree of uncertainty about the outcome of the 1997 election was actually much higher than Nalepa indicates, and it was far from clear to the Democratic Left Alliance that they would lose their dominant position in the new parliament. Finally, it is questionable whether, when considering what kind of lustration law to introduce and support, Democratic Left Alliance legislators really acted like amateur political scientists factoring in the latest (as noted above, far from conclusively negative in any case) opinion polls, trying on the basis of this to anticipate the position of the median member of the new parliament, and then drafting appropriate legislation in accordance with this. Again, Nalepa does not really provide any hard evidence of this and even admits herself (albeit rather cryptically) that 'conclusive inferences cannot be drawn by projecting the results of elections onto expectations about losing power' (Nalepa 2010a, p. 178).

The empirical basis for Nalepa's explanation for why the lustration law was amended and strengthened in 2006 is also rather flimsy and contains some factual errors. Contrary to what Nalepa (2010a, p. 17) argues, it was not Law and Justice that 'promised to make public all of the documentation collected by the dreaded secret police'. Rather, as discussed in Chapter 2, it was Civic Platform – and especially Jan Rokita, the then head of the party's parliamentary caucus and prime ministerial candidate in the 2005 elections – that pushed hardest for a policy of completely opening up the security service files, but this call was restricted to politicians, and Lech Kaczyński actually opposed the idea during the 2005 election campaign (Wroński 2005a).[14] Indeed, as discussed above, the 2006 lustration law was passed with broad cross-party support, except for the Democratic Left Alliance. This included Civic Platform, many of whose leaders were, of course, once prominent figures within the Freedom Union and its predecessor the Democratic Union, who, as heirs to the opposition politicians involved in the 'round table' negotiations, would, according to Nalepa's logic, have been among the political groupings most infiltrated by the communist-era security services. Moreover, it is far from clear that the post of head of the Supreme Audit Office and justice minister really gave Lech Kaczyński the access to security service files that Nalepa implies. She does not provide any evidence for her claim that those parties pushing for the strengthening of the lustration law, such as Law and Justice, comprised new political elites and very young parliamentarians together with those who had a background in low-profile opposition groups that had not been infiltrated by the communist security services and, therefore, contained fewer collaborators. Her claim that the Kaczyński brothers changed party organisations four times and that, among former anti-communist dissidents, they 'were probably those who most frequently terminated one party and created another' (Nalepa 2010a, p. 19) is incorrect.[15] She also provides no real evidence that they 'took liberal advantage of this' to 'purge party ranks of known collaborators' (Nalepa 2010a, p. 19).[16]

Indeed, there was much contrary evidence that Law and Justice was actually dominated by an 'old guard' from the Centre Agreement party whom Jarosław Kaczyński trusted on the grounds that he enjoyed long-standing collaborations with them and that they remained loyal to him even at the end of the 1990s, when the twins found themselves in the political doldrums. The Kaczyński brothers did not (as Nalepa claims) join Lech Wałęsa's Non-Party Bloc to Support Reforms (Bezpartyjny Blok Wspierania Reform: BBWR), which did not (as she also claims) win parliamentary elections and help Mr Wałęsa broaden the powers of the presidency. By 1993, when the Bloc was formed, the Kaczyński brothers had broken away from the then President's political camp and were deeply hostile to him. Nor did they then break with the Bloc to form the Centre Agreement; this political grouping had been formed three years earlier in May 1990. The Kaczyński brothers and the Centre Agreement party did, as Nalepa claims, support the Solidarity Electoral Action electoral conglomerate, which won the 1997 parliamentary election and then abandoned it to form Law and Justice, although Jarosław Kaczyński actually stood as an independent on Jan Olszewski's Movement for Poland's Reconstruction (Ruch Odbudowy Polski: ROP) party list, not for Solidarity Electoral Action, in 1997, and the Centre Agreement split over whether or not to remain part of the latter, with the pro-Kaczyński faction choosing to operate independently as early as 1999.

However, notwithstanding problems with Nalepa's account at an empirical and factual level, one of the biggest difficulties with her so-called 'skeletons in the closet' model is that it posits the notion that the transitional justice issue was almost completely instrumentalised by strategic, office-seeking political elites. The same problems are evident (albeit more implicitly) in some other variations of the 'politics of the present' explanatory framework that focus on strategic political and electoral factors, including, I must admit, my own previous work on this topic. The difficulty with this approach is that it potentially underestimates the importance of normative factors and fails to grasp fully the extent to which the motives of those pushing for lustration and transitional justice may have been, in part at least, genuinely programmatically and ideologically driven rather than being rooted in, and motivated purely and simply by, strategic considerations, partisan interests, and instrumental imperatives to gain an advantage over political competitors. Even those pro-lustration political actors and parties that saw the sponsorship of truth-revelation procedures as a useful power tool to gain an advantage over their competitors were not necessarily solely (or even mainly) strategically motivated; they may also have been committed to these policies for ideological and programmatic reasons. Stan is surely correct when she says that 'it [is] difficult to argue that normative considerations of justice are entirely absent' (Stan 2009a, p269) and that

> to reduce the complexity of the politics of memory to the level of recognizing it only as a manipulating tool used in the cut-throat battles waged by power-thirsty political parties or to relegate it to the grey zone of illusory and unattainable myths ignores the Eastern Europeans' need to know the truth about the communist regime, to confront their own personal history, and to obtain justice and absolution.
>
> (Stan 2009b, p. 4)

Explaining recurrence through ideological-programmatic factors

Indeed, another approach to accounting for different patterns of post-communist lustration and transitional justice – including the recurrence of debates and changes of trajectory, as in the Polish case – places greater emphasis on precisely such ideological-programmatic factors. These accounts are based on the idea that political elites believed, or came to believe, that a more radical approach to such issues was both necessary and desirable from a normative perspective. They also envisage scenarios where some elites who always believed that lustration was necessary came to subsequently find themselves in a position where they were able to implement it. There are a number of examples in the literature on post-communist transitional justice that suggest that a greater emphasis should be placed on precisely such normative, ideological-programmatic factors in explaining the recurrence of debates and changes of trajectory on lustration and truth-revelation procedures in countries such as Poland.

For example, in an analysis of the lustration debate in Poland published at the beginning of the 2000s (and, therefore, not really taking into account post-1997

What drives late truth revelation? 61

developments and failing to foresee the problems with the 1997 law and subsequent attempts to amend it), Calhoun (2002) tries to explain the remarkable ability of the issue to endure, which the Polish case exemplified. She argues that what she termed the 'power politics' explanation – which, she claimed, 'Polish scholars and politicians tend to accept as the most fitting one' (Calhoun 2002, p. 496) – does not account sufficiently for changes of trajectory on the lustration issue, because it ignores why post-Solidarity liberals in parties such as the Freedom Union (as we saw in Chapter 2, a key member of the 'lustration coalition' that secured the passage of the 1997 law) and its forerunners the Democratic Union and Liberal Democratic Congress opposed rather than supported this form of transitional justice for several years after the transition began. Rather, Calhoun tries to explain this pattern of lustration by arguing that it was not simply 'power politics' that shaped Poland's approach to transitional justice but, rather, that liberal democratic ideology provided a guiding, constraining and justificatory framework for debates and political action surrounding the issue. Post-Solidarity liberals strongly opposed rather than promoted lustration for several years after the transition began because it 'violated liberal democratic principles', even though (in contrast to Nalepa's later argument) they 'seemed to have few ulterior motives in adopting this position, and it certainly did not enhance their electoral prospects [to avoid advancing it]' (Calhoun 2002, p. 502). Calhoun argues that liberal democratic ideology provided the conceptual framework for debates on the issue of lustration in Poland, so that they focused on legal procedures, not historical justice and truth; although, as discussed in Chapter 2, my own analysis of the 1997 lustration law debates found that they also encompassed a citizen's 'right to know' and protecting democracy from blackmail by former functionaries and informal 'wild' lustration, together with some elements of historical justice as a secondary feature.

Liberal democratic ideology also constrained the range of acceptable policy options by stressing the importance of political inclusion, condemning collective punishment, preventing the law from working retroactively by only allowing punishment of acts that were legally proscribed at the time, and providing defendants with full prosecution protection. It thus, as Calhoun (2002, p. 497) puts it, gave 'birth to the very idea of an orderly process of lustration rather than a spree of revolutionary violence'.[17] Post-Solidarity liberals created a political identity for themselves linked to this liberal democratic ideology, and 'they were willing to stick with it even if it did not always yield the most popular results' (Calhoun 2002, p. 502).[18] However, at the same time, liberal democratic ideology gave the former communists opportunities to enter procedural debates about lustration with confidence and an opportunity to offer good public reasons to argue against a process that they were naturally inclined to oppose anyway, as well as allowing them to forge an unexpected alliance with post-Solidarity liberals that prevented lustration in Poland during the early years of the transition.

Drawing our attention to the fact that the 1997 lustration law (and, indeed, the subsequent 2006 version) was supported by political elites who, for various reasons, had (apparently) changed their minds on this issue, Calhoun goes on to argue that its later adoption came about through the fact that, over time, many post-Solidarity liberals started to appreciate the subtleties of the relationship between lustration and liberal democracy. At the same time, the ability of individuals linked to the former regime to take advantage of communist-era networks to turn their old political power into economic power prompted many Poles, including some post-Solidarity liberals, to question the virtues of the 'amnesty but not amnesia' option. Consequently, Calhoun argues that Polish lustration debates grew more nuanced as party politicians from the post-Solidarity liberal milieu learned from their own experiences, especially the botched attempt at lustration in 1992, and increasingly weighed other considerations against the civil rights of the accused. These included the importance of the truth and the fact that their constituents had the 'right to know' a political candidate's character. They also concluded that the absence of lustration led to 'unofficial' screening of individuals, thereby creating instability, and that clear procedures were needed to assess the validity of these accusations. As discussed in Chapter 2, my own analysis of the debates during the passage of the 1997 lustration law found that its supporters appeared to be motivated primarily by a desire to achieve openness in public life, protect national security and avoid informal, 'wild' lustration, rather than to secure historical justice and settle scores with the communist past.

According to Calhoun, therefore, by setting up a hierarchy of values, liberal democratic ideology thereby facilitated political learning, as, throughout the post-communist period, Polish political leaders from across the spectrum professed that democracy and individual rights were primary values, but over time post-Solidarity liberals and ex-communist leftists drew different conclusions about whether or not lustration would best promote these values. These post-Solidarity liberals also learned new ideological lessons from international experience as to how to design lustration in order to respect the principles of the rule of law and liberal democracy, both by drawing upon examples from neighbouring countries such as Germany and through explicit guidelines from international organisations like the Council of Europe.

Building on Calhoun's arguments that lustration arose out of an ideological commitment to a new liberal order and 'a way to prevent past political iniquities from polluting or contaminating the new society and polity' (Appel 2005, p. 400), Appel (2005, p. 379) also discusses the ideational motivations behind what she terms 'anti-communist programmes', exploring 'how ideas and beliefs shaped the development of programmes of retrospective justice'. Arguing that 'ideas matter' or 'may matter', she highlights the fact that, due to the methodological challenges of measuring and comparing non-material variables, previous research tended to focus on interests or narrow partisan power calculations and concerns rather than the under-studied areas of broad normative values and conceptions of justice, and thereby 'misses the greatest motivation behind the adoption of these programmes' (Appel 2005, p. 380).

Appel (2005, p. 395) acknowledges that a 'skeptic might find politicians' ideational or ethical motivations suspect', especially given the problems with the implementation of lustration, which was, at times, used as a political weapon and 'given its frequent abuse and exploitation ... it is easy to ... assert that lustration was supported not for reasons of historical justice or anti-communism but for its political utility' (Appel 2005, p. 399). Nonetheless, she argues that anti-communist programmes were much more than this, citing the work of Weber, Goldstein, Keohane, Blyth and Ackerman to draw attention to the fact that ideas and interests are not necessarily mutually exclusive as causal factors. Appel claims that, although they may have served the political interests of some leaders, this did not refute the fact that such programmes had ideational or ethical dimensions. She points out correctly that '[i]n social science analysis ... it is always easier to reduce human motivation to self-serving materialist behaviour' and '[p]erhaps it even seems naïve to attribute lofty goals to politicians or policies', but argues that in national debates on anti-communist programmes, proponents and opponents discussed them explicitly in ideational and even moral terms, claiming that '[d]espite its misuse, lustration nevertheless did arise out of ethical and normative concerns' as a 'way of protecting the inchoate liberal democratic order' (Appel 2005, pp. 399–400).

Truth revelation and post-communist democratisation

A good example of how an academic explanatory debate about the timing of lustration becomes linked with more normative approaches is Horne's (2009) argument that sees the emergence of late lustration as being tied to efforts to improve the quality of post-communist democracy. This directs our attention to the important point that in many countries, such as Poland, examining political discussions about lustration separately from other political developments underestimates the extent to which these issues have often become entwined with other, broader post-communist democratisation discourses on questions such as the public's right to information about the backgrounds of its public representatives, officials and authority figures, and the need to tackle corruption. These relate as much to the relationship between transitional justice and the perceived failures of post-communist democratisation as they do to questions of historical justice and dealing with the communist past, with lustration posited as a project designed to implement democratic renewal and enhance the quality of democracy in these states. This is interesting, because the normative debates on post-communist transitional justice have often posited liberal democratic legal-ethical arguments both for and against adopting a radical approach to lustration: counter-posing questions of securing historical justice and allowing freedom of information, on the one hand, with concerns about ascribing collective guilt and retroactive justice, on the other.[19]

Building on this notion that 'there is a collective sense that the past actively affects the political and economic reality of the present' (2009, p. 357), Horne, thus, sees the fact that countries like Poland embarked upon late lustration programmes as an expression of the perceived need to deepen the democratisation process. The objective of these programmes was to expand the scope of transparency measures associated with transitional justice, such as lustration, to include those in 'positions of public trust' in both the public and private sectors, including journalists, academics and business leaders. As Horne (2009, p. 366) puts it, 'lustration is resonating with a symbolic and institutional sense that something about the democratic transitions in incomplete'.[20] Horne (2009, p. 351) rejects what she calls the 'dominant explanation' that 'lustration is ... a [tool of party politics and] threat to democratic consolidation' and draws a distinction between lustration laws that were 'politically *motivated*' (which, she argues, they all were) and those that were 'politically *manipulated*' (emphasis added) or 'elite driven' and 'wielded against political parties for personal gain' leading to 'personal advantaging of the party in power' rather than advancing a reform agenda. She goes on to argue that the evidence of late lustration in Poland supported neither a strong 'revenge hypothesis' nor a 'limited hypothesis that the laws were timed and designed for direct political party advantage' (Horne 2009, p. 366). Rather, she claims that late lustration was both linked to and driven by legitimate social, economic and political concerns.[21] Thus, post-communist governments – not just in Poland but in other post-communist states such as Latvia, Macedonia, Slovakia and even those that instituted transitional justice measures early on, such as the Czech Republic – continued to grapple with the issue and, in some cases, used late lustration as a means to further and correct some of the problems associated with post-communist transition by addressing public concerns about issues such as corruption, distrust and inequality. The new lustration laws were thereby often re-structured and packaged with other reform measures, specifically anti-corruption programmes.

Horne, as well as Calhoun and Appel, is right to draw our attention to the fact that one cannot assume a priori that lustration is used simply for political manipulation, which some of the 'politics of the present' approaches have a tendency to imply. Although she acknowledges initially that these two explanatory frameworks, power politics and ideological-programmatic, are 'not mutually exclusive' (2009, p. 347), Horne develops her argument by setting out what a lustration programme driven by legitimate concerns would *look* like and then assuming that if these are the kinds of arguments and justifications that are in place, then her case is proven. An example of this is when she says that '[l]ate lustration laws [in these countries] *look* like reformist tools, designed and framed by the government as a way to create an institutional and symbolic break with the past in order to further the democratic transition' (emphasis added) (Horne 2009, p. 359). Horne (2009, p. 366) also presents the fact that there were 'opponents of lustration [who] have changed their mind' as *prima facie* evidence that late lustration was genuinely motivated by programmatic-ideological concerns. Moreover, she argues that 'the party initiating the reforms was adversely impacted by the lustration programmes which works against a traditional argument that lustration laws are tools of party politics designed to confer direct political advantage on the initiating party'.

Conclusions

This chapter has laid the groundwork for further theoretical and empirical analysis to develop our understanding of this phenomenon of late and recurring lustration in the Polish case. The key problem with frameworks that try to explain phenomena such as 'late lustration' through historical and structural factors is, therefore, that, although they may have successfully predicted the lack of an 'early' interest in lustration and transitional justice in countries such as Poland, they are too static and have problems in accounting for and explaining the re-emergence of the issue and the often quite radical changes of trajectory. Explanatory models that try to blend and synthesise communist and post-communist (and sometimes pre-communist) factors to explain variations in transitional justice – and specifically why, in cases such as Poland, the issue recurred strongly, and progressively more radical lustration and file access legislation was introduced – are ambitious, and the frameworks that they produce are often complex and neat. However, they are vague in explaining the precise mechanisms involved in how exactly particular historical legacies in a country like Poland caused *particular outcomes* at *particular times*. In other words, they struggle to explain how and why the transitional justice and truth-revelation issues recurred *in the way that they did* and *at the point in time that they did*. In particular, these models do not take into account the fact that the ebb and flow of the transitional justice issue in cases such as post-communist Poland may, as Horne points out, have been due to political elites actually *changing their stance*.

Many of the attempts to tackle changes of lustration trajectory and the recurrence of the issue – specifically the phenomenon of 'late' lustration and truth revelation – in the academic literature are divided between those who focus on the political and electoral-strategic drivers of its protagonists, and those who ascribe more ideological-programmatic motives to them. My own position on this question – set out in my earlier writings and developed in co-authored work with colleagues working on other countries (Williams and Fowler) – and those of others adopting the so-called 'politics of the present' approach was that the issue recurred because it had become instrumentalised as a political tool in post-communist power struggles. This is even more the case with 'political elite strategy' explanations such as Nalepa's. Other approaches – such those adopted by Calhoun, Appel and Horne – suggest that the motives of those pushing for late lustration and transitional justice could have been more programmatically driven. The next two chapters examine two examples of how the lustration and file access debate re-emerged in post-communist Poland to consider in detail the factors that account for why the issue recurred and the relative importance of instrumental-strategic and ideological-programmatic drivers of late lustration and file access laws and debates.

Notes

1 On communist Poland, see Kolankiewicz and Lewis (1988).
2 Although they also argue that Poland contained elements of the harsher 'bureaucratic-authoritarian' type to be found in the Czech Republic. In his typology of communist

regimes, Offe (1996, p. 139) also argues that the level of repression in Poland was low.
3 Although David (2006, p. 97) acknowledges that the model is only approximate and, rather, provides 'necessary, though not sufficient conditions'.
4 On the Polish transition to democracy see: Sanford (1992), Osiatyński (1996), Castle (2003) and Dudek (2014).
5 See, for example, O'Donnell and Schmitter (1986), Karl (1990), Karl and Schmitter (1991), Higley et al. (2002) and Higley and Burton (2006). Cf. Karl (1987), Hagopian (1990) and Przeworski (1991).
6 Appel (2005, p. 403) also mentions the political power of the former communists as a possible explanatory factor for the intensity of anti-communist programmes, arguing that the 'relationship between the strength of the successor communist party and the strength of lustration programmes is direct'.
7 The reference is to an earlier iteration of our 2005 *Democratization* paper; see Williams et al. (2003).
8 Although it is difficult to find anyone who would argue that these debates and struggles were *exclusively* in the domain of present-day politics. Rather, this was a debate whose contours depended on a number of factors, some of which were to be found in the past. Indeed, together with my collaborators, I agreed with Welsh that the nature of the communist regime explained an 'early' interest in lustration and transitional justice.
9 Although, notwithstanding the problematic definition of 'legitimation' and the way that its existence is inferred from other factors – together with the problem of constructing a causal chain linking this to an interest, or lack of it, in transitional justice – there are dangers of tautology with the last two factors.
10 Nedelsky only examines the period up to the early 2000s and states incorrectly that the passage of a lustration law had to await the return to office of post-Solidarity parties at the end of 1997. Although, as noted above, while the lustration law did not become operational until 1999, it was actually passed in the previous 1993–1997 parliament dominated by regime successor parties.
11 Although, in my view, they mis-characterise lustration as automatically involving exclusion from office by describing it as a process in which 'if they [former communists] were found to be significantly involved in the gross violation of human rights, their participation in the political system could be curtailed for a certain period of time' (Jaskovska and Moran 2006, p. 488).
12 This stood in contrast to countries where the organised opposition to communism was very weak, due to little pre-communist experience with political pluralism, and there was harsh repression of any counter-elites and/or their successful co-optation.
13 The main arguments in the book are reprised in summary form in Nalepa (2010b).
14 Although Jarosław Kaczyński later clarified that it was Law and Justice policy to support opening up politicians' security service files and only opposed making public *all* security service documentation, claiming that the latter was the policy that Lech had in fact opposed. See Wroński (2005b) and Śmiłowicz (2005).
15 Although they were involved in a number of broader electoral coalitions, the Kaczyńskis were only associated with two actual parties, the Centre Agreement and Law and Justice, and their degree of organisational turnover was by no means unusual for those on the post-Solidarity right in the 1990s.
16 Other than an unsubstantiated claim from constitutional law professor Wiktor Osiatyński (whom she wrongly describes as a 'Western journalist[s]') that, when they set up Law and Justice, the Kaczyński brothers 'turned to young people on the far right' (Nalepa 2010a, p. 130).
17 Although some writers, such as Ackerman (1992, p. 96), argue that the legal hurdles in the civil law context of lustration were very low, with the rule of law imposing few constraints (as the functionary in question did not enjoy the full protection of due

process, the ban on retroactivity and equality before the law), and thus recommend it as the preferred form of coming to terms with past injustices.
18 Although Calhoun also acknowledges that this strong commitment to liberalism helped to differentiate these parties from the post-Solidarity centre-right and, thus, formed part of their overall electoral and ideological appeal. So, there may well have been other 'ideological'/non-strategic reasons for them adopting this stance, such as simply feeling that this issue was not a priority and a distraction from other, more pressing ones such as economic reform.
19 For a good comparative overview of competing pro- and anti-lustration discourses, see Łoś (1995).
20 She also considers the argument that lustration policies may have been a response to external cues from international audiences such as the EU, but largely rejects this explanation.
21 Although it is not clear, of course, how exclusive this was to 'late' lustration, and it could well be argued that 'early' lustration also tapped into concerns that were legitimate, or at least appeared legitimate to the public.

Bibliography

Ackerman, B., 1992. *The Future of Liberal Revolution*. New Haven, CT: Yale University Press.
Appel, H., 2005. Anti-Communist Justice and Founding the Post-Communist Order: Lustration and Restitution in Central Europe. *East European Politics and Societies*, 19 (3), 379–405.
Bertschi, C.C., 1995. Lustration and the Transition to Democracy: The Cases of Poland and Bulgaria. *East European Quarterly*, 28 (4), 435–451.
Calhoun, N., 2002. The Ideological Dilemma of Lustration in Poland. *East European Politics and Societies*, 16 (2), 494–520.
Castle, M., 2003. *Triggering Communism's Collapse: Perceptions and Power in Poland's Transition*, Lanham, MD: Rowman and Littlefield.
David, R., 2006. In Exchange for Truth: The Polish Lustrations and the South African Amnesty Process. *Polittikon*, 31 (1), 81–99.
Dudek, A., 2014. *Reglamentowana rewolucja: Rozkład dyktatury komunistycznej w Polsce 1988–90*. Kraków: Wydawnictwo Znak Horyzont.
Dudek, A., 2016. Author interview, 7 June.
Elster, J., ed., 1996. *The Roundtable Talks and the Breakdown of Communism*. Chicago and London: The University of Chicago Press.
Elster, J., 1998. Coming to Terms with the Past. A Framework for the Study of Justice in the Transition to Democracy. *European Journal of Sociology*, 39 (1), 7–48.
Elster, J., 2004. *Closing the Books: Transitional Justice in Historical Perspective*. New York: Cambridge University Press.
Hagopian, F., 1990. Democracy by Undemocratic Means? Elites, Political Pacts, and Regime Transition in Brazil. *Comparative Political Studies*, 23 (2), 147–170.
Higley, J. and Burton, M., 2006. *Elite Foundations of Liberal Democracy*. Boulder: Rowman and Littlefield.
Higley, J., Kulberg, J. and Pakulski, J., 2002. The Persistence of Post-Communist Elites. In L. Diamond and M.F. Plattner, eds, *Democracy after Communism*. Baltimore and London: The Johns Hopkins University Press, 33–47.
Horne, C., 2009. Late Lustration Programmes in Romania and Poland: Supporting or Undermining Democratic Transitions. *Democratization*, 16 (2), 344–376.

Huntington, S.P., 1991. *The Third Wave: Democratization in the Late Twentieth Century*. Norman: University of Oklahoma Press.

Jaskovska, E. and Moran, J.P., 2006. Justice or Politics? Criminal, Civil and Political Adjudication in the Newly Independent Baltics. *Journal of Communist Studies and Transition Politics*, 22(4), 485–506.

Karl, T.L., 1987. Petroleum and Political Pacts. *Latin American Research Review*, 22 (1), 63–94.

Karl, T.L., 1990. Dilemmas of Democratization in Latin America. *Comparative Politics*, 23 (1), 1–21.

Karl, T.L. and Schmitter, P.C., 1991. Modes of Transition in Latin America, Southern and Eastern Europe. *International Social Science Journal*, 128, 269–284.

Kitschelt, H., Mansfeldova, Z., Markowski, R. and Toka, G., 1999. *Post-Communist Party Systems: Competition, Representation and Inter-Party Competition*. Cambridge: Cambridge University Press.

Kolankiewicz, G. and Lewis, P.G., 1998. *Poland: Politics, Economics and Society*. London and New York: Pinter.

Lewis, P.G., 1990. Non-Competitive Elections and Regime Change: Poland 1989. *Parliamentary Affairs*, 43 (1), 90–107.

Linz, J. and Stepan, A., 1996. *Problems of Democratic Transition and Consolidation: Southern Europe, South America, and Post-Communist Europe*. Baltimore: Johns Hopkins University Press.

Łoś, M., 1995. Lustration and Truth Claims: Unfinished Revolutions in Central Europe. *Law and Social Inquiry*, 20 (1), 117–161.

Moran, J., 1994. The Communist Torturers of Eastern Europe: Prosecute and Punish or Forgive and Forget? *Communist and Post-Communist Studies*, 27 (1), 95–109.

Nalepa, M., 2010a. *Skeletons in the Closet: Transitional Justice in Post-Communist Europe*. New York: Cambridge University Press.

Nalepa, M., 2010b. Captured Commitments: An Analytical Narrative of Transitions with Transitional Justice. *World Politics*, 62 (2), 341–380.

Nedelsky, N., 2004. Divergent Responses to a Communist Past: Transitional Justice in the Czech Republic and Slovakia. *Theory and Society*, 33 (1), 65–115.

Nino, C., 1996. *Radical Evil on Trial*. New Haven: Yale University Press.

O'Donnell, G. and Schmitter, P., 1986. *Transitions from Authoritarian Rule: Tentative Conclusions about Uncertain Democracies*. Baltimore: The Johns Hopkins University Press.

Offe, C., 1996. *Varieties of Transition: The East European and East German Experience*. Oxford: Polity.

Osiatyński, W., 1996. The Roundtable Talks in Poland. In J. Elster, ed., *The Roundtable Talks and the Breakdown of Communism*. Chicago and London: The University of Chicago Press, 21–68.

Przeworski, A., 1991. *Democracy and the Market*. New York: Cambridge University Press.

Sanford, G., ed., 1992. *Democratization in Poland, 1988–90: Polish Voices*. Basingstoke: Macmillan.

Śmiłowicz, P., 2005. Pogodzili się w sprawie teczek. *Rzeczpospolita*, 14 June.

Stan, L., 2009a. Conclusion: Explaining Country Differences. In L. Stan, ed., *Transitional Justice in Eastern Europe and the Former Soviet Union*. London and New York: Routledge, 247–270.

Stan, L., 2009b. Introduction: Post-Communist Transition, Justice, and Transitional Justice. In L. Stan, ed., *Transitional Justice in Eastern Europe and the Former Soviet Union*, London and New York: Routledge, 1–14.

Szczerbiak, A., 2002. Dealing with the Communist Past or the Politics of the Present? Lustration in Post-Communist Poland. *Europe-Asia Studies*, 54 (4), 553–572.

Welsh, H., 1996. Dealing with the Communist Past: Central and East European Experiences after 1990. *Europe-Asia Studies*, 48 (3), 413–428.

Wildstein, B., 2014. Okrągły stół jako akt założycielski. *Do Rzeczy*, 23 March.

Williams, K., Fowler, B. and Szczerbiak, A., 2003. *Explaining Lustration in Eastern Europe: 'A Post-Communist Politics Approach'*. Sussex European Institute Working Paper 62. Brighton: Sussex European Institute.

Williams, K., Fowler, B. and Szczerbiak, A., 2005. Explaining Lustration in Central Europe: A 'Post-communist Politics' Approach. *Democratization*, 12 (1), 22–43.

Wroński, P., 2005a. *Teczki dzielą PO i PiS* [online], gazeta.pl, 13 June. Available from: www.gazeta.pl (accessed 13 June 2005).

Wroński, P., 2005b. *PO-PiS drobna korekta poglądów brata* [online], gazeta.pl, 14 June. Available from www.gazeta.pl (accessed 14 June 2005).

4 Truth revelation and post-communist democratisation
The revival of lustration and file access debates in the mid-2000s[1]

In the previous chapter, I argued that the motives of those pushing for more radical transitional justice may not, as 'politics of the present'-type explanations of 'late lustration' suggest, have been motivated simply by partisan interests and instrumental imperatives to gain electoral-strategic advantages over political competitors. Scholars such as Horne say that in countries like Poland, late lustration programmes were linked to other, broader post-communist democratisation discourses and were an expression of a perceived need to deepen, improve the quality of, and correct some of the problems associated with post-communist democracy. They were, it was argued, driven by – and aimed at addressing – social, economic and political public concerns about issues such as corruption, distrust and inequality, and were often packaged with other reform measures, specifically anti-corruption programmes.

In order to test this proposition, in this chapter I examine in detail the revival of the lustration and file access debate in the mid-2000s. As discussed in Chapter 2, this culminated in the passage of a more radical lustration and file access law in 2006, which significantly expanded their scope, although its provisions were not fully enacted, and many of them were either amended subsequently or struck down by the constitutional tribunal in 2007. The main empirical focus of this chapter is an examination of the arguments used by the supporters and opponents of more radical truth revelation, primarily in the parliamentary and media debates leading up to the passage of the 2006 law, supplemented by data from interviews that were undertaken by the author subsequently. The chapter examines controversies over the apparent failure of the Polish lustration model; the relationship between truth revelation and democracy, especially calls for greater openness and transparency; communist security service links with post-communist elites; and the relationship between lustration and file access, elite turnover and the so-called 'Fourth Republic' project.

The (apparent) failure of the Polish lustration model

Many of the strongest arguments in favour of a new, revised lustration law were rooted in the idea that Polish truth-revelation procedures in their current form – that is, the 1997 lustration and 1998 file access laws, together with the ways in which these were interpreted through court judgements – had not proved themselves. As the justificatory statement attached to the 2006 Law and Justice draft law, which formed the basis for the eventual legislation, argued,

> After nearly 9 years of being in force, it transpires that the current lustration law does not fulfil the tasks placed upon it by the legislators. Above all, it does not protect the interests of the state sufficiently and, at the same time, does not give enough protection to the person undergoing lustration.

It continued by stating that none of the three objectives that the introduction of lustration declarations was expected to ensure – swift trials, unambiguous and widely accepted verdicts, and wide access by interested parties to those materials covered until then by a secrecy clause – were achieved in practice (Sejm RP 2006a, p. 32).

Introducing the Law and Justice draft during the March 2006 debate on the new lustration law, party spokesman Arkadiusz Mularczyk argued that '[t]he necessity of introducing new regulations arises from the ineffectiveness of the current law' (Sejm RP 2006a, p. 137). On a later occasion, Mr Mularczyk (2016) argued that the earlier lustration and file access laws were 'a kind of rotten compromise' that 'did not resolve the matter'. Speaking in the same March 2006 debate, Law and Justice deputy Zbigniew Girzyński claimed that

> [o]nly when the vision of lustration was unavoidable, as the 1997 election approached [and] when it was clear that the political pendulum would reverse, in April 1997 a lustration law was passed but even when it was passed everything was done to torpedo it.

The 1997 law was, he claimed,

> meant to satisfy the conscience of the political class ... deceive public opinion into thinking that lustration was occurring ... [and] create[d] a mechanism which, instead of allowing historians access to these archives in a de facto substantive way, led to a situation where these historians ... had problems obtaining the IPN files.
> (Sejm RP 2006b, pp. 144–145)

Self-Defence spokesman Mateusz Piskorski also argued that 'in spite of numerous subsequent amendments to the second of these laws (the 1998 file access law) the lustration process and access to the SB files has not been regulated in a civilised way' (Sejm RP 2006b, p. 130).

Similarly, speaking in the July 2006 debate on the new law, Polish Peasant Party deputy Tadeusz Sławecki claimed that 'after nine years of the lustration law functioning, the Polish model of lustration does not safeguard the interests of the state and, at the same time, does not give sufficient protection to those undergoing lustration' (Sejm RP 2006c, p. 303). Writing in support of the new law, veteran Solidarity activist and commentator Krzysztof Wyszkowski (2006) also argued:

> From the outset it was clear that the [1997] law was poor, protecting excessively the interests of those people entangled with collaborating with the communist security services. It was a similar story with the creation of the Institute of National Remembrance. As a result of opposition from the Freedom Union a crippled monster emerged limiting the possibility of society discovering the truth about the PRL [Polska Rzeczpospolita Ludowa: PRL; the (communist) Polish People's Republic].

On a later occasion, historian Sławomir Cenckiewicz (2016) argued that lustration 'as a process of checking various politicians or public officials became an ineffective tool for eliminating these people from politics'. The opponents of lustration, he said,

> tried to use various procedures and circumstances – the lack of files, the five conditions that have to be fulfilled [in order] to meet the definition of collaboration stipulated by the constitutional tribunal, the use of court procedures ... prevent lustration, even though there was the façade that it happened.

Similarly, commentator Piotr Semka (2016) said that 'The criteria set by the constitutional tribunal for [someone to have undertaken] collaboration [with the communist security services] ... created a net that it was very easy to slip through.' The lustration process carried out under the auspices of the 1997 law was, he claimed, 'actually a way of hiding agents under the pretence of lustration .... They [lustration opponents] said: let's give the [political] right the parody, imitation of lustration to keep them quiet.'

One of the main reasons why the current lustration legislation was not felt to have met its objectives was the fact there were no negative legal consequences arising from the act of having been a communist security service functionary or collaborator: it was only submitting a false declaration that led to any sanctions being imposed upon an individual. As Arkaduiusz Mularczyk put it in the March 2006 debate, the lustration law 'has not succeeded in realising its basic objectives, specifically: revealing materials which were secret up until now, ensuring the effectiveness and swiftness of court proceedings'. The Polish lustration law adopted 'a solution ... which was unknown in other states of the former communist camp', whereby 'the basic task of the court is to check the truthfulness of lustration declarations', as opposed to monitoring what the security services and the persons who collaborated with them actually did. In other words, under the Polish lustration system, 'failing to disclose work, service for or collaboration with the security services is sanctioned much more harshly than simple collaboration' (Sejm RP 2006b, p. 137).

As the justificatory statement attached to the 2006 Law and Justice draft law points out, the 1997 law was underpinned by the notion that fear of having compromising documents revealed would encourage former security service agents and collaborators to own up and, as a result, reveal facts that were not found in the extant archive material. Defenders of the current law argued that simply revealing collaboration or service both represented a certain act of atonement and eliminated the danger of former security service functionaries being blackmailed. Another perceived advantage of this solution was that it appeared to free the courts from having to take into account 'extra-legal considerations relating to normative judgements on events of a historical, ideological or political character' and allow them to limit themselves to one simple criterion of judgement: the truthfulness or otherwise of the lustration declaration. These hopes were not, it was argued, realised in practice. Given that those undergoing lustration could 'own up' to collaborating with the security services generally without specifying the precise nature of that collaboration, they were still potentially left open to blackmail if the blackmailer had proof confirming that they had undertaken particular actions. As the justificatory statement put it,

> It turns out that the concept of a 'lustration declaration' did not, in the majority of cases, encourage those persons undergoing lustration to reveal the truth, nor did it free the courts from making normative judgements about the activities of secret collaborators.
>
> (Sejm RP 2006a, pp. 32–33)

Another reason why it was felt that that the current system of lustration and file access was not working was that it was very difficult to bring a successful case to conclusion in the lustration court. This was because either the law and court judgements were too generous to those suspected of lying in their lustration declarations or the trials were conducted in secret, dragged on for years and, as the justificatory statement attached to the 2006 Law and Justice draft law put it, often ended 'in a judgement which simply pose[d] hypotheses and [did] not determine the facts unambiguously' (Sejm RP 2006a, p. 32). Writing just before he released his infamous 'list', pro-lustration commentator Bronisław Wildstein (2005) argued that

> it is clear that in these kinds of cases, Polish courts function not just in a very sluggish way, but are exceptionally understanding in relation to the accused. In the case of [Marian] Jurczyk[2] that fact that his [security service] reports did not particularly harm the opposition, the Supreme Court recognised as proof that he was not an SB collaborator. In addition, the SLD managed to introduce an amendment to the law which meant that a final verdict would only come into effect after cassation in the Supreme Court. This is not just a mockery of the principles of a state governed by the rule of law (where appeal to the higher court instance is an exceptional path) but, at the same time, dragged out an already years-long procedure.

Similarly, speaking during the March 2006 parliamentary debate on the new lustration law, League of Polish Families deputy Rafał Wiechecki said:

> In Poland ... [we] have a long lustration court process, where the criminal procedure is used, where there is a presumption of innocence, where all doubts are resolved in favour of the person undergoing lustration, where collaboration does not carry any consequences.
>
> (Sejm RP 2006b, p. 133)

Historian Antoni Dudek (2016), generally a supporter of the court-based lustration model, also noted how, although the 'infamous' Jurczyk case was

> a model example of how all the [relevant] documentation – a personally signed agreement to collaborate, signed receipts for money [received for denunciations] – was retained but the [supreme] court ruled that [even] after two [lower court] verdicts that he was a lustration liar ... still overturned this saying although that maybe Jurczyk was [formally] an agent, but he did not harm anyone so he was not [in fact] an agent.

Critics of the existing lustration law also felt it was absurd to conduct lustration trials using a criminal procedure based on the principle of a presumption of innocence, with all doubts resolved in favour of the accused. Such far-reaching protection was felt to provide the accused with too many safeguards and produced absurdities in terms of the way that verdicts were reported and perceived. For example, the media often reported a 'not guilty' verdict as meaning that someone was not a security service collaborator rather than showing that the Public Interest Spokesman had not been able to prove beyond reasonable doubt that they had submitted a false lustration statement. As Law and Justice deputy Tomasz Markowski put it, speaking in the March 2006 parliamentary debate,

> the trial of the prominent representative of the post-communist left [former Democratic Left Alliance prime minister and party leader] Józef Oleksy ... probably best shows how flawed the existing [lustration] law is in practice.... The problem lies in the fact that lustration proceedings are based on the ... procedures of criminal law in which protection for the accused goes considerably further than in other procedures.
>
> (Sejm RP 2006b, p. 162)

On a later occasion, Law and Justice spokesman Arkadiusz Mularczyk (2016) said that

> the model based on lustration declarations ... was a faulty model because admitting or not admitting [security service collaboration] in a declaration was verified in court in a criminal procedure which established guilt completely based on other principles which serve to determine the [guilt of]

perpetrators of crimes, where there is a presumption of innocence and all doubts are determined to the advantage [of the accused].

He argued that determining whether someone had collaborated with the communist services was completely different, because 'it is [not] about determining the scale of a crime ... or where there are doubts, [someone is] found to be innocent'. Rather, 'it was about whether people who served in the communist state ... who supported it through secret collaboration ... should not work in a democratic Polish state.' Similarly, historian Sławomir Cenckiewicz (2016) argued:

> In this legal system [of very narrow criteria for determining whether someone had collaborated], developed by the constitutional tribunal following its 1998 ruling, and [given] the state of the [communist security service] archives, court-based lustration ... [was] ... completely ineffective while giving the Polish state and security services the illusion of verification, the illusion of lustration.

Moreover, lustration verdicts were often determined by evidence from former communist security service functionaries who appeared at lustration trials and, as the justificatory statement attached to the 2006 Law and Justice draft law put it, 'in most cases submitted testimony advantageous to those undergoing lustration'. The statement argued that the experience of the current system showed that links between secret informers and their handling officers outlasted the formal period of collaboration. The common interests developed between a secret informer and their handling officer in communist times – through, for example, moving money across the border or setting up and nurturing businesses – were continued into the post-communist period (Sejm RP 2006a, pp. 35–36). This meant that those covered by the lustration law might be aware of what archival materials had been destroyed and, therefore, whether or not they needed to own up to their collaboration. Indeed, as Janusz Kurtyka (2006), Institute of National Remembrance chairman from 2005 to 2010, put it, 'In our current process of lustration we often have a situation where the handling officers speak on behalf of the agent that they were once handling. The officer will always protect their agent.' He continued that '[t]he lack of specific mechanisms to verify archival documents, by (for example) calling witnesses who know and understand archival procedures, is also striking; this can have an influence on the result of a trial'. Indeed, even when proof of collaboration existed 'on paper, they [the spy handlers] deny it saying that it [such proof] was entered falsely'.

At the same time, the definition of what constituted collaboration with the communist security services was progressively narrowed. As the justificatory statement attached to the 2006 Law and Justice draft law pointed out,

> The Polish lustration law adopts a solution not known in any other former communist state.... The court has to ascertain, if the information obtained by secret collaborators was useful for realising the tasks being implemented

by the security services of the Polish People's Republic and, specifically, if it could lead to people subject to invigilation being harmed.

(Sejm RP 2006a, p. 32)

As discussed in Chapter 2, even before the Public Interest Spokesman and lustration court began their work, in its November 1998 judgement the constitutional tribunal defined collaboration extremely narrowly, ruling that simple registration as an informer in the operational evidence of the security services did not represent sufficient proof of collaboration, for which several other conditions had to be fulfilled for it to have 'materialised'. As the justificatory statement put it, 'In this situation, the threat of revealing compromising material became illusory and ... it did not pay for those undergoing lustration to reveal the truth in their lustration declarations' (Sejm RP 2006a, p. 33). As a consequence of the constitutional tribunal's narrow definition of collaboration, not all those whose declarations were subject to screening by the Public Interest Spokesman could complete the full lustration process. As noted in Chapter 2, between 1999 and 2004 the Spokesman only directed 153 statements that he suspected of being false to the lustration court for evaluation. According to the 2006 Law and Justice draft law justificatory statement, he could not proceed with court actions against a further 588 declarations of which he had justified suspicions on formal grounds that they were false, as the names were recorded in the security service operational records, but the only evidence that he had was a personal (and not an operational) file; this was therefore insufficient to meet the burden of proof for collaboration set out in the lustration law and subsequent constitutional tribunal and Supreme Court judgements. This meant that 80 per cent of those whom he suspected of submitting false declarations evaded responsibility, a group that included 47 parliamentary deputies, 43 representatives of the media, 16 ministers and deputy ministers, 12 provincial governors and deputy governors, and two employees of the Presidential Chancellery. According to the Law and Justice justificatory statement, 'one can assume that these people received prior warning that the relevant documents had been destroyed' (Sejm RP 2006a, p. 36).[3] Mr Kurtyka and the Institute's lawyers also felt that the judgements of the Supreme Court and the constitutional tribunal were too restrictive and blocked the potential to use the lustration and file access laws to cleanse Polish public life (Burnetko 2006).

At the same time, in October 2000 (in the so-called 'Jurczyk case', as discussed in Chapter 2), the Supreme Court ruled that, when deciding whether or not someone had collaborated, the authorities had to 'take into account the possibility of fake collaboration', a formulation that was repeated in a September 2002 amendment to the lustration law which came into force in November of that year. Moreover, in an October 2002 verdict (hearing a further appeal from Mr Jurczyk), the Supreme Court also declared that the information passed on to the security services by a secret collaborator had to be 'helpful and useful' in assisting them in implementing their responsibilities (Sejm RP 2006a, p. 32). The October 2003 constitutional tribunal judgement had a very negative evaluation of the very concept of the enforcement of declarations regarding possible collaboration with the communist security services, describing them as an 'unacceptable game with citizens' (Sejm RP 2006a, p. 39). Finally, the tribunal's October 2005 verdict threw the whole lustration process into turmoil by allowing those persons recognised as secret collaborators to examine their own personal files. Previously, it was only those who had been invigilated, and had not themselves at any time collaborated, who were allowed such access (Gazeta.pl 2005a; Kaczyński 2005). As Law and Justice spokesman Arkadiusz Mularczyk put it, 'This verdict changes the chemistry and atmosphere surrounding lustration. We are in a different situation than a few years ago' (Smoleński 2005).

The Polish lustration model was also felt to be somewhat chaotic, with a number of competing systems apparently operating alongside each other. As Bogdan Borusewicz (who was elected in 2005 as a Law and Justice-backed Senator but later switched to Civic Platform) put it,

> Today there are two [lustration] orders: the Public Interest Spokesman and the lustration court for political elites ... [and] the IPN – which, according to the [1998 file access] law, issues statements [declaring] if someone who approaches the Institute was persecuted by the previous regime or not. In practice, this [the latter] is para-lustration and a person who is not recognised as having been persecuted, which suggests that they were a secret collaborator, effectively does not have the possibility of appeal against [what is, in effect] an administrative decision.
> (Smoleński 2005)

Commentator Bronisław Wildstein (2005) also drew attention to these parallel lustration orders, which, he argued, were an attempt by opponents of the process to cause confusion and undermine the system:

> Verdicts on the question of collaboration by public persons ... belong to the courts. In the case of other people, the IPN simply reveals the name of the secret collaborator hidden behind a pseudonym.... [T]his inequality was forced through by opponents of lustration who, in this way, wanted to forcefully make carrying it [the process] out more difficult.

As the 2006 Law and Justice draft law justificatory statement pointed out, various attempts to try to amend the 1997 lustration law led to a situation of legal chaos, where analogous actions undertaken by persons undergoing lustration at the same time were evaluated according to different criteria. For example, as discussed in Chapter 2, amendments to the lustration law relating to the definition of collaboration with the state security organs (that is, whether or not it included co-operation with the intelligence, counter-intelligence and border security services) were passed in February and September 2002, both of which were struck down by the constitutional tribunal. This meant that, in the course of one year alone, the basic clause determining who was covered by lustration was changed four times, with four different definitions of collaboration being applied (Sejm RP 2006a, pp. 37–39)!

At the same time, the establishment of the Institute of National Remembrance and other lustration-linked institutions created a greater appetite for further revelation. This was partly achieved by showing that giving the public access to communist security service files did not necessarily lead to the disaster that many critics predicted. As commentator Tomasz Wiścicki (2005) pointed out,

> An important cause of the change in the climate surrounding the revelation of communist interior ministry documents is the activity of the Institute of National Remembrance, Public Interest Spokesman and lustration court.... It turns out that there was no catastrophe, wave of suicides nor even divorces, and the Polish political scene was not plunged into a 'war of files' which was supposed to be caused by reaching for the UB [Urząd Bezpieczeństwa, the Security Office, the SB's predecessor] materials.

According to Mr Wiścicki, the new lustration and file access regime also meant that '[t]he climate surrounding the revelation of the contents of the communist interior ministry archives located in the IPN has changed markedly ... It is no longer possible to recognise all supporters of opening up these files as freaks.' Mr Wiścicki argued that the Institute 'has played a particular role in the practical weakening of anti-lustration hysteria' and was

> the most powerful cause encouraging the change in the public atmosphere surrounding the revelation of security service materials. Compared to the specific effects of the activities of the Institute, it is very difficult to maintain most of the arguments for keeping these documents secret.

However, the new Polish truth-revelation regime also threw into sharp focus frustrations about the limitations and contradictions of how the current provisions were working, highlighted by the release of the 'Wildstein list'. As Tomasz Wiścicki (2005) put it, 'Supporters of the publication of the inventory of [the IPN] archives see this [the Wildstein list] as a symbol around which those who support opening up the communist security service files can coalesce.' Similarly, as Law and Justice deputy Zbigniew Girzyński put it, speaking in the March 2006 debate on the new lustration law,

> [I]n spite of the enormous restrictions, the Institute of National Remembrance started to function, historians – especially those from the Institute, which had greater access to these files – started to write books, write articles, which unveiled the reality of communist Poland. Thanks to this, things are now coming into the open which unveil the truth about what happened, [and] also unveil the truth about [what] this anti-lustration front [represents].

Referring to the 'Wildstein list' specifically, Mr Girzyński argued that the journalist

> undertook a certain act of civic bravery providing access to the wider public to the contents of the IPN materials, a list of the names of those people who were contained in the IPN materials, which led to a situation where even a Sejm dominated by the left had to add certain resources to the IPN to finally begin the process of unveiling the truth.

Moreover, thanks to being given access to the files, former opposition activists 'were [now] able ... thanks to their contents ... to un-mask the people who had informed upon them. All of this, maybe a bit against the intentions of those who passed the legislation, reveals the truth about these times' (Sejm RP 2006b, p. 145).

On the other hand, opponents of more radical lustration in general, and the 2006 draft law in particular, defended and argued against moving away from the existing court-based lustration system – which, they argued, de-politicised and 'civilised' it by subjecting it to a judicial process – to one based on certificates issued by Institute of National Remembrance historians and archivists. For example, speaking during the March 2006 debate on the draft lustration bill, Ryszard Kalisz, the spokesman from the Democratic Left Alliance, the only parliamentary grouping to vote against the new law, argued that while his party 'support[ed] the continuation of lustration', this had to be 'judicial lustration', so that 'everyone has the right to a just, open consideration of their case in front of an independent, unbiased court' (Sejm RP 2006b, p. 152). Similarly, speaking in the July 2006 debate on the new law, Democratic Left Alliance deputy Tadeusz Iwiński argued that under the current system 'the burden of proof rested on an organ which questioned the veracity of a lustration declaration', whereas now the individual concerned 'has themselves to prove that they are not a camel' (Sejm RP 2006c, p. 307).

According to commentator Mirosław Czech (2006), who was a Freedom Union deputy at the time when the 1997 law was passed, the 2006 law 'combine[d] a drive to establish "justice and a moral order" with a contempt for the basic principles of a law-based state and good legislation'. Similarly, Jan Lityński (2007a) from the non-parliamentary liberal 'Democrats' party – which was formed in 2005 as the organisational successor to the Freedom Union, of which Mr Lityński was a parliamentary deputy when he spoke in favour of the 1997 law – also said that it was 'a mistake to shift the burden of the lustration process from judges to IPN officials ... first a verdict will be given and then you have to defend yourself, appeal to the courts'. On another occasion, Mr Lityński (2007b) argued that, under the 2006 law, lustration had

> developed the form of an inquisitorial process in which the criteria of evaluation are unclear, the accused has the right to defence only after the verdict has been delivered, [and] what is more even if he achieves a verdict clearing

him [he] remain[s] on the lists of accused, and therefore on the lists of shame.

Critics of the 2006 lustration law warned about the dangers of giving so much power to Institute of National Remembrance archivists. Speaking during the March 2006 debate, Mr Kalisz argued that the new law 'gives the archivists from the Institute of National Remembrance the possibility ... to create an algorithm allowing them to create, without possibility of contradiction, with 100 per cent certainty the material truth' (Sejm RP 2006b, p. 151). Similarly, in the July 2006 debate, he said that under the new law there was 'a presumption of guilt' and 'the supremacy of the Institute of National Remembrance archivists, who issues certificates that will be published. And how is an ordinary person to defend themselves ... given that at that moment everyone knows what is written in their declaration.' He also criticised the Institute's power of discretion, whereby 'on one side ... [we have] an ordinary person who stands against the state machine – a whole large bureau – on the other side', which could 'issue some [people] with a certificate very quickly and some [only] after many years' (Sejm RP 2006c, pp. 300–301). Speaking in the March 2006 debate, Mr Iwiński also complained that 'the state of the IPN archives is a mess, which means that the work of its archivists is not credible' and questioned

> how then is the IPN meant to be able to take on all of these new, one hundred times greater responsibilities when it can't cope with its current ones ... and we are to introduce the lustration of hundreds of thousands of people?
>
> (Sejm RP 2006b, p. 160)

Truth revelation and democratisation

Calls for a more radical lustration and file access law also became bundled up with broader critiques, and an ongoing process to improve the quality, of post-communist democratisation. An important justification for pushing forward with a more radical law was the idea of lustration as a key element of a policy package to renew and cleanse politics and public life. For example, commentator Bronisław Wildstein (2005) argued:

> The Third Republic was constructed on [the basis of] a fundamental inequality. A democratic state constructs the basic equality of citizens on the basis of equal access to information. Citizens have the right to know the past of those who want to represent them and have a right to know about the activities which were undertaken against them by the totalitarian regime. They have a right, and even an obligation, to know their recent past which, in large part, is contained in the secret documents of the PRL secret services.

Similarly, according to Civic Platform deputy Stefan Niesiołowski (2005), 'revealing the names of communist security service employees and agents is an important element of building an independent democratic Poland'. Sociologist Barbara Fedyszak-Radziejewska (2005) also said:

> I regard lustration as an important instrument of democracy, understood as something more than just putting a voting card into a ballot box once every four years. The true sense of democracy exists in the possibility of making a choice – if we don't know who to choose between, then that choice is an illusion. Without good journalists, we know less than nothing.

Mrs Fedyszak-Radziejewska defended the release of the 'Wildstein list' on the grounds that, 'by speeding up the lustration process, Wildstein has strengthened the democratic system in the Third Republic'.

Speaking in the March 2006 debate on the new lustration law, Law and Justice spokesman Arkadiusz Mularczyk argued: 'This draft fully realises the principle that the Polish Republic is a democratic state ruled by law that realises the principle of social justice' (Sejm RP 2006b, p. 137). Another Law and Justice deputy, Zbigniew Girzyński, argued that

> in 1989 when we began systemic changes and [a process of] transformation, one really serious thing was neglected, which today has repercussions in our public life, the neglect associated with the transparency of the Security Service archives, with questions of lustration.
> (Sejm RP 2006b, p. 143)

Marek Suski, another Law and Justice deputy, also argued that

> the question of opening up the SB and other communist state service archives now in this parliament is one more attempt to bring Poland in line with normality, with a democratic, sovereign and, what is more, just state. Because the law emerges from a system of values and without a just state you cannot talk about full democracy and sovereignty. The history of the last few years shows that although Poland is a sovereign and democratic state it is, at the same time, deeply unjust. This is undoubtedly a shameful, still untreated boil from the times of the Polish People's Republic.
> (Sejm RP 2006b, p. 137)

Another Law and Justice deputy, Stanisław Pięta, argued that 'by presenting this bill, we are developing the foundations of democracy.... We are forming the foundations of a democratic Polish Republic' (Sejm RP 2006b, p. 163). Similarly, supporting the introduction of a new lustration law in the July 2006 debate, League of Polish Families spokesman Daniel Pawłowiec said: 'In order for a normal state to exist it needs understandable regulations, [that are] accepted [by], and apply throughout, the whole of society ... it needs a certain coherence between the theory and practice of power.' The existing lustration law was, he argued, 'an open example that [in Poland] there are [the] equal and [the] more equal, and that the latter are obviously [including] communist agents' (Sejm RP 2006c, p. 302).

A key specific benefit of pushing ahead with a more radical lustration and file access law, linked to these broader concerns about the need for more far-reaching post-communist democratisation, was felt to be that it responded to the need for greater openness and transparency in public life. In particular, it would satisfy the public's 'right to know' the backgrounds of its public officials and authority figures who occupied positions of public trust. For example, commentator Bronisław Wildstein (2005) argued that making public the communist security service archives held by the Institute of National Remembrance would 'end the whole problem of checking lustration declarations, as everyone can make up their own mind on the subject'. It would 'have a cleansing character' that would be more effective than any South African-style reconciliation commission, which was unrealistic in Polish circumstances, as this required 'the recognition of guilt and goodwill on the part of the perpetrators of the evil of the communist security service', which was lacking in the Polish case. On a later occasion, Mr Wildstein (2016) argued that

> the basic issue is this: who should decide if citizens have the right to look into their past? ... who gives us the right to look at or into our archives? The old nomenklatura know about it, the old Security Services and others know about it, they know about it in Moscow – and probably in Berlin too! It's just that we aren't allowed [to see] it.... We have a right [in a democracy] to know about our past.

Similarly, speaking during the 2005 parliamentary election campaign, Civic Platform prime ministerial candidate Jan Rokita argued that 'absolute transparency' and 'openness of politicians' biographies' was a 'fundamental aspect of [an honest] state'. Mr Rokita said that, '[a]s long as the biography of even one politician is hidden in some secret archive and cellar, then you don't have an honest state' (Gazeta.pl 2005b). Even commentator and historian Adam Leszczyński (2016), who was opposed to radical lustration, admitted on a later occasion that

> opponents of lustration made a mistake in thinking that you could completely avoid it, that you can leave this matter unresolved, you can leave it to historians ... this was unrealistic. The moral argument relating to openness and cleansing was incredibly strong and you could not simply dismiss it in this way.

According to the Law and Justice draft law justificatory statement, it

> represent[ed] an extremely important element in [ensuring] openness in public life in Poland broadly interpreted, through allowing society to judge

facts from the past of those people participating actively in public life, for whom these facts can be recognised as compromising.

(Sejm RP 2005a, p. 31)

Introducing the draft law in the March 2006 parliamentary debate, Law and Justice spokesman Arkadiusz Mularczyk said that it was underpinned mainly by the idea of 'openness and transparency of public life' and that its main purpose was to 'reveal the past of those people fulfilling public functions' (Sejm RP 2005b, p. 136). Similarly, Civic Platform parliamentary caucus leader Jan Rokita said that 'it is high time to finish with the secrets, pretend-secrets, pseudo-secrets, gossip and tittle-tattle that have accompanied the lustration procedure in recent years' and that the way to tackle these various problems was 'openness, only openness' (Sejm RP 2005b, p. 139). Speaking in the same debate, Law and Justice deputy Marek Suski argued: 'The efforts of Polish society for openness, [and to] reveal the agents of the Polish People's Republic are a fight for justice.' This, he said, was 'the key to constructing a justice-based state – [and in determining] if Poland is honest, or [if Poles are being] lied to' (Sejm RP 2006b, p. 31).

Speaking in the July 2006 debate on the draft law, Law and Justice deputy Zbigniew Girzyński said that the new legislation 'introduces a ... completely new principle for ... lustration'. He continued: 'We have not passed a lustration law, we have passed ... a law for revealing information contained in the documents of the communist state security service organs' (Sejm RP 2006c, p. 295). Indeed, Mr Girzyński argued that

> this law ends the lustration process. We are not passing new principles for lustration. We are approving the revelation of all of these materials. We want to finally end the game of files. Every public person will have to reveal their file.
>
> (Gazeta.pl 2006)

Speaking in the same debate, Civic Platform spokesman Sebastian Karpiniuk also argued that thanks to the 'full openness' of the archives which the new law would facilitate, Poles would 'finally be able differentiate victims from executioners, decent people from informers or apparatchiks of the Polish People's Republic's security service apparatus', thereby 'guaranteeing decency in politics and public life' (Sejm RP 2006c, p. 296). On another occasion, Mr Karpiniuk said that the new law was 'all about the complete openness of public life. The biographies of those who are active in public life have to be screened adequately' (Smoleński 2006). Similarly, also speaking in the July 2006 debate, Self-Defence spokesman Mateusz Piskorski argued that through the new law '[w]e want to achieve full openness of public life as a value in itself' (Sejm RP 2006c, p. 299). While admitting that the new process would be 'difficult, costly and, for many, unpleasant', League of Polish Families spokesman Daniel Pawłowiec argued that 'this is a price that we have to pay for peace, for honesty and for truth' (Sejm RP 2006c, p. 302).

This need for openness was justified on the grounds that the Polish public had a 'right to know' the background of its public representatives and authority figures. Bronisław Wildstein (2005) argued that the Polish Third Republic 'was constructed on a fundamental inequality', namely that

> [a] democratic state builds the basic equality of citizens on the basis of equal access to information. Citizens have the right to know the past of those who want to represent it and have a right to know about the activities which were undertaken against it by the totalitarian regime. They have a right, and even an obligation, to know their contemporary past, which, in large part, is contained in the secret documents of the PRL [Polish People's Republic] secret services.

The 2006 Law and Justice draft law justificatory statement also drew attention to 'the [Polish] constitutional guarantee that gives citizens a right to information about persons occupying such functions [positions and professions requiring public trust]' (Sejm RP 2006a, p. 31). Similarly, speaking during the March 2006 debate on the new law, League of Polish Families spokesman Rafał Wiechecki said that 'this [law] is about the honest right of citizens to information. This is about openness in public life' (Sejm RP 2006b, p. 133). Moreover, speaking in the later July 2006 debate, Sebastian Karpiniuk argued:

> The time has finally come ... for a reckoning with the past [when] Poles finally have the right to know both their executioners as well as the functionaries representing the repressive apparatus of the Polish communist republic. Poles finally have a right to see who imprisoned them and who was imprisoned. They finally have a right to know who collaborated and by what methods they were recruited to collaborate.
> (Sejm RP 2006c, p. 296)

Greater openness was also justified on the grounds that it would put an end to so-called 'wild' lustration, taking smears and the danger of blackmail based on the documents located in the communist security service archives out of politics. Explaining why he felt that openness of the files was so important, during the 2005 election campaign, Civic Platform prime ministerial candidate Jan Rokita said that he could not imagine that a government could be effective 'in conditions where every week some group of functionaries, politicians, investigative journalists or provocateurs removed consecutive secret materials on anyone, whether it was a politician from the governing camp or an opposition politician'. 'This', he said, was 'a situation in which governing is absolutely impossible'. A condition of effective governance was thus 'full openness and full information about biographies, especially of people active in politics. Without this you cannot govern' (Gazeta.pl, 2005b). Similarly, speaking in the March 2006 debate on the new law, Self-Defence leader Andrzej Lepper argued that '[we have to] once and for all end this wild lustration, once and for all adopt a law which will be clear, understandable and which will mean that Poland is not hell, but that we have survived hell' (Sejm RP 2006b, p. 148). Speaking in the same debate, his party's spokesman Mateusz Piskorski also said: '[Our intention] is to liquidate the possibility of taking advantage of the materials which are at the IPN's disposal to carry out ... dirty ... political games' (Sejm RP 2006b, p. 131). League of Polish Families spokesman Rafał Wiechecki also claimed:

> In Poland we ... have had wild lustration, with people 'playing' the files before every parliamentary election, every local government election, but also when filling public positions.... We have to reveal the contents of the IPN archives and [reveal them] to everyone; to finally end this anarchic dance ['chocholi taniec'], to finally lance this boil that is bringing down Polish democracy.... We have to end wild lustration.
> (Sejm RP 2006b, p. 133)

Similarly, speaking in the July 2006 debate, Law and Justice deputy Zbigniew Girzyński said:

> We want to finally end the situation which has meant that up until now you could play with the files, that you could take advantage of leaking information against people in order to ruin their political careers, or ruin them in every other area of public life in which they function.
> (Sejm RP 2006c, p. 295)

Civil Platform spokesman Sebastian Karpiniuk also said that

> only full openness of the archives...will lead to a situation in which no person performing a public role or fulfilling an occupation of public trust can be blackmailed by so-called smears ['haki'] in the files ... the more openness, the fewer half-truths and understatements.
> (Sejm RP 2006c, p. 296)

He continued: '[p]ersons fulfilling, or seeking to fulfil, public functions cannot work honestly when they are being blackmailed by potential security service materials relating to their past. We have to definitively finish with this' (Sejm RP 2006c, p. 298). Criticising what he called 'a gurgling lustration swamp' and 'the game of files', Self-Defence spokesman Mateusz Piskorski also said:

> We want to avoid wild lustration.... We want to avoid phenomena like the voluminous Wildstein list.... We want to avoid what we have had to deal with over the [last] 10–20 years, unconfirmed allegations.... We want to be in a position where there will not be a situation in which any public functionaries can be blackmailed by files that allegedly exist on them.
> (Sejm RP 2006c, pp. 298–299)

On another occasion, Civic Platform spokesman Sebastian Karpiniuk drew on his experience as a local councillor when he said that he had often wondered whether some of the decisions taken in his town were due to blackmail based on the manipulation of secret knowledge contained in the communist security service files (Smoleński 2006). Law and Justice spokesman Arkadiusz Mularczyk (2016) also argued that

> [t]he objective of lustration is, above all, openness of public life and ensuring that the key posts in public life are occupied by people on whom there are no documents and who cannot be blackmailed … and cleansing the state from people who are vulnerable to blackmail.

It would 'ensure that public figures or those carrying out public functions were motivated by the public good and not fear of the threat of blackmail'. Similarly, historian Sławomir Cenckiewicz (2016) said that '[i]f you hide this information then it ends in a great scandal particularly if that person advances and becomes a moral authority'. It was 'in politicians' interests to ration and take advantage of [this] knowledge', and '[a] lack of openness and transparency allowed [them] to use this knowledge instrumentally'. Commentator Bronisław Wildstein (2016) also argued: 'People talked about a "game of files". You can't play [that game] when everything becomes open. Then all the games, all the blackmail ends.'

Communist security service links with post-communist elites

Another recurring theme that ran through the discourses of calls for more radical lustration and file access laws was often bound up with the idea that these processes were required to end the entanglement of the communist security services with post-communist economic, political and cultural elites. At the same time, calls for more radical lustration were often linked to the fight against political corruption, which became a more salient issue in Poland in the early to mid-2000s following the emergence of the so-called 'Rywin affair' at the end of 2002. Lew Rywin, a prominent Polish film producer, offered Adam Michnik – a veteran anti-communist opposition strategist who in post-communist Poland became proprietor of the Agora media empire, which published the influential liberal-left daily *Gazeta Wyborcza*, of which Mr Michnik was founder and editor-in-chief – that, in exchange for a bribe, he would arrange for a change in a draft law aimed at limiting the print media's influence on radio and television (which would have been in Mr Michnik's favour). Mr Rywin claimed that he was acting on behalf of what he called the 'group in power', which wanted to remain anonymous but possibly included the then prime minister and Democratic Left Alliance leader Leszek Miller. The incident took place in July 2002, and six months later, at the end of December, the paper printed a partial record of Mr Michnik's conversation with Mr Rywin, thus starting the actual scandal (Smoleński 2002).

In January 2003, the Polish parliament created a special committee to investigate the circumstances of the affair, which eventually helped to bring down Mr Miller in May 2004. Although Democratic Left Alliance deputies on the commission were able to vote through a final report, which came to the conclusion that Mr Rywin had been acting on his own,[4] in September 2004 the Sejm unexpectedly voted to accept a dissenting minority report that departed radically from the majority one, naming five leading government and media figures linked to the Democratic Left Alliance as the 'group of power' masterminding Mr Rywin's mission. In addition to Mr Miller, this included Aleksandra Jakubowska, the deputy culture minister, who was in charge of the amendment that would have benefited Agora; Lech Nikolski, the head of Mr Miller's prime minister's chancellery; Robert Kwiatkowski, the head of Polish public TV, whose TVP2 second channel was considered a possible target for a post-privatisation Agora takeover; and Włodzimierz Czarzasty, another influential media policy-maker, who was secretary of the National Radio and Television Council (Krajowa Rada Radiofonii i Telewizji: KRRiTV), the Polish regulatory body that issued radio and television broadcast licences, ensured compliance with the law by public broadcasters, and indirectly controlled state-owned TV and radio stations.

The Rywin affair was followed by a raft of further scandalous revelations involving politicians and officials from the ruling party, which meant that the corruption issue moved to the top of the political agenda. One of the most serious of these was the so-called 'Orlen affair' surrounding the privatisation of the partly state-owned oil company PKN Orlen. The scandal began in February 2002 with the arrest by the Office of State Security of PKN Orlen's chief executive Andrzej Modrzejewski on the order of the attorney general's office. The arrest was carried out on the eve of a PKN Orlen directors' meeting, and, although Mr Modrzejewski was released two hours before it took place, the board removed him from his position. In an April 2004 interview for *Gazeta Wyborcza*, Wiesław Kaczmarek, who was treasury minister at the time of the arrest, claimed that its real purpose was to provoke Mr Modrzejewski's dismissal and, as a consequence, not allow the signing of a $14 billion contract for oil supplies. The decision to arrest Mr Modrzejewski was, he claimed, taken during an official meeting that he had attended in the prime minister's office involving Mr Miller, justice minister Barbara Piwnik and the head of the Office of State Security, Zbigniew Siemiątkowski (Kublik 2004; Śmiłowicz 2004; Wielowieyska 2004). The 'Orlen affair' attracted considerable publicity and, because of its perceived potential for undermining the security of Poland's energy supply, appeared to have even more far-reaching effects; by the end of 2004 it had already overshadowed the Rywin affair.

As a consequence, the Polish parliament voted to initiate another independent parliamentary investigative commission. This did not reach a conclusion but discovered a number of new threads, including the publication of notes from the Intelligence Agency (Agency Wywiadu: AW) describing a meeting between Jan Kulczyk, the wealthiest Polish businessmen and a minority shareholder in PKN Orlen, and Russian businessman and reputed spy Vladimir Alganov. At the meeting, Mr Kulczyk explained the importance of his contacts with Mr

Kwaśniewski, who, he claimed, could enable a privatisation of the Rafineria Gdansk oil refinery on terms advantageous to the Russians. For his part, Mr Alganov said that a Russian oil company had paid a large bribe to a Polish minister and industrialist to ensure that the Russians would win the tender for the refinery (*Economist* 2004). The parliamentary commission and linked protracted criminal investigation pointed to, as Łoś (2005) put it, 'an octopus like structure' involving powerful Russian and Western interests 'that had its tentacles in all influential power networks in Poland'.

Indeed, as part of its inquiry, in January 2005 the commission voted to request from the Institute of National Remembrance access to the communist security service files of 37 individuals linked to the affair. These were mainly those who had given, or were due to give, evidence before the commission, and included Mr Kwaśniewski, prime minister Marek Belka, former Solidarity Election Action prime minister (between 1997 and 2001) Jerzy Buzek, and Mr Siemiątkowski. They also included staff from the President's office; Mr Kulczyk's circle; other members of the Miller, Belka and Buzek governments; PKN Orlen itself; and the security services (Gazeta.pl 2005c, 2005d). On the basis of these files, one right-wing commission member, Antoni Macierewicz, claimed that former communist security service functionaries had exercised behind-the-scenes influence on Mr Kwaśniewski (Kublik and Czuchnowski 2005). These files also revealed that, before taking a study trip to the USA in 1984, Mr Belka had agreed to seek out potential informers for the communist security services and inform them if he was approached by US intelligence officers. In June 2005, opposition members of the commission called upon Mr Belka to resign, arguing that at an earlier hearing the prime minister had denied collaborating with the communist security services. Requesting that his file be de-classified, Mr Belka refused to step down, claiming that it was not unusual for scholars undertaking trips abroad during communist times to be approached by the security services, and that he had not provided them with any information of importance on his return home (Deutsche Welle 2005; *Rzeczpospolita* 2005; Śmiłowicz 2005a, 2005b).

These scandals, in which both former and current security service operatives seemed to be actively engaged, were felt to exemplify the corrupt and croneyistic network that had allegedly colonised Polish capitalism. It was widely felt that, through their connections with the world of business and politics, which stemmed from (often corrupt) communist-era networks, many former communist security service functionaries and other officials linked to the previous regime enjoyed privileged positions in the Polish state.[5] As we shall see in Chapter 6, they convinced increasing number of Poles that politicians, policy-makers and opinion-formers were involved in a web of large-scale business deals as part of a 'shadow economy' linked to organised criminal networks whose origins were to be found in the communist security services. This prompted many citizens and political figures to question the virtues of the 'amnesty but not amnesia' option and led to calls for more radical lustration and revelation of former communist security service networks as a means of breaking this corrupt nexus.

These discourses often included explicit references to the various scandals that were linked to the processes of privatisation, awarding of contracts, and interference with the legislative process that emerged in Poland at the beginning of the 2000s. They were felt to shed light on the ability of networks linked to former communist service functionaries to exercise influence in various formal and informal power structures. For example, commentator Bronisław Wildstein (2005) argued that the work of the parliamentary investigative commission into the so-called 'Orlen affair' showed that 'communist security service networks are still alive' and this 'game of files' was possible 'precisely because this knowledge is [only] available to [the] chosen ones, and this situation is optimal for former functionaries (including those in Russian intelligence) who have this knowledge.'

Defending Mr Wildstein's actions in releasing his infamous list, Piotr Skwieciński (2005) argued that

> various structures of a business-financial character have an 'SB' (and 'military') provenance and, in addition to former communist security service functionaries, their membership also includes former [security service] collaborators. These structures carry out an active economic, financial and political game, and secret collaborators participate in this game.

He described this 'corrupt network' as 'the core of the real social system of the Third Republic', which the 'post-UB mafia' was committed to defending against attempts by the then opposition to try to break it up. Defending the importance of more radical truth revelation, Mr Skwieciński argued that

> the possible revelation of the existence of agent entanglements in the media and business communities would be a change whose importance it is difficult to overestimate.... This would allow the discovery of the prior sources of part of the existing financial and financial-mafia construct. And also one of the sources of the support that the oligarchic system still enjoys in part of the media.

He said that Mr Wildstein was 'acting in a state of higher necessity' as 'the revelation of at least part of the post-UB entanglements' was necessary because it 'increased the chances of breaking up that [Third Republic network] system'.

Similarly, sociologist Barbara Fedyszak-Radziejewska (2005) argued that

> [t]he work of the three [Sejm] investigative commissions (Rywin, PZU[6] and Orlen) shows how much our present reality is immersed in the past. And among the more important elements of this past are the assets of the IPN archives.

She bemoaned the fact that – while there were a substantial number of historians carrying out research and writing important books, and those who had been invigilated could learn the truth about what the communist regime meant for them personally – very few journalists took advantage of this possibility. She put this down to the fact that 'the elite "holding power and government over our souls" has blocked the articulation of these demands [for lustration and decommunisation] in public debate, in spite of the clear and stable support of Polish society for these processes.' She interpreted the fact that 'the milieu holding senior positions in the formal and informal structures of power' had blocked these processes as being due to the fact that 'hidden behind this there is a defence of (their vested) interests'.

Two other sociologists, Radosław Sojak and Andrzej Zybertowicz (2005), also argued that lustration was 'the one procedure thanks to which we can get to know important mechanisms of systemic transformation. The mechanisms that are responsible for the chronic illness of the Third Republic.' Again, linking the need for lustration with recent scandals, they asked:

> Is it possible (after the Rywin affair) to write about the functioning of the media without taking into account the behind-the-scenes dimensions? Is it possible (from the time of the Orlen and PZU commissions) to analyse the improprieties of small and large-scale privatisation without analysing the [communist security service] agent dimension? Is it possible (after the Starachowice affair)[7] to write monographs about local Polish milieu without taking into account the politico-criminal networks?

Arguing that the Polish state could not afford to ignore the way that the hidden, behind-the-scenes aspect of the country's systemic transformation had played out, they claimed that '[w]ithout lustration we cannot correctly diagnose Polish problems. Without staring into the eyes of communist evil we cannot be in a position to deal with today's weaknesses.'

Similarly, commentator Tomasz Wiścicki (2005) argued that the climate surrounding the revelation of the communist security service archive contents had changed and was much more favourable to greater file access due to

> the revelations of the scale of the scandals in which the communist secret services played the main role. Through the common effort of journalists, parliamentary deputies in the investigative commissions, certain public prosecutors we have learned how the 'privatisation of the police state' was not the imaginings of fantasists.

At the same time, 'weaknesses and internal disputes in the post-communist camp have meant that the notorious unity of this group has started to crack and some of them have started to '"fess up"'. Law and Justice leader and prime minister Jarosław Kaczyński also argued that lustration was designed to 'eliminate dangerous people from public life, break up old links between officers and agents, who – according to our knowledge – to this day play a considerable role in our political and economic life' (Leszczyński 2006).

Speaking in the March 2006 debate on the new lustration law, Self-Defence leader Andrzej Lepper argued that

> if you examined the careers of the chairmen of state treasury companies after 1989, chairs of supervisory boards, those who took over our national assets to then pass them on to others, in the communist party and the preceding communist system, then you immediately come to the conclusion that the majority of them are in fact the [former communist security] service [functionaries], these are collaborators, these are people who – whether they wanted to or not – did something in the previous system, they were not pushed aside from power, [they] were just given responsible tasks.

'These people', he continued, 'have certainly benefited from these changes' because 'no government, no legislature, no Sejm after 1989 has done what it should have, that is: it has not adopted an appropriate law which would ensure openness of these [communist security service] archives.' He argued that post-1989 privatisation scandals were linked to the need for a lustration law and that 'it is time to finally break it [this link] so that we can have a reckoning of all these privatisations, these scandals, knowing who is who. And then we will have openness' (Sejm RP 2006b, pp. 149–150). In the same debate, League of Polish Families leader Roman Giertych claimed that the 1989 round table agreement between the communist regime and sections of the democratic opposition had 'identified certain [security] services, certain milieu which are, to this day, untouchable'. In an allusion to veteran democratic opposition activist and post-communist media magnate Adam Michnik and his Agora conglomerate, Mr Giertych argued that this untouchability was 'built on fictional moral authorities' who were actually 'caricatures of that period [of anti-communist opposition]' and who 'as a result of a conspiracy, grabbed media capital and power' (Czuchnowski 2006).

Speaking in the same debate, Law and Justice deputy Marek Suski argued that

> [t]he extremely privileged position of people linked to the repressive apparatus of the Polish People's Republic is proof of the strong legal-mental link between the Third Republic and the People's Republic. This is an important element of the post-communist [system].

'These people', he claimed, 'are still taking advantage of their acquired rights, rights that are still invoked, when we try and take away something [of the] entitlements of the former functionaries of the services of the repressive apparatus of the Polish People's Republic.' For example, a 'sizeable proportion' of the most successful businessmen in post-communist Poland, such as those who ran the PKN Orlen company,

> are in part people whose origins are to be found in the communist and People's Republic security services. Opening up the archives would certainly have prevented the plotting with the head of the KGB for Poland [of] the

sale of our strategic businesses to a foreign power that had enslaved Poland for several decades.

He argued that a proportion of the communist security services 'undoubtedly continued their activity in free Poland ... but this footprint, this influence on the pace of events is also hidden, made secret, like the SB archives.' He continued,

> the more we find out about the activities of these services, the more we understand the complexity of the contemporary social and economic situation, because undoubtedly the influence of the [communist security] services on our economy – as the Orlen affair showed – is huge.

The fact that these scandals were found to be linked to the communist security services showed that

> a lack of lustration also greatly harms the economy. A failure to push these people – for whom betrayal was, for years, a method of functioning, a kind of way of living – aside from positions of influence, is continually, and increasingly, coming back to take its toll upon us.
> (Sejm RP, pp. 157–158)

League of Polish Families deputy Rafał Wiechecki also argued that

> everyone knows full-well that the connections in Poland between the secret services and the world of business and politics still exist. We know that files are still held, that people who were employees, functionaries of the security organs, have certain information, have certain documents and are holding on to these documents.

These documents are 'a sword which is hanging over certain people. [They are told that] [y]ou have to do this because if you don't we will reveal them.' This was, he argued, one of the mechanisms that caused corruption within the post-communist Third Republic, but thanks to the lustration bill, '[t]his sword will no longer be there' (Sejm RP 2006b, pp. 135–136).

On a later occasion, Law and Justice spokesman Arkadiusz Mularczyk (2016) argued that

> [communist] Security Service functionaries ... had many possibilities ... to [participate in the] sell-off of the Polish state ... [which] led to gangster, mafia activities ... in the 1990s it was clearly evident that a large section of the criminal world took advantage of its influences in the old Security Services.

The scandals that emerged at the beginning of the 2000s contributed to the revival of the topic, because, he claimed, it could be seen that the [1997 lustration] law had not cleansed public life ... that many Security Service collaborators were continuing to function in public life, political, local government, media, economy – this gave a strong political headwind to carrying ... through ... the [2006] law.

Similarly, commentator Piotr Semka (2016) argued that 'the demand for lustration and the scale of the opposition ... showed that the situation was not normal ... [that] there is a problem that people know that hidden mechanisms operate but [people] cannot prove it'. Sociologist Andrzej Zybertowicz (2016) also claimed that

> at a certain moment it became clear that without ... explaining how the [communist] Polish People's Republic functioned – that it was a police-state, that security services were one of the key regulators of the social sphere, the party regulated one set of processes and the secret services regulated another type of process – ... we will not understand the structure of certain [social phenomena]. There [were] certain types of links which generate[d] the temptation for consciously planned conflicts of interests which no prosecutor, no policemen, no journalist can uncover without lustration. Lustration makes the development of hidden conflicts of interests more difficult.

Prof. Zybertowicz claimed that, while working as a national security adviser in the presidential chancellery at the end of the 2000s, he headed up a team that monitored around 80 post-1989 scandals and found that 80 per cent of these were 'linked in some way to the security services: either as current functionaries, previous ones or secret collaborators'.

Interestingly, historian Antoni Dudek (2016) argued that 'the majority of the various pathologies which arose in the Third Republic have their roots after 1989 and not before ... [and] did not have a clear link with the communist security services'. He estimated that of the 100 richest people in Poland, 'around 20 had some kind of links with the [communist] apparatus of power, although not necessarily the Security Services'. Similarly, speaking on a later occasion, commentator Bronisław Wildstein (2016) also offered a somewhat more nuanced argument, saying that although among the individuals involved in the scandals of the early to mid-2000s, such as the Rywin and Orlen affairs, there 'were clearly [those] who grew up under the communist system, this was a post-communist network [układ], [but] this was not [linked directly to] lustration itself because these were communists'. Although '[t]his (business network) ... ensured that these privileged businessmen had a quasi-monopoly and, in this way, destroyed their competition' and 'sometimes it was revealed that someone was a [communist security service] agent ... generally these were just individuals who were important figures in the [communist] Polish People's Republic'.

Lustration and elite turnover

Closely linked to the notion of lustration as an element of democratisation and the cleansing of politics and public life was the idea that public positions should be held by those who have behaved honourably. Historian Antoni Dudek (2016) has argued that one of the key objectives of lustration was to 'serve as a tool to change social elites, especially the older ones' so that 'the agents of the [communist] security services were to be annihilated from public life, not just parliament, government but also academia, the media ... they were supposed to be completely pushed aside from any important sphere'. For example, writing in the mid-2000s, Tomasz Wróblewski (2005) argued that

> the verification of [public] authority figures is the outright key to changing the consciousness of Poles. The more examples that we have of the reflexive defence of well-known figures from public life in spite of the principles that they espouse every day, the faster that public opinion loses trust.

Tomasz Wiścicki (2005), another commentator, also argued that there was a need to 'take advantage of the current favourable atmosphere and political conjuncture' to broaden the scope of lustration so that 'members of professions that involve public trust should be free from suspicion that they collaborated with the [communist security] services.' On a later occasion, historian Sławomir Cenckiewicz (2016) argued that lustration

> was an element of a more general anti-communist moral cleansing, it raised questions about all politicians ... who had had some previous involvement in the communist regime – revealing their role in this process ... [and] ... past collaboration ... [which] would have been a severe blow to them.

Similarly, sociologist Andrzej Zybertowicz (2016) argued that although '[l]ustration was a [truth] revelation process', those promoting it were 'fully conscious of [its] political objectives, including elite change'. Commentator Bronisław Wildstein (2016) justified this on the grounds that, citing one example, as a result of the elite pacted nature of the Polish transition to democracy, judges linked to the previous communist regime – which 'was not a law-based state, so [they] were not appointed in line with the rule of law' – had 'an entry point advantage' in the new, post-1989 judicial system.

In the draft lustration law justificatory statement, Law and Justice argued:

> The basic aim of this draft law is to protect and strengthen democracy in the Republic of Poland through leading us to a position in which the most important state positions, the fulfilment of which combines a requirement to possess not just meritocratic but also moral qualifications, will be filled by people whose past does not raise doubts in the realms of their service, work or those kind of contacts with state security organs whose moral evaluation must be negative.

The statement also argued that

> [we have to have a guarantee that those who occupy] functions, positions and professions requiring public trust by people through their conduct up until now gave and continue to give a guarantee of honesty, honour, a feeling of responsibility for their own words and actions, civic determination and righteousness.
> (Sejm RP 2006a, p. 138)

Speaking in the March 2006 debate, Law and Justice spokesman Arkadiusz Mularczyk said that the proposed certificates that individuals would have issued under the new law outlining the nature of their collaboration 'will have a significant impact upon the evaluation of that person's moral qualifications that are essential for fulfilling public functions' (Sejm RP 2006b, p. 138). On a later occasion, Mr Mularczyk (2016) argued:

> The opposition to the more radical model of lustration [contained in the 2006 law] was linked to the defence of certain interests ... who either feared [it for what it would say about] themselves or were concerned at what would be found generally in those documents.

He said that

> many people who worked for or collaborated with the [communist] Security Services continued to perform public functions ... there are still places like the media, judiciary and academia where they still fulfil prominent functions and still have an influence on the ... selection of people for these functions.

Speaking in the same March 2006 parliamentary debate, Civic Platform parliamentary caucus leader Jan Rokita argued that

> public figures who are in professions or functions where a certain public trust and credibility is required; these should be treated exactly the same by the lustration law.... [A]ll those who perform public functions, functions based on trust – and who, in connection with that, in a democratic state should have fully open, and not hidden, biographies – all of these should be obliged to submit a lustration declaration.
> (Sejm RP 2006b, p. 139)

Mr Rokita argued that by ensuring that 'politicians cannot hide their biographies', the new lustration law would 'guarantee the decency of politics and public life' (Sejm RP 2006b, p. 142). Similarly, Dariusz Lipiński, another Civic Platform deputy, also said:

> We are today debating a little about the past, but also the wholly contemporary need to fill functions, positions and professions which require

public trust with people who are supposed to give a guarantee of honesty, worthiness, a feeling of responsibility for their words and actions, civic determination, integrity.

(Sejm RP 2006, p. 159)

Law and Justice deputy Marek Suski said that the process of opening up the communist security service archives would 'reveal who is loyal towards our country' and determine whether the Polish state was 'democratic with a human face, or with the face of a chimney sweep', because this 'depends on what kind of opinion-forming class we have'. Lustration was thus 'a specific activity to repair the state', because a country 'does not want to be notoriously betrayed, has to condemn betrayal, and deplore traitors', and 'a law which, thus, shows who was a traitor and who was a hero' would be 'a milestone in the history of constructing a just state' (Sejm RP 2006b, p. 158). Tomasz Markowski, another Law and Justice deputy, also argued that 'we need to finally, and in a manner that conforms to reality, establish a catalogue of functions, positions, occupations, which require public trust. Too many sensitive segments of the state and society found themselves beyond the verification of lustration.' The lustration law would 'in line with social intuition, and what society expects from us, significantly widen the group of occupations requiring public trust' (Sejm RP 2006b, p. 162). Stanisław Pięta (Law and Justice) argued that

> the Polish nation must have the certainty that [members of] the state administration, [parliamentary] deputies, [and] the government are people who are committed to the interests of the nation and interests of the state, that no one has any compromising materials [held on them].

He also said that

> cleansing [the state] administration, cleansing local government, cleansing state institutions, cleansing many occupations, from people who collaborated with the communist security apparatus is a condition of the re-birth of the Polish state elite. Without this we cannot construct a normal, honest Poland.

(Sejm RP 2006b, p. 163)

Andrzej Szlachta (Law and Justice) also claimed that '[c]leansing the Polish state by eliminating people from public life whose past raises moral reservations is an obligation, a historical necessity, a national imperative' (Sejm RP 2006b, p. 164).

Interestingly, although they obviously used somewhat different arguments, opponents of more radical lustration also said that the proposal to extend its scope was motivated in large part, if not solely, by a desire to achieve elite turnover. For example, speaking during the March 2006 debate on the new lustration law, Democratic Left Alliance spokesman Ryszard Kalisz argued that the authors of the new law 'regard lustration as the destruction of people' (Sejm RP

2006b, p. 151). Speaking in the same debate, Democratic Left Alliance deputy Katarzyna Piekarska claimed that 'the moral qualifications [set out in the Law and Justice draft law] ... will ... be the only criteria determining if a person is suitable for a particular role' (Sejm RP 2006b, p. 178). Similarly, speaking in the July 2006 debate, another Democratic Left Alliance deputy, Joanna Senyszyn, argued that the communist security service files were 'used selectively according to political requirements' and that '[e]very so often a file of a person which they want to be eliminated from public life is discovered' (Sejm RP 2006c, p. 305).

Commentator Jerzy Baczyński (2005) argued that the objective of radical lustration was 'excluding certain groups of people from public life'. Similarly, Jacek Żakowski (2005) said that the objective of what he called '[t]he "Wildstein avalanche"' was to strengthen 'the feeling of ... the lack of credibility of the elites – whose representatives found themselves among the thousands of people of unclear status'. On another occasion, Mr Żakowski (2007) argued that 'new [intellectual and cultural] elites' wanted to use lustration to 'disown the old elites and the instrument to change them is to be unveiling the biographical truth about the past'. Intellectuals who felt that they had 'missed out' saw '"lustration revelations"' as a way to 'break through to the position to which they aspire ... for years they saw in the security service files their last chance for places which they could occupy to be vacated'.

Commentator Janina Paradowska (2005) also argued that thanks to lustration, the '"who" becomes more important than [the] "what"', so that only 'people who are morally without accusation will come to power', who 'will be in a position to overcome the wicked and shameful remnants of the Polish People's Republic'. The process would thus 'verify the existing balance of forces according to unclear lustration criteria' and 'hit political formations that emerged from the Polish People's Republic' but also 'above all ... those newly emerging milieu and parties that emerged after 1989, who have a restrained attitude towards lustration (in other words, have betrayed the idea of a clean and moral Poland)'. On another occasion, Ms Paradowska (2016) said that

> the 2006 law was supposed to bring about a change of elites ... [that was] one of its basic aims.... When Law and Justice came to power in 2005 they were convinced that they could change the intellectual elite, the founders of the Third Republic ... through lustration.

Similarly, another commentator, Krzytsztof Burnetko (2005), said that the kind of lustration proposed by Law and Justice was 'an excellent method to clear out positions in the state to create spaces for its people.' Political scientist Jacek Raciborski (2005) claimed that 'the intention of the supporters of universal lustration is really about de-communisation, sometimes understood very simply as removing from influence in political life people linked to the previous regime'. Constitutional lawyer Wiktor Osiatyński (2007) said that the 2006 lustration law was 'a potential scourge [to be used against] almost everyone who participated in social, academic and cultural life or in the opposition during the PRL period, and would now like to be active in public life'. Commentator Ewa Siedlecka (2016) also argued that lustration was 'a tool through which one group is trying to eliminate another ... a tool for re-furnishing the Polish political scene'. The lustration process was, she said, part of a 'battle to change elites ... we have a narrative [from Law and Justice] that those who held positions ... – who ... were [public] authority figures ... – that you have to replace them'.

Lustration and the 'Fourth Republic' project

Sometimes (although perhaps not as often as one might have expected), the need for greater lustration and file access was linked to, and became entwined specifically with, the so-called 'Fourth Republic' project. Against the background of the various scandals that emerged in the early to mid-2000s, politicians and commentators, particularly from the Law and Justice party, began to call for a moral revolution that would replace the corrupt post-1989 Third Republic state with a strong and moral new 'Fourth Republic'. The 'Fourth Republic' project was based on a harsh critique of the post-communist state, which was considered to be inherently weak, morally bankrupt, controlled by corrupt cliques and requiring far-reaching moral renewal and political reform. Specifically, it was rooted in the notion that political life in the post-communist period was manipulated by the former (but still influential) communist-era security services – and, more broadly, the perceived ability of elites linked to the former regime to take advantage of their communist-era networks to turn their old political power into economic power; what Lipiński terms the 'propertisation' of the nomenklatura (Lipiński 2013, p. 243)[8] – which prompted many Poles to question the virtues of the so-called 'thick line' approach towards transitional justice.

Rejecting key elements of the settlement agreed at the round table negotiations and entrenched as a result of the Mazowiecki government's 'thick line' policy, Law and Justice-linked politicians and supporting intellectuals often argued that Poland's apparent post-1989 economic success and political stability were illusory and that the country's key institutions were often simply a façade to hide the machinations of a vast, all-encompassing and powerful web of inter-locking secret, informal networks. This exploitative 'układ' (roughly translated as 'system' or 'mechanism') generated by the post-1989 settlement comprised an entrenched, corrupt nexus which brought together organised crime with politicians, businessmen, interest groups, cultural elites, the legal establishment and others associated with the previous regime or linked to the former communist security services, and which, through its power and wealth, exerted a baleful influence on political and economic life in post-1989 Poland.[9] As historian Andrzej Paczkowski (2016) put it, the call for radical lustration was based, in large part, on the notion that 'the officers who ran these secret collaborators ... and the [communist security] services more generally ... had a significant influence on what happened after the collapse of communism' and that those old ties would have been utilised ... so that the most important players in the economic, political and cultural spheres were linked with each other through the old structures – the secret collaborators and their handling officers. This is where the concept of the 'układ' originated, and to this was added the [former communist] nomenklatura.

Lustration was thus a key element of the 'Fourth Republic' project, at least in a rhetorical sense, because it fitted with the analysis of an elite bargain that protected (and created) certain old-new elite groups, and the idea that opening up the files was needed to reveal these hidden mechanisms.

This idea that the Polish state was politically corrupt and morally bankrupt was not simply political rhetoric. It was the key to understanding Law and Justice's worldview, with the notion of a radical project of reconstruction to confront and break the power of these networks underpinning the party's programme of moral and political renewal. This formed the core of the party's programme for government, although, arguably, the 'Fourth Republic' was more of a slogan than having been fully and systematically thought through, and the party was less clear about how it would actually be operationalised. Originally an idea and critique that enjoyed quite broad political support (including from politicians and intellectual milieu associated with Civic Platform), the 'Fourth Republic' renewal project came to be associated primarily with the 2005–2007 Law and Justice-led governments, and, together with anti-corruption measures and a radical reconstruction of the Polish state, included a re-affirmation of traditional patriotic and religious values and a more solidaristic social and economic policy, which, its supporters argued, better reflected the original ideas of the anti-communist Solidarity movement.[10] The broadening of the scope of lustration and communist security file access was, in many people's minds, a key element of such a renewal project, and the 2006 law came to be seen as one of this government's flagship legislative reforms embodying the 'Fourth Republic' project, together with the formation of a powerful new central anti-corruption bureau (Centralne Biuro Antykorupcyjne: CBA) with wide-ranging powers to prosecute public officials at all levels; the root-and-branch reform of the Military Information Service counter-intelligence agency, which was felt to be corrupt and still dominated by functionaries linked to the previous communist regime; and enhancing the role of the Institute of National Remembrance as a key body in promoting traditional patriotic values.

For example, sociologist Andrzej Zybertowicz (2016) argued that these were all necessary and complementary

> to break the spine of ... the post-communist system. The central anti-corruption bureau's objective was to monitor how the elite, especially the political one, behaves, [to see if it] is honest, check asset declarations, and the Institute of National Remembrance was the institution whose aim was to research the biographies of the elites. [The Institute's role] is to cleanse the elites of those whose biographies ... have characteristics that are not necessarily themselves

shameful but show [that they are people who have] a weakness to carry out behind-the-scenes instructions, while the central anti-corruption bureau['s role] was to reduce current temptations.

In fact, commentator Janina Paradowska (2016) even claimed that the central anti-corruption bureau quickly replaced lustration as the key institution in the political battle to build a 'Fourth Republic', because it 'emerged that lustration did not affect the governing elites to a great extent.... Corruption and the central anti-corruption bureau were, on the other hand, much more important.'

In debates on the new lustration and file access law, this was reflected in calls for the dis-entanglement of the ruling elite from such secret networks. For example, according to Law and Justice spokesman Arkadiusz Mularczyk (2016),

> [lustration] was an important element [of the Fourth Republic project] because the Polish state, after years of 'post-communist' governments was in fairly bad condition ... people saw that post-communist governments had taken the country to a certain level of ruin ... [and] citizens expected [that Law and Justice and Civic Platform would undertake] a general cleansing of public life, with lustration being one of these elements.

Similarly, speaking in the March 2006 debate in support of the proposed new lustration law, Law and Justice deputy Marek Suski argued:

> Knowledge about the people who make up the elite, who was on the side of darkness and who was on the side of light, is the dawn of the Fourth, just Republic. This dawn, this [new] beginning, [is what] Law and Justice is seeking.
>
> (Sejm RP 2006b, p. 158)

Similarly, Stanisław Pięta, another Law and Justice deputy, argued that 'without truth and justice there is no honest Poland. Without these values there will be no Fourth Republic' (Sejm RP 2006b, p. 163).

Krzysztof Wyszkowski (2006), a veteran communist-era Solidarity opposition activist, also drew attention to this link, arguing that the lustration law was 'a matter that could determine the ability of the current Polish government to build the Fourth Republic'. Mr Wyszkowski argued that, in the run-up to the 2005 elections, 'those parties invoking the Solidarity ethos and a will to build the Fourth Republic, declared as one of their main slogans a will to completely open up and give wide access to the IPN archives'. While there were major differences between the two parties (Law and Justice and Civic Platform) on many issues, 'on the question of the new [lustration] law both parties [have] co-operated surprisingly well'. Mr Wyszkowski saw the Law and Justice party and President Lech Kaczyński's determination (or lack of it) to carry through the lustration law as a test of the credibility of the Fourth Republic project:

The President faces an alternative. Does he want to build a Fourth Republic with those who will sooner or later take power and will evaluate, and possibly lengthen, his presidency? Or with those who are tired by the curious war of the so-called opposition with the SB and WSW [Wojskowa Służba Wewnętrzna, the Internal Military Service – Poland's communist-era military counter-intelligence agency], exhausted by permanent compromises, used to continual defeats.

Interestingly, this explicit link was more often made by commentators rather than politicians, and frequently by opponents of lustration and Law and Justice and the Fourth Republic project more generally. For example, commentator Jacek Żakowski (2005) saw demands for lustration in general, and the 'Wildstein list' in particular, as part of what he termed 'the conservative-republican revolution' (rewolucja konserwatyno-republikańska: RKR). 'The motor of the RKR' was, he argued,

> universal frustration at the state of politics and the state. Its vehicle is meant to be lustration and de-communisation. Its fundamental principle is breaking the evolutionary continuity reaching back to the years of the PRL. Its effect: excluding a large segment of the elite, changing the rules of the game, releasing energy.

The objective of the Wildstein list was, therefore, according to Mr Żakowski, to 'achieve such a temperature in public life, such a boiling of emotions, that would justify implementing the politically, culturally and socially radical turn about which the supporters of the Fourth Republic dream.' What he termed 'the Wildstein avalanche' helped to achieve this, because it

> fuels the demand for radical change. It strengthens the feeling of uncertainty and ambiguousness, lack of credibility of the elites – whose representatives found themselves among those thousands of persons of an unclear status – the weakness of institutions, the tardiness of procedures, stiffness of the legal corset.

Similarly, Janina Paradowska (2005) saw the drive for more radical lustration and file access laws as 'the next stage of the pre-[2005] election offensive of groupings of the so-called Fourth Republic and attempt to polarise the political scene, strengthen the extremes and crush the liberal centre'. Seeing 'political tactics and hypocrisy' as lying behind the call for moral renewal, she saw this as an attempt to divide Poles into pro- and anti-lustration camps, with those in favour being 'for moral renewal, for cleansing public life, for good and against [communist security service] agents'. On another occasion, Ms Paradowska (2016) argued that 'the curse of lustration in Poland was that it was [used as] a political tool'. Another commentator, Krzysztof Burnetko (2005), also argued that, for Law and Justice in particular, lustration was 'not just a condition of [its] credibility but also an element of a useful tactic after the wave of "bread or circus" electoral promises. It fits superbly with the mechanism of progressing the revolution.'

More generally, critics of more radical lustration attacked it specifically, and the Fourth Republic project in general, as socially divisive and politically destructive. For example, commentator Jacek Żakowski (2005) argued that the objective of the Wildstein list was 'about achieving such temperature in public life, such heating up of emotions, which will justify implementing a radical political, cultural and social turn which the supporters of the Fourth Republic hope for.' Similarly, political scientist Jacek Raciborski (2005) argued that the radical lustration supporters' aim was to 'demolish the current hierarchy of social values, to seize control of the symbolic sphere from the supporters of the Third Republic'. Speaking during the March 2006 debate on the new lustration law, Democratic Left Alliance deputy Tadeusz Iwiński also argued that 'right-wing forces' reached for the lustration issue as a distraction when 'they come to power [and] encounter enormous difficulties solving basic problems such as unemployment' and accused its supporters of promoting 'a new wave of lustration madness' (Sejm RP 2006b, p. 160).

Opponents of radical lustration also criticised the assumptions upon which the 'Fourth Republic' project and the concomitant demand for radical lustration were based as opportunistic and false. Speaking in the same March 2006 debate, Mr Iwiński argued that however one evaluates the 1989 round table negotiations, 'you cannot consider the history of Poland in conspiratorial categories' (Sejm RP 2006b, p. 160). Similarly, Democratic Left Alliance Katarzyna Piekarska responded to arguments that the objective of more radical lustration was to protect an emerging democracy by saying that 'democracy in the states of Central and Eastern Europe is [now] so solidified that further lustration proceedings are beside the point' (Sejm RP 2006b, p. 178). Commentator Jerzy Baczyński (2005) also argued that lustration would 'not solve any Polish problems, even the much sought-after "breaking up of the suspected political-business networks"'. Political scientist Jacek Raciborski (2005) said that

> even if one accepted the overall thesis about such an appropriation [of the state and the economy by elites linked to the previous communist regime] then by what miracle will a thousand ordinary 'Kowalskis' ['Smiths'] investigating informers find an explanation in the [communist security service] files into who 'stole' Orlen or PZU, and why?

Conclusions

Many of the arguments used by supporters of more radical lustration and truth revelation were inter-linked and often overlapped with one another, but it is possible to draw out a number of clear themes. The impetus for the revival of the lustration debate and revising the lustration and file access law in the mid-2000s came in large part from the fact that the truth-revelation procedures that were established at the end of the 1990s, and became operational at the beginning of the 2000s, were not felt to be working well and functioning effectively. At the same time, the revelations that accompanied the formation of the Institute of National Remembrance, and the opening up of communist security service files to journalists and historians and other individuals, themselves created a greater appetite for a more radical lustration and file regime. In addition to this, the re-emergence of the issue and discussions about the idea of pushing forward with more radical lustration and communist security service file access often became entwined with other, broader debates about the perceived failures of the post-communist democratisation process more generally. Calls for more radical lustration and communist security file access were felt to be indicative of the need to, and were often linked to projects designed to, implement post-communist renewal and deepen and improve the quality of democracy more generally. In particular, they were often linked to a perceived need to tackle corruption as an endemic feature of post-communist Polish politics and society, and the importance of freedom of information and satisfying the public's 'right to know' the backgrounds of its public officials and authority figures. This was often bound up with the notion that elites and officials linked to the former regime had taken advantage of their communist-era networks, including those rooted in the former security services, to turn their old political power into new economic influence, which prompted many citizens and political elites to question the virtues of the 'thick line' approach towards transitional justice adopted by the first post-1989 governments. Such critiques of post-communist democratisation and calls for greater transparency were exemplified by the so-called 'Fourth Republic' project, most associated with the 2005–2007 Law and Justice party-led governments, but actually part of a broader, radical critique of post-1989 Poland as corrupt and requiring far-reaching moral and political renewal.

The analysis presented here, therefore, supports the notion that 'politics of the present'-type approaches to explaining the recurrence of lustration and file access and changes of trajectory, which posit the notion that they became instrumentalised in post-communist power struggles, need to be modified to take account of the fact that the (at least declared) motives of those pushing for more radical lustration and transitional justice were, in part at least, programmatically and ideologically driven. In this sense, it supports the arguments of authors such as Horne, who see the emergence of late lustration as being tied to efforts to improve the quality of post-communist democracy. This directs our attention to the important point that in many post-communist states, such as Poland, examining discussions about lustration and transitional justice separately from other political developments can lead one to underestimate the extent to which these issues need to be analysed in conjunction with other debates and factors, given that they often became bundled up with other, broader post-communist democratisation discourses. These were related as much to the relationship between transitional justice and the perceived failures of post-communist democratisation as they were to questions of coming to terms with the communist past, with lustration posited as a project designed to implement democratic renewal and enhance the quality of democracy.

There are clearly limitations to the approach adopted here, not least the danger of 'cherry picking' statements to fit with a purported narrative. Moreover, examining the *declared* motives of lustration supporters may not reveal their *actual* intentions. In order to overcome these problems here, I attempted as far as possible to locate and draw out consistently recurring themes that were developed by several different speakers and contributors to this debate, rather than simply picking individual, sporadic statements that fitted with my overall argument. Moreover, the fact that there was a clear and consistent programmatic rationale presented by a range of different contributors to the debate suggested (although it does not, of course, prove) that such statements were, to some extent at least, properly thought through and not simply grafted on as a justificatory after-thought. This, together with the fact that the 2006 lustration law enjoyed (initially, at least) overwhelming cross-party support, which obviously reduced the scope for using the issue as a means of strategic positioning, provided prima facie evidence that there was at least some programmatic underpinning to the motivations of lustration supporters.

Nonetheless, it is instructive to compare and confront the arguments used by lustration supporters with those advanced by opponents of its more extensive use as a transitional justice method. Opponents of radical lustration focused many of their arguments on defending the court-based model adopted in 1997, as being better able to safeguard the provisions of the rule of law, and the shortcomings of the proposed alternatives contained in the 2006 law, which, in its original form at least, shifted the emphasis from self-declarations verified by a judicial process to one based primarily on certificates outlining the nature of security service collaboration issued by Institute of National Remembrance historians and archivists. Nonetheless, critics of more radical lustration also focused on the alleged instrumental-strategic motivations of its proponents, accusing them, and supporters of the 'Fourth Republic' project more generally, of weaponising the issue in a socially divisive and politically destructive way as a means of achieving elite turnover: an objective that supporters of extending truth revelation themselves openly acknowledged. This could also be seen in the fact that supporters of more radical truth revelation also posited elite turnover as one of their motivations – and the strongest proponents of it in parliament included younger deputies (as noted in Chapter 2, from virtually all parties) who potentially stood to benefit from such turnover – together with the fact that the most bitter resistance to the 2006 law emerged from specific interest groups who felt that they had the most to lose from such turnover, namely journalists and academics.

So, there were clearly elements of both ideological-programmatic and instrumental-strategic motivations evident here on both sides of the debate. However, the objective here is not necessarily to argue that one set of motives was dominant (even if, in practice, it was), as it is clearly difficult to separate these different motives out and identify them empirically. Rather, what the analysis in this chapter shows is the need to bring 'programme-ness' back into the equation, suggesting that at least *some* ideological motivations may have been significant in at least the *declared* motives of lustration supporters. Neither supporters nor opponents of radical lustration were solely (or even mainly) programmatically and ideologically motivated, and it is obviously impossible to know unambiguously whether a particular statement was ideological or instrumental. In practice, as in the case of virtually every political action, the protagonists were likely to have been motivated by an inter-play of both instrumental-strategic and ideological-programmatic factors.

Notes

1 An earlier version of this chapter was published as Szczerbiak (2016). I am grateful to Taylor and Francis publishers (www.tandfonline.com) for their permission to reproduce material from this article in this book.
2 Veteran Solidarity activist and regional leader who was accused of submitting a false lustration declaration (see Chapter 2).
3 For more on this, see Kaczyński (2006) and Nizieński (2006). According to Mr Nizieński's final report as Public Interest Spokesman, the list also included six Senators. See Sejm RP (2005a, p. 31).
4 In April 2004 the criminal court sentenced Mr Rywin to 30 months in prison, but also concluded that allegations that senior Democratic Left Alliance figures had put him up to the bribe attempt could not be proven (*Rzeczpospolita* 2004).
5 See, for example, Zybertowicz (1993, 2013) and Łoś and Zybertowicz (2000).
6 PZU (Powszechny Zakład Ubezpieczeń) was a monopolist communist-era state insurance agency, which was later converted into a state-owned company and established a number of subsidiaries. These included PZU Życie, which appeared to be particularly active in diverting large sums of public money into private investments, the mass media and political parties. The company seemed to have corrupt connections to many important political and business figures, and the scandal involved both former and current security service officers (Łoś 2005). A Sejm investigative committee set up in January 2005 found in its September 2005 report that the state treasury had lost billions of złoties in the 1999 sale of shares in PZU by the then Solidarity Electoral Action-led government to the Dutch insurance company Eureko and Polish Gdańsk BIG bank. It called for former treasury ministers Emil Wąsacz and Aldona Kamela-Sowiński to be summoned before the State Tribunal to account for their role in the sale.
7 In the Starachowice affair, Democratic Left Alliance parliamentary deputy and local party boss Andrzej Jagiełło was implicated in a scandal involving Starachowice local government officials who co-operated with local criminals. He tipped off fellow party members on the city council to warn them of a planned operation by the Central Bureau of Investigation (Centralne Biuro Śledcze: CBŚ) in which they would be detained by the police, apparently quoting information obtained from the party-nominated deputy internal affairs minister Zbigniew Sobotka.
8 For more on this see, for example, Łoś and Zybertowicz (2000).
9 See, for example, Kaczynski (2007). For interesting analyses of the politics of the 'układ', see Janicki and Władyka (2006), Wnuk-Lipiński (2006) and Matyja (2007).
10 The 'Fourth Republic' concept was first developed by political scientist Rafał Matyja (1998) in a niche conservative journal at the end of the 1990s, although it actually came to prominence in public discourse when the Civic Platform-linked academic (and future parliamentary deputy) Paweł Śpiewak (2003) used it in the wake of the Rywin affair. For a good summary of the debate on this concept, see Matyja (2004). For critical accounts of the Fourth Republic project, see, for example, Hall (2005), Reykowski (2005), Śpiewak (2010) and Bugaj (2010).

Bibliography

Baczyński, J., 2005. Lustracja niczego nie załatwi. *Rzeczpospolita*, 4 February.
Bugaj, R., 2010. Osierocona idea IV RP. *Rzeczpospolita*, July 6.
Burnetko, K., 2005. Dogrywka. *Polityka*, 10 December.
Burnetko, K., 2006. Żegnaj TW, witaj OŹI. Polityka, 5 August.
Cenckiewicz, S., 2016. Author interview, 6 June.
Czech, M., 2006. *Archiwista prokuratorom* [online], gazeta.pl, 20 August. Available from: http://serwisy.gazeta.pl/wyborcza/2029020,34474,3558371.html (accessed 21 August 2006).
Czuchnowski, W., 2006. Wszytkie partie chcą otwarcia archiwów bezpieki. *Gazeta Wyborcza*, 11 March.
Deutsche Welle, 2005. *Past Catches up with Polish PM* [online]. Deutsche Welle, 23 June. Available from: www.dw.com/en/past-catches-up-with-polish-pm/a-1626267 (accessed 18 January 2016).
Dudek, A., 2016. Author interview, 7 June.
Economist, 2004. Another week, another bribe. *Economist*, 21 October.
Fedyszak-Radziejewska, B., 2005. Dlaczego pikieta? *Gazeta Wyborcza*, 7 February.
Gazeta.pl, 2005a. *TK: dostęp do teczek dla agenta, ale nie do wszytkich* [online], gazeta.pl, 29 November. Available from: www.gazeta.pl (accessed 30 November 2005).
Gazeta.pl, 2005b. *Rokita: wraca szansa na wspólne rządy PO i PiS* [online], gazeta.pl, 13 June. Available from www.gazeta.pl (accessed 14 June 2005).
Gazeta.pl, 2005c. *Kieres: nie wykluczam, że poproszę marszałka Sejmu o spotkanie* [online], gazeta.pl, 14 January. Available from: http://wiadomosci.gazeta.pl/kraj/2029020,34308,2494188.html (accessed 14 January 2005).
Gazeta.pl, 2005d. *Lista osób, które komisja chce zlustrować* [online], gazeta.pl, 14 January. Available from: http://wiadomosci.gazeta.pl/wiadomosci/1,114873,2493080.html (accessed 14 January 2005).
Gazeta.pl, 2006. *Nowa lustracja nadchodzi* [online], gazeta.pl, 21 July. Available from www.gazeta.pl (accessed 22 July 2006).
Hall, A., 2005. IV Rzeczpospolitej raczej nie będzie. *Rzeczpospolita*, 27 October.
Janicki, M. and Władyka, W., 2006. Układ. *Polityka*, 1 April.
Kaczyński, A., 2005. Kto zajrzy do teczek. *Rzeczpospolita*, 30 November.
Kaczyński, A., 2006. Cztery razy lustracja. *Rzeczpospolita*, 8 March.
Kaczynski, J., 2007. *Nie obiecujemy cudów – obiecujemy konkrety* [online], dziennik.pl, 8 October. Available from www.dziennik.pl/Load.aspx?TabId¼2097lsnf¼p&f¼63180 (accessed 9 October 2007).
Kublik, A., 2004. *Orlengate: nowe rewelacje Kaczmarka* [online]. wyborcza.pl, 7 April. Available from: http://wyborcza.pl/1,75248,2009698.html (accessed 8 April 2004).
Kublik, A. and Czuchnowski, W., 2005. *Co jest w teczkach prezydenta i premiera?* [online]. gazeta.pl, 10 June. Available from: http://wiadomosci.gazeta.pl/kraj/2029020,34308,2758818.html (accessed 10 June 2005).
Kurtyka, J., 2006. Nie przeproszę Przewoźnkia. *Gazeta Wyborcza*, 7 January.
Leszczyński, A., 2006. *Lustracyjne wolty szefa PiS* [online]. wyborcza.pl, 5 July 2006. Available from: http://wyborcza.pl/1,75515,3460171.html (accessed 27 July 2006).
Leszczyński, A., 2016. Author interview, 8 June.
Lipiński, A., 2013. Meanings of 1989: Right-Wing Discourses in Post-Communist Poland. In K. McDermott and M. Stibbe, eds, *The 1989 Revolutions in Central and Eastern Europe: From Communism to Pluralism*. Manchester: Manchester University Press, 235–252.

Lityński, J., 2007a. Lustracja przyniesie krzywdę tysięcy ludzi. *Dziennik*, 15 March.
Lityński, J., 2007b. O tym, jak Semka odkrył spisek Geremka. *Rzeczpospolita*, 30 April–1 May.
Łoś, M.W., 2005. *Reshaping of Elites and the Privatization of Security: The Case of Poland* [online]. Reflections on Policing in Post-Communist Europe, 2. Available at: http://pipss.revues.org/351 (accessed 15 January 2015).
Łoś, M.W. and Zybertowicz, A., 2000. *Privatising the Police State: The Case of Poland*. Basingstoke: Macmillan.
Matyja, R., 1998. Obóz Czwartej Rzeczypospolitej. *Debata*, 3.
Matyja, R., 2004. *Druga..., trzecia..., czwarta..., czyli o państwie Polaków* [online], fakt. pl, 4 August. Available from: www.e-fakt.pl/artykuly/artykul.aspx/Artykul/30956 (accessed 19 December 2005).
Matyja, R., 2007. *Układ w Polsce cały czas istnieje* [online], 9 July, dziennik.pl. Available from: www.dziennik.pl/Load.aspx?TabId¼2097lsnf¼p&f¼51870 (accessed 13 July 2007).
Mularczyk, A., 2016. Author interview, 8 June.
Niesołowski, S., 2005. Lustracja totalna. *Gazeta Wyborcza*, 20 January.
Nizieński, B., 2006. Prokurator ludzkich sumień. *Rzeczpospolita*, 3 August.
Osiatyński, W., 2007. Lustracyjna pułapka. *Polityka*, 24 March.
Paczkowski, A., 2016. Author interview, 9 June.
Paradowska, J., 2005. Politeczka. *Polityka*, 19 February.
Paradowska, J., 2016. Author interview, 6 June.
Raciborski, J., 2005. Elity wyruszyły na wojne. *Rzeczpospolita*, 11 February.
Reykowski, J., 2005. 3 razy 60 proc. *Polityka*, 29 October.
Rzeczpospolita, 2004. Lew samotnym wilkiem. *Rzeczpospolita*, 27 April.
Rzeczpospolita, 2005, Instrukcja stypendysty Marka Belki. *Rzeczpospolita*, 22 June
Sejm RP, 2005. *Informacja Rzecznika Interesu Publicznego o działalność w latach 1999–2004*. Warsaw: Sejm RP.
Sejm RP, 2006a. *Projekt ustawy o ujawnieniu informacji o dokumentach organów bezpieczeństwa panstwa komunistyznego z lat 1944–1990 oraz treści tych dokumentów oraz o zmanie innych ustaw. Druk nr 360*. Warsaw: Sejm RP.
Sejm RP, 2006b. *12. Posiedzenie Sejmu w dniu 9 marca 2006r*. Warsaw: Sejm RP.
Sejm RP, 2006c. *22. Posiedzenie Sejmu w dniu 20 lipca 2006r*. Warsaw: Sejm RP.
Semka, P., 2016. Author interview, 6 June.
Siedlecka, E., 2016. Author interview, 8 June.
Skwieciński, P., 2005. Wildstein i wyższa konieczność. *Rzeczpospolita*, 3 February.
Śmiłowicz, P., 2004. Kto nasłał UOP na Modrzejewskiego. *Rzeczposolita*, 3 April.
Śmiłowicz, P., 2005a. Teczki dzielą i łączą. *Rzeczpospolita*, 13 June.
Śmiłowicz, P., 2005b. Teczkowy fortel premiera. *Rzeczpospolita*, 17 June.
Smoleński, P., 2002. *Ustawa za łapowkę czyli przychodzi Rywin do Michnika* [online]. wyborcza.pl, 26 December. Available from: http://wyborcza.pl/1,75478,1237212.html#ixzz3qVE3SIV1 (accessed 28 December 2002).
Smoleński, P., 2005. Inkwizycja zamiast sądu. *Gazeta Wyborcza*, 3 December.
Smoleński, P., 2006. *Młodzi lustrują* [online]. wyborcza.pl, 5 August. Available from: http://wyborcza.pl/1,76842,3529550.html (accessed 7 August 2006).
Sojak, R. and Zybertowicz, A., 2005. Lustracja dla chóru. *Rzeczpospolita*, 22 February.
Śpiewak, P., 2003. Koniec złudzień. *Rzeczpospolita*, 23 January.
Śpiewak, P., 2010. Pięć lat po czwartej. *Polityka*, 26 June.
Szczerbiak, A., 2016. Deepening Democratisation? Exploring the Declared Motives for 'Late' Lustration in Poland. *East European Politics*, 32 (4), 426–445.

Wielowieyska, D., 2004. *Kaczmarek: Miller nasłał UOP na szefa Orlenu* [online]. gazeta. pl, 2 April. Available from: http://wiadomosci.gazeta.pl/wiadomosci/1,114873,2001505. html (accessed 3 April 2004).
Wildstein, B., 2005. Cały ten antylustracyjny zgiełk. *Rzeczpospolita*, 14 January.
Wildstein, B., 2016. Author interview, 9 June.
Wiścicki, T., 2005. Poszerżyć zakres lustracji. *Rzeczpospolita*, 17 March.
Wnuk-Lipiński, E., 2006. W sieci układu. *Rzeczpospolita*, 22–23 April.
Wróblewski, T., 2005. Weryfikacji autorytetów. *Rzeczpospolita*, 4 February.
Wyszkowski, K., 2006. Gra pozorów czy lęk prezydenta. *Rzeczpospolita*, 6 November.
Zybertowicz, A., 1993. *W uścisku tajnych służb: Upadek komunizmu i układ postnomenklatury*. Warsaw: Wydawnictwo Antyk Marcin Dybowski.
Zybertowicz, A., 2013. *III RP: Kulisy systemu*. Warsaw: Wydawnictwo Słowo i Myśli.
Zybertowicz, A., 2016. Author interview, 7 June.
Żakowski, J., 2005. Czyja Polska? *Polityka*, 19 February.
Żakowski, J., 2007. Walcza kłamstwem. *Gazeta Wyborcza*, 13 March.

5 The 'Bolek' affair

Using truth-revelation procedures for political legitimation and de-legitimation

This chapter examines another example of how the lustration and file access issue had the capacity to recur as a topic of political debate: the stormy, indeed often ferocious, national political debate and divisions within the political elites that emerged from the Solidarity independent trade union and mass anti-communist opposition movement over claims that its one-time legendary leader, and the first democratically elected President in post-1989 Poland, Lech Wałęsa had collaborated with the communist secret services in the early 1970s as an informer codenamed 'Bolek'; and the nature and significance of this apparent collaboration. The 'Bolek' affair and different assessments of Mr Wałęsa's historical role show how post-communist debates about how to deal with the legacy of the communist past, and specifically truth-revelation procedures and the lustration and file access issue, became entwined with broader post-communist political struggles.

In particular, they illustrate the process of defining individuals as historical heroes or villains in order to establish them as public authority figures, and then to use them as authoritative sources to legitimate or de-legitimate the post-1989 state, political system and narratives underpinning it; particular political actors and formations; and the transitional justice process itself.[1] The 'Bolek' affair, therefore, shows how the question of truth revelation recurred because it was an instance, probably the most controversial and high profile, of how the communist security service archives were used to legitimate and de-legitimate the post-communist state's genesis and foundational myths, specific political actors and formations, and the transitional justice process itself. This differed from the way that some of the existing literature posits the lustration issue as being used to gain strategic advantage through, for example, presenting political opponents as being insufficiently (or too) radical in terms of their approach to vetting, or calculating that revealing or not revealing files about individual politicians is likely to support a particular party and/or damage its political opponents. It was more about using the contents of communist secret files, and the debates surrounding them, to locate that party within a particular historical narrative that it considered advantageous.

This chapter begins by examining the background to the 'Bolek' affair and discussing how the question of Mr Wałęsa's alleged communist security service collaboration surfaced and re-surfaced on a number of occasions in post-communist Poland. It then moves on to outline the arguments used by Mr Wałęsa's defenders and critics. The next section explains in detail how the 'Bolek' affair was used as a means of legitimation and de-legitimation at a number of levels: of the post-communist state, of particular political actors and formations, and of the truth-revelation process itself. Public attitudes towards Mr Wałęsa's alleged collaboration are examined separately and in detail in Chapter 6.

What was the 'Bolek' affair?

Allegations that Mr Wałęsa was a paid informant of the communist security services in the early 1970s codenamed 'Bolek' (the undercover moniker his handlers assigned him) first appeared in the public domain at the beginning of the 1990s and were to re-surface on a number of occasions in the post-communist period. Agent 'Bolek''s activity began with the anti-communist protests on the Baltic coast at the end of 1970 and the beginning of 1971, when Mr Wałęsa was a member of the strike committee in the Gdańsk shipyard. The alleged informer went on to provide information to Poland's communist-era secret police in the early 1970s on the views and actions of his colleagues in the shipyard. Mr Wałęsa, of course, became an icon of the struggle against Poland's communist regime, leading the Solidarity trade union and anti-communist opposition movement from its formation in 1980 until he was elected President in Poland's first fully free post-communist election at the end of 1990. Nonetheless, several of Mr Wałęsa's former colleagues from the Free Trade Unions of the Coast (Wolne Związki Zawodowe Wybrzeża: WZZ), an anti-communist opposition organisation operating in the coastal region in the late 1970s, backed the theory that he had been recruited as an agent. These included one-time leading Solidarity activists Andrzej and Joanna Gwiazda, Krzysztof Wyszkowski and the late Anna Walentynowicz.[2] However, Mr Wałęsa side-lined them within the union, and their claims were generally dismissed as conspiracy theories by most politicians and the mainstream media.

As discussed in Chapter 2, the allegations received their first high-profile airing in June 1992, when the by then President Wałęsa was included on the so-called 'Macierewicz list', and then re-surfaced at various points, including dramatically in June 2008 when, amid huge public interest, the Institute of National Remembrance published an academic monograph on Mr Wałęsa's alleged communist security service links by two of its historians, Sławomir Cenckiewicz and Piotr Gontarczyk (2008a), with the blessing of the Institute's then chairman Janusz Kurtyka. While the accusations themselves were not new, the authors presented what Mr Wałęsa's opponents said were previously unknown communist security service files, which contained strong, new circumstantial evidence that linked the former Solidarity leader and President to a very active collaborator codenamed 'Bolek'. Agent 'Bolek' was an ordinary worker who was recruited by the communist security service apparatus while under arrest during the coastal strikes in December 1970 and went on to inform on his fellow Gdańsk shipyard workers in the early 1970s.

Although most documents concerning agent 'Bolek' were destroyed, the book contained evidence of his collaboration from the remaining materials, including papers from the communist security service archives, excerpts of memoirs from participants in the political events of the 1970s and 1980s, and files from the 1990s concerning vetting procedures for the State Security Office and the public prosecutors' office. From these documents, the authors argued that agent 'Bolek' was a very effective and active agent between 1970 and 1972 but was apparently removed from the operating files in 1976. While not conclusive, given that some of the key documents went missing during Mr Wałęsa's 1990–1995 presidency, the authors claimed that the evidence contained in the book, based on the sources that they had uncovered from the incomplete 'Bolek' file and supported by testimony from security service officers who were his handlers, exposed his role as an informer. The book also claimed that, in the wake of the publication of the 'Macierewicz list', Mr Wałęsa had, while President, accessed some of the documents among the archived communist security service files that recorded his collaboration and arranged for them to be doctored, removed and even destroyed.

The book received substantial coverage in both the Polish and international media, sparking a heated national public and political debate on Mr Wałęsa's alleged collaboration.[3] Moreover, the authors questioned the lustration court's August 2000 verdict when Mr Wałęsa ran for President again during that year's presidential election campaign, which, as discussed in Chapter 2, declared that he had not lied when he stated in his declaration that he had never collaborated with the communist security services (Cenckiewicz and Gontarczyk 2008b). The evidence contained in the book also questioned the Institute's November 2005 decision to officially designate Mr Wałęsa as falling into the category of being 'persecuted' by the former communist regime (Cenckiewicz 2009). In doing so, it appeared to effectively clear him of collaboration, as this was a status not open to communist security service functionaries and informers, even if the latter had also been invigilated themselves. Interestingly, in September 2008, after the book was published, the Institute did not include Mr Wałęsa in a list of 2,000 people who were persecuted under communism, saying that his case was 'complicated', although it included some of the former President's main Solidarity adversaries, who accused him of having been a communist security service agent, including the Gwiazdas and Ms Walentynowicz (Czuchnowski 2008; Kubiak 2008).

Then, as discussed in Chapter 2, in February 2016 the Institute released copies of original documents which apparently filled in the missing pages from the incomplete 'Bolek' file and confirmed unequivocally that Mr Wałęsa had collaborated with the communist security services in 1970s as a paid secret collaborator (Czuchnowski 2016a; Gajca 2016). The files were hidden illegally in the home of General Czesław Kiszczak, a one-time high-ranking security services officer and communist interior minister who died in November 2015. Together with the then communist leader General Wojciech Jaruzelski, General

112   The 'Bolek' affair

Kiszczak was responsible for imposing the December 1981 martial law crackdown that crushed the Solidarity movement. Both of them were also leading figures on the regime side during the February–April 1989 round table negotiations between the communist government and the Solidarity opposition movement that led eventually to the collapse of the regime in Poland. About three months after General Kiszczak's death, his widow Maria, who claimed that her husband had hidden the documents to protect Mr Wałęsa's status as a national hero,[4] tried to sell them to the Institute for a cash payment of 90,000 złoties. However, acting upon a law that gave it the right to appropriate important historical documents, the Institute instructed the authorities to seize them immediately.

The dossier, which covered the period 1970–1976, contained two folders. The first bundle was a 'personal file' that included a one-page hand-written agreement to co-operate with the communist security services as an informant signed by hand with the name 'Lech Wałęsa' and the codename 'Bolek'[5] and dated 21 December 1970, at a time when he had been working as an electrician and was under arrest as a strike leader of the worker protests at the Gdańsk shipyard. The second batch was a 'work file' containing numerous reports by agent 'Bolek' on his co-workers in the shipyard and notes of his meetings with communist security service functionaries. The documents showed that agent 'Bolek' co-operated as a paid informant and was most active from the beginning of the December 1970 strikes until December 1972. At first, he eagerly provided information about the situation at the shipyard that could potentially have harmed his friends and fellow workers: on their opinions and actions; preparations for strikes, lockouts and demonstrations; and the names of the instigators of unrest among the workforce and those leafleting the plant. The files also included confirmations of the receipt of regular payments of money for his denunciations signed by Mr Wałęsa, together with his discharge from collaboration. After a while, agent 'Bolek''s enthusiasm diminished as he became disenchanted with the political situation, he tried to avoid meeting with security service officers, and, as the quality of his information declined, he was no longer deemed a valuable asset, and collaboration with him terminated formally in 1976. In January 2017, a forensic handwriting expert's report commissioned by the Institute confirmed the authenticity of the files (Czuchnowski 2017; Kozubal 2017).

Mr Wałęsa's own statements regarding the truthfulness of these allegations, and his response to the documents that purported to prove them, were confusing and contradictory.[6] At some points, he came close to admitting that he had collaborated. In his autobiography *A Way of Hope*, for example, Mr Wałęsa (1990) acknowledged: 'I did not emerge from these confrontations [with the communist security services following the December 1970 strikes] entirely clean. They gave me a condition: sign! And then I signed!' Then again in June 1992, in a statement to the Polish Press Agency on the day that the Macierewicz list was released, he said: 'in December 1970 I signed three or four documents' to escape from the security services (Cenckiewicz and Gontarczyk 2008a, p. 436), although he withdrew this statement later that day, when it became clear that the Olszewski government would be removed. However, even then Mr Wałęsa implied that what he signed was not a collaboration agreement as such but simply a document expressing loyalty to the communist regime (what he termed a 'lojalka'), and denied that he ever acted upon it by informing on anyone or accepting any payments.[7] Sometimes Mr Wałęsa claimed that he had fooled the system and outwitted his interrogators to

> familiarise himself with his enemy, strive for victory, minimalise losses, particularly to rescue clever and brave people ... [and harm] provocateurs, drunks and trouble makers, pushing them into scuffles, losses and lost causes. If you can see any collaboration here, then in this concept the Security Service was collaborating with me!
> (Stankiewicz 2016a)[8]

On other occasions, Mr Wałęsa denied vehemently that he had ever been an informant and dismissed the incriminating files as forgeries created by the communist security services to discredit him. Indeed, for a number of years he was involved in an ongoing lawsuit against fellow one-time Solidarity and Free Trade Unions of the Coast activist Krzysztof Wyszkowski, who alleged that Mr Wałęsa had been a collaborator. He also denied removing incriminating documents from the security service archives during his presidency. Indeed, until 2008 he claimed that he had never seen his secret police file, and it was only after the publication of the Cenckiewicz–Gontarczyk book that he admitted borrowing it, although he also insisted that nothing had been removed. When the accusations against him re-surfaced with the discovery of the Kiszczak dossier in February 2016, Mr Wałęsa once again denounced the files as forgeries: 'It is believed that I allowed myself to be broken, that I did in fact in spite of everything slightly collaborate, inform and take money in the 1970s. NO. NO. NO' (Stankiewicz 2016b).

What arguments were used by Mr Wałęsa's supporters?

Some of Mr Wałęsa's staunchest supporters, who included many of his erstwhile Solidarity colleagues, argued that the supposedly incriminating documents might have been fabricated, or at least questioned whether it was possible to make unambiguous judgements about the nature of his involvement on the basis of them. For example, commentators Wojciech Czuchnowski and Agnieszka Kublik (2016) argued that 'the files ... are incomplete and carry traces of numerous interferences in their contents' because 'the Security Services specialised in falsification, societal disinformation activities and breaking up the opposition ... you cannot treat the Security Service materials as an oracle and the revealed truth. You have to approach them with suspicion.' Mr Wałęsa's defenders drew attention to the fact that false documents relating to his collaboration were created at the beginning of the 1980s in order to discredit him with his fellow oppositionists and (as it turned out in the end, unsuccessfully) prevent him being awarded the Nobel Peace Prize (Czuchnowski 2016b).

However, especially after the release of the Kiszczak files, most commentators, even those sympathetic to Mr Wałęsa, accepted that it was difficult to question the authenticity of the documents and that he almost certainly did collaborate with the communist security services between 1971 and 1976. They acknowledged that it would be impossible (and unnecessary) to fabricate such elaborate and detailed accounts of the situation in the Gdańsk shipyards as set out in Mr Wałęsa's files years after the actual events took place simply in order to discredit the former Solidarity leader. While the later reports were much rarer and more laconic, agent 'Bolek''s initial accounts were very detailed, describing not just the general sentiment in the shipyards but particular individuals at length. For example, even generally pro-Wałęsa historian Andrzej Friszke (2016) accepted that while 'we cannot rule out that maybe some of these were falsified ... [t]his would mainly affect receipts for money paid ... [b]ut ... not ... the sections containing information'. 'These testimonies', he argued, 'were not thought up by some security service functionary behind a desk in Warsaw or even in Gdańsk; there are too many details in them.' On another occasion, Prof. Friszke argued: 'There is no possibility to reconstruct such an extensive, detailed account of the situation in the shipyards years later to ... discredit Mr Wałęsa as leader of Solidarity. No one would be capable of doing this' (Leszczyński 2016a). Similarly, commentator Andrzej Stankiewicz pointed out: 'It is very unlikely that the head of the security services (General Kiszczak) would have wasted space in his home safe on false papers – Kiszczak almost certainly collected solely authentic papers, because he wanted to have effective smears ['haki'] on people who were important during the 1989 velvet revolution. Only such papers would represent an insurance policy' (Stankiewicz 2016c). The Institute of National Remembrance itself not only insisted that an expert archivist had certified that the Kiszczak files were authentic papers produced by the communist security services at the time (Kozubal 2016), but, as noted above, commissioned a forensic handwriting expert's report, which, in a January 2017 report, also confirmed their authenticity.

Consequently, rather than dismissing the allegations outright, most of Mr Wałęsa's supporters tended to focus not on the authenticity and contents of the files but on how deeply he was implicated, and the interpretations of his actions, particularly the notion that they were difficult to evaluate from a post-communist perspective. As commentator Jarosław Kurski (2016) put it, '[the files contained] the truth about Wałęsa ... but only the partial truth'. First, Mr Wałęsa's supporters tried to relativise his involvement and actions by positing various mitigating circumstances. They argued that when he was coerced by the security services into signing a co-operation agreement Mr Wałęsa was a young, isolated worker in a brutal political system with no broader support network, fearing persecution and harsh reprisals against him and his large family. They said that the only reason why he was interrogated in December 1970 was because he had been active in worker protests as one of the leaders of the shipyard strike, while those who never stood up to the regime did not have to deal with the state's coercive apparatus in the same way. As commentator Piotr Moszyński (2016) put it,

> [This is the] story of a worker with a large family, squeezed effectively by the then all-powerful security services literally the day after the massacre of workers on the coast, when it was obvious to everyone that the threat was not theoretical, because the authorities were prepared to kill if they felt that this was appropriate.

Similarly, veteran opposition activist Karol Modzelewski argued that

> Wałęsa in 1970 was an ordinary [worker] … without any experience. When they arrested him in December 1970 for five days, he did not have a clue that he even had any rights. He had every reason to be afraid. Shortly before then his colleagues had been beaten up and buried in nylon body bags in anonymous graves. He did not know if he would also be killed. He signed because they told him to sign. He did not have a clue whether he could not sign. It didn't enter into his head.
>
> (Stasiński 2016)

Bogdan Lis, a veteran of the August 1980 Gdańsk shipyard strike that led to Solidarity's formation, said: 'The 1970 period is a very difficult one to evaluate. I myself spent time in prison and know how hopeless a person is when confronting the security apparatus. You don't have anyone to appeal to, there was no opposition' (Czuchnowski 2016c). Historian Andrzej Friszke (2016) also argued:

> [In 1970] when he was being interrogated, the corpses of the victims were still not buried. Three days earlier he saw how people were killed.… You can't hold the first interrogation against Wałęsa. He was arrested not long after there had been shooting on the streets.

They also tried to locate his actions within a broader historical context, arguing that they were difficult to evaluate from a post-communist perspective and that only those who found themselves in similar circumstances could judge him on the moral choices that he made at the time. For example, Bogdan Lis argued that only those who 'went through the "paths of health"[9] in 1970, [and who] were among the workers who were run over by tanks' could evaluate Mr Wałęsa's decisions (Leszczyński 2016b). Another veteran Solidarity leader, Władysław Frasyniuk, argued that

> making a great sensation out of the 'Bolek' affair without knowing the context of the times in which he was supposed to have allowed himself to be broken is the behaviour of a son-of-a-bitch.… In the police stations they

were executing people, and there was no Workers' Defence Committee,[10] no lawyers, underground press, contacts with the West. And someone today wants to make a judgement that someone else wanted to avoid being crippled?! That they wanted to protect their family?!

(Harłukowicz 2016a)

Similarly, commentator Janina Paradowska (2016) said: 'I understand a worker who is frightened, signs something, has a few meetings, and even takes some small change [as a payment]. It was a different climate in the 1970s.'

Second, they tried to minimise Mr Wałęsa's period of collaboration with the security services, arguing that he should be judged according to the whole of his life's achievements and not just the (understandable, they argued) weaknesses of his youth. They said that it was only an 'episode' that lasted for a short period, from which he soon found the strength to extricate himself. The final document in his file was dated 1976, and there was, they argued, no hard evidence that Mr Wałęsa's collaboration continued beyond then, when he was engaged in anti-regime opposition activity. For example, Karol Modzelewski argued that

> it is false to say that if someone once signed something, then you can write them off for their whole life.... It has happened that well-known oppositionists started to collaborate with the Security Service and then spent time incarcerated and became respected oppositionists.

(Stasiński 2016)

Arguing that '[e]ven if Bolek was Wałęsa, Wałęsa is not Bolek ... he is a hundred times greater than him', commentator Adam Szostkiewicz said that while Mr Wałęsa 'made mistakes, took bad decisions and did stupid things ... the same Wałęsa [also] did great things' (Szostkiewicz 2016). Another commentator, Wojciech Maziarski (2016), argued: 'This is the story of a young worker who, in the deep darkness of communism, decided to collaborate with secret police but later, through his own strength, lifted himself up from the fall and bravely broke off those links.' Similarly, commentators Wojciech Czuchnowksi and Agnieszka Kublik (2016) said that 'the agent "Bolek" files ... only give extracts from [a fragmentary picture of] Lech Wałęsa's activities', while historian Andrzej Friszke argued that Mr Wałęsa's communist security service file 'cannot be regarded as the key to understanding [his] whole [life] history' (wPolityce 2016b). While admitting that the contents of the Kiszczak files contained 'things that seriously compromise Lech Wałęsa', commentator Adam Leszczyński (2016c) argued that 'they affect a very short and very early period of his [political] activity. His collaboration really ends in 1973–74 ... in other words a long time before the start of his opposition activity.'

Third, Mr Wałęsa's supporters also argued that his earlier period of collaboration was just a part of the story that should be viewed within the context of, and did not detract from, his later historical achievements. In other words, they claimed that ultimately his behaviour in the 1970s was irrelevant, because Mr

Wałęsa compensated for his earlier transgressions. Through his remarkable negotiating skills, charisma and stubborn bravery under house arrest during martial law, Mr Wałęsa, they said, played a pivotal role in helping to bring about the collapse of communism and democratisation in Poland. Historian Antoni Dudek (2016) has argued that 'those who defend Wałęsa ... [do so] because Wałęsa is a symbol of a certain myth which they wanted to defend, [and they are] concerned that if Wałęsa's myth collapses then so does that of the legend of Solidarity'. In that sense, 'he is important to them ... [because] it is difficult to separate the Wałęsa myth from the Solidarity myth'.

For example, Bogdan Lis argued that 'it is thanks to Lech Wałęsa that Poland is free today' and 'no one will tear [this] down, no file and no accusation about collaboration' (Leszczyński 2016b). Similarly, commentator Jarosław Kurski (2016) said: 'A scandal from forty six years ago when in the tragic December of 1970 a young worker undertakes an unclean game with the communist security services cannot change the positive balance of his achievements.' Historian Jan Skórzyński also argued: 'An episode of possible collaboration with the Security Services will not have a great impact on the overall assessment of Lech Wałęsa's achievements as one of the fathers of the third Polish independence' (Skórzyński 2016). Indeed, some of Mr Wałęsa's supporters even claimed that his earlier collaboration helped him to understand how the system worked from the inside – and, therefore, how to fight it more effectively – which made him an even greater threat to the communist regime. As commentator Piotr Moszyński (2016) put it,

> [F]rom the coolly practical point of view of our common interest, this whole dramatic turn of events shaped a person who knew the system and the threats that were contained within it from the inside, and who was then able to take advantage of this knowledge in his [later] activities.

Nor, his supporters argued, was there any solid evidence that his earlier collaboration with the communist security services meant that he remained under their control, or that they had any influence on him subsequently during his later periods of opposition activity in the 1980s, when he was leader of the Solidarity movement. Indeed, they said that Mr Wałęsa was both a genuine, authentic and heroic leader who acted independently against the regime's wishes and a legendary figure of international standing who embodied and symbolised Poland's courageous struggle for freedom and democracy and eventual victory over communism. For example, in an open letter titled 'The Institute [of National Remembrance] is harming Poland', which came out a month before the publication of the Cenckiewicz–Gontarczyk book, a number of signatories drawn from the Third Republic political and cultural elites and linked to the liberal wing of the Solidarity movement argued:

> The role of Solidarity and its historical leader Lech Wałęsa in the fight for a free Poland and returning European unity is Poland's moral capital ... the archives of the communist security services are to become an instrument for

wiping out the image and authority of the worker leader of Solidarity, Nobel Peace Prize winner and the first President of the newly independent Poland.

The signatories, who included Solidarity intellectual Tadeusz Mazowiecki – who, as noted in Chapter 2, in August 1989 became Poland's first post-war non-communist prime minister – and former veteran anti-communist opposition activist, theoretician and, in post-communist Poland, editor of the *Gazeta Wyborcza* newspaper, Adam Michnik – appealed for Poles to counter '[this] campaign of hatred and slander being directed at Lech Wałęsa which is damaging Poland's national memory' (Cenckiewicz 2016a).

Similarly, following the publication of the Kiszczak files, commentator Jarosław Kurski (2016) described Mr Wałęsa as 'the victor over communism, our greatest contemporary historical symbol'. Józef Pinior, a one-time Solidarity leader, argued that 'Wałęsa is a symbol of our road from dictatorship to freedom and democracy. An important figure for both the history of Poland and – alongside Nelson Mandela, perhaps – also the history of the whole world.' 'People like him are not', he argued, 'judged by people but by history' (Harłukowicz 2016b). Commentator Aleksander Hall (2016) said that 'regardless of what materials are found in files stored by Czesław Kiszczak ... Lech Wałęsa is one of the most distinguished and honoured Poles of the twentieth century'. Another commentator, Wojciech Maziarski (2016), described Mr Wałęsa as 'not just Poland's national capital but also a living embodiment of the passage from the dark to the bright side'. Sociologist Ireneusz Krzemiński (2016) also described him as 'a representative and symbol of the Polish transformation and Polish victory over the previous regime ... a symbol of the victory of freedom and democracy, integrating Poland and Poles into the West'.

What arguments were used by Mr Wałęsa's critics?

Mr Wałęsa's critics, on the other hand, argued that his actions in the early 1970s mattered, even if they were only part of the story of his public life. They pointed out that his collaboration as a communist security service informant was not simply an 'episode' but lasted for several years. The documents showed, they argued, that at first Mr Wałęsa was an ardent informer who eagerly and shamelessly betrayed and provided information about the opinions and actions of his friends and fellow workers at the Gdańsk shipyard. This served as the basis of repression and persecution against them, and his victims deserved an apology. Mr Wałęsa was remunerated financially for the information that he provided, accepting 13,300 złoties in total for his services during his six years of collaboration (the average wage at the time was around 2,000 złoties per month) (Czuchnowski and Leszczyński 2016).

For example, commentator Bronisław Wildstein (2016a) argued that, '[although] he probably was able to disentangle himself from it later ... the fact is that he informed on his colleagues and behaved badly', noting (2016b) that from the documents revealed in the Kiszczak files 'it emerges that Wałęsa was driven by material motives and also that he did not hold back from anything in his denunciations', On another occasion, Mr Wildstein (2016c) said that he 'would not hold it against him that he signed something in those circumstances [in the aftermath of the 1970s strikes]', but 'when you see [how] he really denounced people, it was not [just] saying any old thing, there were real denunciations' and 'now he even talks contemptuously about his victims'. Similarly, historian Sławomir Cenckiewicz said that

> [Wałęsa's] collaboration was neither a 'few months long incident' in his biography nor did his 'real collaboration' only 'probably last until 1972' ... but [it] lasted several years, was directed at specific people (around thirty) and he was financially rewarded for it.
>
> (wPolityce 2016c)

Commentator Rafał Ziemkiewicz (2016) argued:

> Talking about a 'moment of weakness' and 'signing a scrap of paper' is simply grotesque when we have more than 250 hand-written denunciations in the space of six years and receipts for a considerable amount of money for that time, particularly compared with a worker's income.

Marcin Fijołek (2016), another commentator, also argued: 'You cannot just dismiss the fate of those people whose lives were broken (or at least fractured) as a result of the information that Secret Collaborator Bolek sold to the security services.'

They also argued that – although Mr Wałęsa stopped collaborating by the second half of the 1970s, several years before he became Solidarity leader – fear that his earlier period of communist security service collaboration would be revealed raised questions about whether this could have been used to influence his later political decisions. Most commentators, including most (although not all) of his critics, appeared to accept that Mr Wałęsa was probably acting independently when he was Solidarity leader in the 1980s; or, at least, that there was no hard evidence that he was under the control of the security services.[11] However, his critics claimed that fear of being blackmailed by representatives of the outgoing regime explained Mr Wałęsa's seemingly erratic behaviour during the transition to democracy and early years of post-communist Poland, particularly as its first freely elected President in 1990–1995, when, they argued, he made a series of questionable personnel and policy choices. Having earlier quarrelled with Solidarity liberals and leftists, Mr Wałęsa jettisoned his temporary right-wing allies as soon he was elected, and some of the people he then chose to collaborate with and surrounded himself with as advisers, and eventually grew to accept and befriend, were, his critics argued, highly dubious officials and individuals linked to the former communist military intelligence and security services. They also pointed to some of the policy decisions that he made as President, which, his

120   The 'Bolek' affair

critics argued, appeared to betray Solidarity's ideals. These included moves that left Poland within Moscow's sphere of influence, such as his proposal to establish joint Polish–Russian stock companies on the territory of former Soviet military bases in Poland and develop a second-class NATO membership category for Poland, termed 'NATO-mark two' ('NATO-bis'); his rather ambiguous reaction to the August 1991 coup against reformist Soviet communist leader Mikhail Gorbachev by hard-liners; and his role in helping to precipitate and facilitate the downfall of the radical anti-communist Olszewski government in 1992.[12]

For example, commentator Piotr Zaremba (2016a) argued that although

> Mr Wałęsa ... was not a puppet [and] had his own aims and interests ... he [also] had to deal with a formidable partner (General Kiszczak) who had a box of papers on him under his bed. And it is then that the most horrendous things started to happen. After he secured the presidency in 1990.

On another occasion, Mr Zaremba (2016b) argued that these included:

> His abandonment, immediately after the 1990 presidential election, of his programme of anti-communist acceleration. His removal of independent right-wing politicians from his chancellery and their replacement with figures who were often registered as [communist security service] secret collaborators. Keeping Mieczysław Wachowski,[13] a secretive and dark figure, at his side.... Forcing joint Polish-Russian companies which would be a path to [Moscow's] penetration of Poland. Nurturing communist networks in the army and security services. Promoting the idea of 'NATO-mark two' aimed at halting Poland's pro-Western path.

Similarly, sociologist Mateusz Fałkowski (2016) argued that

> Lech Wałęsa's personnel choices during the period of his presidency, his role in relation to the army, ideas of 'NATO-mark two' or his reaction to Genady Yanayev's [anti-Gorbachev] coup, his activity relating to lustration and de-communisation themselves – all of this can be evaluated afresh, knowing now not just Wałęsa's open interests and views but also the documents revealed [in the Kiszczak files].

Michał Karnowski (2016), another commentator, argued that 'questions about the possibility of Wałęsa's activity as an agent, about the possibility that he was blackmailed' emerged

> after 1990 [when] he betrayed the whole Solidarity movement in favour of an agreement with the communist torturers. Questions about his unusual advisers, about his support for the ex-communists, about him aligning himself with the fiercest opponents of the anti-communist camp.

His critics also raised questions about whether, during his presidency, Mr Wałęsa – or, more likely, former communist security service and military intelligence officers acting on his behalf – illegally removed, and then attempted to destroy, the incriminating classified records of his collaboration contained in the 'Bolek' file; returning incomplete files to the State Security Office several months later.[14] The public prosecutor's office initially launched an inquiry into this incident and pressed charges against Mr Wałęsa's interior minister Andrzej Milczanowski and State Security Office heads Jerzy Konieczny and Gromosław Czempiński, accusing them of losing classified files. However, the investigation was discontinued in 1999; formally on the grounds that no offence had been committed but, according to Mr Wałęsa's critics, more likely for political reasons. All of this, they argued, deserved condemnation, even if the culprit was a national hero or an internationally recognised public figure. For example, historian Sławomir Cenckiewicz argued:

> One of the facts confirming the level of Wałęsa's collaboration, and the consequences of this for free Poland, was the organised annexation and robbery of the 'Bolek' documents by high-level state functionaries from the interior affairs ministry, the State Security Office and the presidential chancellery in the years 1992–95.
>
> (wPolityce, 2016c)

Similarly, historian Mikołaj Mirowski (2016) said that Mr Wałęsa 'removed documents from the Agent Bolek file, [and] in doing so form[ed] an informal alliance with people of a security service-army provenance'. Commentator Bronisław Wildstein (2016b) also claimed that

> [d]uring the course of his presidency ... Wałęsa destroyed documents held on him to which he had access, and so committed an actual crime. The activities of Lech Wałęsa, from the moment that he won the presidency, were dedicated to one objective: hiding the truth about a shameful episode in his life.

How was the 'Bolek' affair used as a means of legitimation and de-legitimation?

Both sides of the political debate over the nature and meaning of Mr Wałęsa's collaboration accused each other of instrumentalising the 'Bolek affair' and trying to develop an image of the former Solidarity leader that was politically advantageous to them. There were three main, inter-linked arenas in which this could be seen.

The (true?) nature of the post-communist Third Republic

First, the 'Bolek affair' went to the heart of one of the most divisive questions and disputes in Polish politics, which ran throughout the entire post-1989 period and was used to both legitimate and de-legitimate the post-communist Third Republic state's genesis and foundational myths. It was a key element of the debates about the nature of the Polish transition from communism to democracy and different attitudes towards and interpretations of the events of 1989, especially the role of the so-called 'round table' negotiations between the communist government and anti-communist opposition, which, as discussed in Chapter 3, led to the semi-free elections that precipitated the end of the previous regime. Many observers felt that the role played by Lech Wałęsa, who was a key figure in these negotiations and processes (historian Andrzej Paczkowski (2016) described him as the 'father of the Third Republic'), explained many of the choices and decisions taken during this transition period. Without understanding these, and Mr Wałęsa's role in them, it was not possible to make sense of the broader process of post-communist transformation and the main issues and lines of division that went on to dominate contemporary Polish politics and society.

Supporters of the Third Republic status quo viewed the post-communist period as one of success marked by economic growth, democracy and Poland's successful integration into Euro-Atlantic political, economic and military international structures.[15] For the post-1989 political, business and cultural elites that emerged from the transition process, the 'round table' process embodied the peaceful transfer of power from the previous to the new regime;[16] as discussed in Chapter 3, for many it represented the 'foundational myth' of the new, democratic post-communist Polish state. They argued that, by accusing Mr Wałęsa of being a communist security service informer, the opponents of the Third Republic status quo were attempting to undermine, de-legitimise and ultimately destroy his legend as one of the fundamentals of the post-1989 state and replace him with a new hierarchy of moral authority figures and pantheon of anti-communist heroes who were more sympathetic to their analysis of the shortcomings of the Polish post-communist transformation. Historian Antoni Dudek (2016) argues that the defence of Mr Wałęsa was, therefore, 'a question of the defence of the process of [post-communist] transformation because Wałęsa as the first President of the early 1990s symbolised these economic, political and social changes'. As commentator Ewa Siedlecka (2016) put it, 'Wałęsa is ... an incredibly important symbol' for the supporters of the Third Republic. Although 'these people do not have any illusions ... everyone is critical of Wałęsa', she drew a distinction between 'Wałęsa the person, with his shortcomings, and Wałęsa the symbol. We are tied to Wałęsa the symbol and we don't want anyone to take him away.' By arguing that the transition process was conducted under the direction of the communist security services and those potentially beholden to them, such as Mr Wałęsa, the Third Republic's critics were, it was argued, trying to promote their own, alternative vision of post-communist transformation by proving that that the state established in 1989 was not an authentic creation and was rotten from the outset.

For example, the signatories of the open letter 'The Institute Is Harming Poland' signed by figures from the Third Republic's political and cultural elites (see above) argued:

The role of Solidarity, and its historical leader Lech Wałęsa, in the fight for a free Poland and restoring European unity, is Poland's moral capital ... the archives of the communist security services are to become an instrument for wiping out the image and authority of the worker leader of Solidarity, Nobel Peace Prize winner and the first President of the newly independent Poland.

They appealed for Poles to counter '[this] campaign of hatred and slander being directed at Lech Wałęsa which is damaging Poland's national memory' (Cenckiewicz 2016a). Similarly, after the revelation of the Kiszczak files, commentator Jarosław Kurski (2016) argued that

[b]y attacking [Mr Wałęsa as] the symbol [and foundational myth of the Third Republic his critics] want to question the success of the last 26 years.... This is about laying a bomb under the foundations of the Third Republic, about establishing a new hierarchy and new authority figures. About writing Polish contemporary history anew.

Another commentator, Marek Beylin (2016), argued that, for Mr Wałęsa's opponents, the Kiszczak files 'represent a good pretext to re-heat hypotheses such as Jarosław Kaczyński's (formulated at the beginning of the 1990s) that a network emerging from the former communist [security] services was continuously controlling both Wałęsa and the Third Republic'. This 'melange of revenge and devious, conspiratorial imaginings' represented the 'founding myth for this milieu' of enemies of Mr Wałęsa and those who felt that they were marginalised by the Third Republic.

Former Solidarity activist Józef Pinior argued that the 'Bolek' affair was 'nothing less than trying to colonise Polish history by the milieu associated with Jarosław Kaczyński' (Harłukowicz 2016b), while Bogdan Lis, another one-time leading union activist, argued that Mr Wałęsa's opponents were 'trying to cancel out the Polish road to independence, cancel out Wałęsa's role within it, depreciate him, ruin the symbol, who cannot be rubbed out from Polish history' (Czuchnowski 2016c). Referring to Mr Wałęsa as Poland's 'symbolic Moses' on the country's 'road to freedom', commentator Adam Szostkiewicz (2016) claimed that

by destroying Lech Wałęsa's legend [Law and Justice and other critics hoped] to negate the whole of the Third Republic and create new heroes of independence ... to discredit him in order to strike down the foundational myth of the Third Republic.

The defence of Lech Wałęsa thus became 'a defence of our common road to freedom ... we cannot agree to removing Wałęsa from it ... [with writing our] contemporary history anew with the help of Kiszczak's documents'. Sociologist Ireneusz Krzemiński (2016) argued: '[D]evaluing Lech Wałęsa as a hero and symbol has the objective of devaluing the act that he symbolised. This is about re-writing national history and introducing new figures on the scene of national symbols.' Commentator Janina Paradowska (2016) also argued that the 'Bolek affair' was 'all about ensuring that he [Wałęsa] was not a symbol of Solidarity ... many people would like to position themselves as the leaders of Solidarity.'

Critics of the 'round table' agreements and later 'thick line' policy, on the other hand, saw them as fatally flawed, allowing the former ruling elites to make a smooth transition into the new political and economic system and entrench their power and influential positions within it. To these critics of the Third Republic status quo, the 'Bolek affair' exemplified the way that the military and security services clustered around Generals Jaruzelski and Kiszczak agreed an unequal political pact that entrenched former elites and co-opted a number of their opponents, some of whom, they said, were security service collaborators masquerading as oppositionists and operating under their influence. Former (but still influential) communist-era security service functionaries had, they argued, entrenched themselves and remained active in Polish public life, controlling the economy and society from behind the scenes so that those with links to the previous regime maintained their wealth, influence and a dominant position among the post-communist business, cultural and political elites.[17] For example, sociologist Mateusz Fałkowski (2016) argued that 'if it was not for [the contents of] "Kiszczak's safe", [then] reforms of state institutions would possibly be much more advanced and the functioning of the state itself much more transparent'. Similarly, commentator Piotr Semka (2016b) argued that the discovery of the 'Bolek' files in General Kiszczak's home

> throws a light on the system of secret control of many social and political processes in the Third Republic by the communist Polish People's Republic's elites. [These were] [p]henomena which many Poles felt instinctively but were deafened by the mockery and attacks from critics of the 'round table order'.

Many of Mr Wałęsa's critics also raised questions about the conduct of the 1989 'round table' negotiations themselves, pointing out that these did not just involve public discussions but also informal, private meetings of the so-called 'Magdalenka' group, which included the communist state elites and the leadership of the Solidarity opposition (notably Mr Wałęsa) with senior Catholic Church officials as observers. These meetings were little noticed at the time, but subsequently, especially in more radical versions of this account of the transition, became the source of accusations of underhand dealings, with some observers coming to see them as playing a decisive role in the transfer of power.[18] Historian Antoni Dudek (2016) argues that 'this is a kind of vision [of events] that [says that] it started with betrayal in Magdalenka and then the [communist security service] agents and their handling officers prepared a systemic transformation for us which was one great swindle'. Similarly, commentator Adam Leszczyński (2016c) argued that lustration was 'an element of a certain story about the genesis of the Third Republic'. For many on the political right, 'the "round table" was a betrayal ... it was the result of an ... agreement between a section of the communist elite and a section of the opposition elite', which was linked to the question of lustration because 'there was always that question ... how much they were really oppositional'. 'Talking about lustration was', therefore, 'a comfortable, useful political tool for certain groups in Poland because it helped them to de-legitimise the order.... It is one of the instruments for de-legitimating this "round table" order and the Third Republic'. These groups argued not only that the post-1989 settlement was 'based on the treachery in Magdalenka ... on some horrific agreements' but also that 'an element of this betrayal was ... the presence of various [communist security service] agents in various spheres of (post-1989) Polish public life'.

Mr Wałęsa was, according to his and the Third Republic status quo's critics, the key to understanding this process. As historian Sławomir Cenckiewicz put it, 'Lech Wałęsa's collaboration as an agent of the Security Service had a significant subsequent meaning ... [and] influence on the shape of the systemic reforms after 1989' (wPolityce 2016c). He had already compromised with the communist regime to side-line Solidarity radicals such as the Gwiazdas and Anna Walentynowicz before the 'round table' talks began and, over time, grew to accept and befriend his former enemies. As commentator Konrad Kołodziejski (2016) put it,

> It is difficult to escape from the impression that those who always regarded the round table as the original sin of the new independent Poland are today right ... it was above all about protecting communist influence both formal (control over the 'power' ministries, the semi-free elections, the economy) as well as informal, whose contents we can work out by observing the later hysteria of many post-Solidarity milieu in response to the slogans of lustration and de-communisation.

'The communists themselves', he argued,

> chose their interlocutors from the Solidarity side, obviously not just former agents, but it is possible to assume that these represented the most welcomed and influential group.... Their interest was obviously: not to permit the revelation of the truth. Communists – as the holders of secret information – appeared to be the one guarantee of this implicit agreement. The files hidden in Kiszczak's house only confirm this hypothesis.

For Mr Wałęsa's critics, therefore, the 'Bolek' affair revealed how the entire post-1989 political order was a sham, with the former Solidarity leader portrayed, as commentator (and one-time Civic Platform prime ministerial candidate) Jan Rokita (2016) put it, as the 'icon of a system of lies'. This was, according to Mr Rokita, part of 'a radical alternative historiography' developed by Law and Justice's supporting media and intellectuals, which attempt[ed] to turn the fact that Mr Wałęsa's denunciations of workers in the shipyards at the beginning of the 1970s was a fact, into a key piece of evidence about the necessity of completely redefining the heroic history of Solidarity and the first twenty five years of independence.

As historian Antoni Dudek (2016) put it, to critics of the Third Republic, concealing Mr Wałęsa's security service was 'lie number one', and they felt that if 'we can unmask the lie of the Wałęsa affair – that Wałęsa was not a hero, but actually a traitor – then we can un-mask [the] other lies on which the Third Republic was built'. Similarly, Andrzej Paczkowski (2016), another historian, argued that the dispute over Mr Wałęsa 'was an important element of this dispute' about the origins of the Third Republic, with its critics arguing: '"Poland is in ruins" [and] "Poland arose on the basis of a con" ... these two things are linked: Poland is in ruins (today) because it arose as a con ... if there was no con, there would be no ruins.'

According to its critics, therefore, the Third Republic was the 'bastard child' of the communist security services (Stankiewicz 2016c), and this was used to justify their calls for a far-reaching re-structuring of Polish state institutions. For example, writing about the Cenckiewicz–Gontarczyk book, sociologist Andrzej Zybertowicz (2008) talked of 'a system of lies built in the Third Republic' and 'the mechanisms of manipulation and lies operating in the 1990s and 2000s'. On a later occasion, Prof Zybertowicz (2016) talked about the process of the 'Bolek-isation of the Third Republic', which involved 'creating a false myth of freedom based on a [communist security service] agent'. Similarly, according to commentator Michał Karnowski (2016), the Kiszczak files contained 'the truth about how the Third Republic was built ... [and was] the essence of the foundations of this construct. This ... [was] ... the real constitution of the Third Republic.' Commentator Bronisław Wildstein argued that the Bolek files revealed 'how we were lied to for twenty five years' and 'the mechanism, through which former security service functionaries held people in their grip' (wPolityce 2016a). The Kiszczak files, he said on another occasion, unveiled 'the whole truth about the Third Republic' and proved that it 'was built on silencing, lies and behind-the-scenes intrigues ... [a]nd that the, constantly mocked, conspiracy theories on this subject were deeply justified' (Wildstein 2016b). On another occasion, Mr Wildstein (2016c) argued that for the Third Republic establishment, Mr Wałęsa was meant to 'overshadow Solidarity' and re-inforce the idea that 'there is an elite thanks to whom we achieved our freedom and, as a result of this, they have special entitlements, they are authority figures'. Mr Wałęsa was built up as 'an idol who gave us freedom, it was not Solidarity, the 10 million [members of the movement]' and, in that sense, he was 'a very comfortable figure for the Third Republic establishment ... because he always claims that "*I* defeated communism, not *we* but *me*"'.

Historian Sławomir Cenckiewicz (2016a) also argued that the defenders of the Third Republic 'knew that the system is built on a network of [communist] agents and lies ... that Wałęsa was a figurehead for them, behind whom were hidden the dark interests of the beneficiaries of post-communism'. On another occasion, Mr Cenkiewicz (2016b) said that 'Wałęsa has a "systemic" meaning to this milieu, the beneficiaries of the Third Republic ... [they] have to stick together...they are all defenders of the system that they developed after 1989.' Mr Wałęsa was, in other words, 'a symbol, a guarantor of that system'. Similarly, commentator Łukasz Adamski (2016) argued that the 'Bolek' affair affected 'the essence of the Third Republic ... [a] country built on a stinking compromise with communists and lies', Another commentator, Piotr Semka (2016c), argued that because 'Wałęsa was an idol, a symbol of the best years of Solidarity' he enjoyed a 'transactional' relationship with the Third Republic elites: 'This particular political camp fetes Wałęsa as a role model, and [in return] Wałęsa supports this political camp.'

A key issue dividing the main post-2005 political actors

Second, although politicians often tended to let commentators and supporting intellectuals lead the charge for their side, the 'Bolek' affair was also used to legitimate and de-legitimate specific political actors and formations, particularly after the 2005 parliamentary and presidential elections. With the collapse of the communist successor left, these elections re-aligned the political scene around two post-Solidarity parties that were to dominate Polish electoral politics for the next decade: Law and Justice and Civic Platform. As noted above, the latter was originally a liberal-conservative party but was later to evolve into an ideologically eclectic centrist grouping. Certainly, Mr Wałęsa's political significance declined following his defeat in the 1995 presidential election; he secured a humiliating 1 per cent of the vote when he stood again five years later. However, in the 2000s Mr Wałęsa was drawn increasingly into the battle over lustration and other challenges to the Third Republic, and attitudes towards the 'Bolek' affair emerged as an important issue dividing Law and Justice and Civic Platform, both their leaders and (as we shall see in Chapter 6) their supporters. Although both parties contested the 2005 elections on the basis of a sharp critique of the Third Republic status quo (albeit having a somewhat different emphasis in terms of the issues that they highlighted) and were originally seen as natural coalition partners, they became bitter rivals after the election when, as discussed in Chapter 2, Law and Justice formed a minority government and then a coalition with two smaller radical, anti-establishment parties.

Law and Justice blamed post-communist Poland's political, economic and societal shortcomings upon the country's apparently flawed post-1989 transition to democracy. As noted in Chapter 2, having helped to run his 1990 presidential election campaign and then worked in his presidential chancellery, Lech Kaczyński and his twin brother Jarosław, who went on to form and lead the Law and Justice party, had been in a bitter dispute with Mr Wałęsa since the early 1990s and had accused him of being a communist security service agent from the time that these allegations first emerged following the publication of the 'Macierewicz list' in 1992. They were also among the prime advocates of the notion that the 'Bolek' affair exemplified the way that the communist military and security services had agreed an unequal political pact that entrenched the former ruling elites and co-opted some of their opponents, For example, speaking shortly after the release of the Cenckiewicz–Gontarczyk book, Law and Justice leader Jarosław Kaczyński argued that the Third Republic's social hierarchy was

> based on lies, you can say radical lies, which rejected both the reality of the real situation that existed before 1989 and the post-1989 reality. [T]his book is a blow to this picture which serves the establishment and hence its hysterical defen[sive reaction to it].
>
> (Paradowska 2008)

Similarly, Law and Justice parliamentary caucus leader Ryszard Terlecki claimed that '[former communist security service] spies remained in public life, in the justice system and in educational establishments' (Ferfecki 2016). Law and Justice foreign minister Witold Waszczykowski said that the Kiszczak files 'cast a shadow over the creation of an independent Poland and its political elites', raising the possibility that the communists had guided Poland's transition to democracy and that, as President, 'Mr Wałęsa could have been a controlled puppet' (Rzeczpospolita.pl 2016a). Antoni Macierewicz, who became Law and Justice defence minister in 2015, claimed:

> The Lech Wałęsa affair shows in miniature what the Third Republic system was based on ... it was based on the fact that people were blackmailed with the help of the [communist security service] files. And a whole group of people was transformed into a slow operating tool of the communist apparatus, which constructed its later power and influence [based] on these people.
>
> (Kublik 2016)

Law and Justice parliamentary deputy Jacek Sasin also argued that Poles had a right to ask whether the activities of those governing them in the 1990s 'were not caused by the fact that Lech Wałęsa, and maybe other persons who represented the post-1989 elites, feared that certain decisions could lead to the revelation of materials that were compromising to them'. A lack of lustration and a failure to undertake a reckoning with the communist past, he said, raised questions 'about what were the real causes of the decisions that were undertaken at its [the Third Republic's] foundation and the omissions that took place then', which involved 'turning a blind eye to the communist nomenklatura appropriating national assets' that 'belonged to all of us but became the way that the few who had access to these assets were able to enrich themselves' (Rzeczpospolita. pl 2016b).

At the same time, Mr Wałęsa's reputation was defended by Civic Platform, who argued that the publication of the Cenckiewicz–Gontarczyk book was the latest move in a political war being waged against him by Law and Justice. Although while in opposition Civic Platform had supported moves to extend lustration and file access, after 2005 it evolved increasingly into a party representing the Third Republic status quo, its critics argued, and 'took him [Mr Wałęsa] out of the historical showcase ... dusted him off' as a '*deus ex machina* to rescue the Third Republic' (Wildstein 2016b) and 'hid[ing] behind his false legend' (Zaremba 2016a), thereby trying to use Mr Wałęsa's moral authority to legitimate themselves and de-legitimise their Law and Justice opponents. As part of this, Civic Platform leaders were in the vanguard of those politicians and commentators who defended Mr Wałęsa in 2008 over the allegations contained in the Cenckiewicz–Gontarczyk (and later in the 2009 Zyzak) book and again in 2016 following the publication of the Kiszczak files,[19] arguing that, as a result of its conduct during these events, the Institute of National Remembrance was being used as a political tool by the pro-lustration right.[20]

Civic Platform argued that, by attacking Mr Wałęsa – who, they claimed, symbolised Poland's international reputation as being in the forefront of a historical struggle for political freedom in the former Soviet bloc – Law and Justice and his critics were damaging an important Polish trademark, or 'positive myth', and thus the country's image abroad. For example, commenting on the Cenckiewicz–Gontarczyk book, the then Civic Platform leader and prime minister Donald Tusk said that he would 'do everything to defend the good name of Lech Wałęsa and the ideas of August [1980]', because it was 'a great duty for people like me ... to defend the myth, because every nation needs positive myths ... to defend the historical fact of Lech Wałęsa's pivotal role in some of the most important events in Polish history' (Kurski 2008). Subsequently, following the publication of the Kiszczak files, Civic Platform leader Grzegorz Schetyna described Lech Wałęsa as a 'symbol of Polish history, a symbol of Polish victory' (wPolityce 2016d), and argued that his opponents hoped to use the 'Bolek affair' to '[kill] his [Mr Wałęsa's] legend' and '[show] that the foundations of the Third Republic were something evil' (Rzeczpospolita.pl, 2016b). Indeed, at the party's October 2016 programmatic convention, at which Mr Wałęsa was a keynote speaker, Mr Schetyna went so far as to pledge that Civic Platform would abolish the Institute of National Remembrance if the party was returned to office (Wachnicki 2016).

In fact, for his part, Mr Wałęsa supported Civic Platform against Law and Justice in the bitter struggle that these two parties had been engaged in since they came to dominate the Polish political scene in 2005. The former Solidarity leader and President thus played a role in helping to legitimate Civic Platform in the eyes of many Poles who identified with the Solidarity tradition. To the extent that he was discredited as a symbol of the anti-communist democratic opposition, he was, of course, less well able to perform this function for the party. His apparent 'un-masking' by the Institute of National Remembrance at the end of the 2000s and mid-2010s thus helped to ensure that the issue of lustration and file access once again became entwined in party political conflicts.

The post-communist truth-revelation process

Third, the 'Bolek affair' was used to legitimate and de-legitimate the truth-revelation process itself as either vitally necessary or dangerously politicised. On the one hand, opponents of truth revelation argued that the Institute of National Remembrance's conduct, both during the publication of the Cenckiewicz–Gontarczyk book and subsequently when the contents of the Kiszczak files were revealed, showed how the file access process had been politicised. Indeed, the publication of the Cenckiewicz–Gontarczyk book was one of the factors that prompted the then Civic Platform-led government to introduce legislation passed in 2010 that, as discussed in Chapter 2, reformed the way that the Institute's leadership was selected, at least partly in the hope of preventing further publications of this kind. Historian Antoni Dudek (2016) argues that

> Wałęsa became a very comfortable tool [when] developing a certain historical policy.... When the question of lustration and the Institute of National Remembrance ... [came up his critics] could say: 'Look, a Nobel Prize Winner, a hero, the best known Pole in the world apart from Pope John Paul II they want to pin some files on him' ... for a milieu that was completely opposed to lustration, he was the ideal shield, better than anyone else.

Opponents of truth revelation thus accused the Institute of allowing itself to be used as a tool in a vengeful political war being waged by right-wing politicians against Mr Wałęsa. For example, commentators Wojciech Czuchnowksi and Agnieszka Kublik (2016) argued that

> the activities of the Institute of National Remembrance in the Lech Wałęsa affair are characterised by political dislike towards him and lead to falsifying the role that he played in contemporary Polish history. The materials on Lech Wałęsa are being released uncritically and the Institute, which is an organ of the Polish state, is leading public opinion into error.

Moreover, according to some supporters of lustration and file access, the 'Bolek affair' also gave opponents of truth revelation an opportunity to relativise collaboration with the communist security services by arguing that if such a heroic historical figure as Mr Wałęsa was an informer, then it was an activity that potentially anyone could have succumbed to. As commentator Bronisław Wildstein (2016b) put it,

> When it turned out that Wałęsa had problems with his past he became even more useful (to opponents of truth revelation). His example could be used to discredit lustration and present it as damaging those who gave us freedom and an instrument of resentment, in other words envy of heroes.

Similarly, another commentator, Piotr Semka (2016c), claimed that there was 'a sort of orchestra effect':

> Those who feared their own lustration [such as Mr Wałęsa] spoke up in defence of others to maintain the overall principle that the files were not credible, that you cannot draw conclusions [on whether or not someone collaborated] based on them.

Supporters of truth revelation, on the other hand, argued that the 'Bolek affair' both exemplified and explained the lack of willingness to deal with the communist past, given that those who were collaborators with, or had links to, the former security services had remained active and entrenched themselves in public life after 1989. As noted above, according to Mr Wałęsa's critics, the outgoing Polish communist leadership could have used his security service collaboration to blackmail him into negotiating a transition that was favourable to the outgoing elites, paving the way for them to co-opt a section of the Solidarity opposition and retain their power and influence after 1989. Then, as discussed in Chapter 2, rather than prosecuting and excluding what many saw as traitors and criminals from public life, the first post-communist government, led by Solidarity intellectual Tadeusz Mazowiecki, adopted the communist-forgiving 'thick line' policy, as a result of which, it was argued, the former ruling elites were able to dodge responsibility for their crimes and misdeeds. Moreover, in spite of his promises to 'accelerate' post-communist transformation, when elected President, Mr Wałęsa did nothing to move forward the de-communisation and truth-revelation processes. Indeed, as noted above, he both allied himself with officials and individuals linked to the former communist military intelligence and security services and actively blocked one such attempt at introducing lustration by the Olszewski government. For example, commentator Konrad Kołodziejski (2016) argued that Mr Wałęsa's and many important Solidarity opposition figures' fear of lustration and truth revelation 'was one of the causes of the conflicts and pathologies that affect today's Poland'. Lustration

> was really about the shape of Poland. Whose vision it would comply with: [Adam] Michnik's or [Jarosław] Kaczyński's. The person who tilted the scales in favour of 'Michnik's vision' was Lech Wałęsa. He did this – everything indicates – as a result of his file. And this is what today's argument is about.

Bronisław Wildstein (2016b) also said: 'The battle over Wałęsa became a battle with lustration and a war to maintain the Third Republic status quo.'

The discovery of the Kiszczak files also raised the question of how many other former communist security service functionaries kept personal archives in their homes, which they could have used to blackmail politicians, businessmen, lawyers, academics, and other persons in position of power and influence (Szułdrzyński 2016). For such critics, the contents of the Kiszczak files were the missing link for their narrative on the nature of Poland's flawed transition. Indeed, the very fact that they had remained in the hands of a former communist interior minister for more than a quarter of a century was as important as the actual content of the written denunciations themselves. Many right-wing politicians and commentators believed that the rest of the secret archives were also hidden somewhere and contained an immeasurable wealth of leverage which post-communist communist elites were using to control politics, the economy and society from behind the scenes. For example, commentator Bronisław Wildstein (2016b) argued that communist leaders kept 'smears ['haki'] on their former opponents, then [their] partners in the round table ... for the possibility of blackmail, and ... behind-the-scenes pressure on public figures. In this way they could realise both their political and material objectives.' Similarly, another commentator, Piotr Zaremba (2016b), noted how General Kiszczak, 'a former head of the communist police almost slept on [security service] documents that were held on the founder of the new state', which revealed 'a truth about the political mechanisms governing the Third Republic' and raised questions as to whether this was 'a mechanism that could have occurred in many other areas of public life. How many other "private" archives dictated political decisions?' Law and Justice spokesman Arkadiusz Mularczyk (2016) also argued that the materials found on Lech Wałęsa in General Kiszczak's home raised the question: '[O]n how many [more] minor activists of the democratic opposition were there documents and archives [held] in the [private homes of the more] minor heads of the Security Services at the parish, county or regional level?'

The 'Bolek' affair thereby demonstrated the necessity of both clarifying Mr Wałęsa's role in relation to the communist security services in particular and the truth-revelation process more generally in helping Poles to understand the nature of the post-communist transformation. For example, commentator Paweł Lisicki (2016) claimed that 'the history of the revelation of the [Bolek] files is a specific indictment against the [post-1989 state's] whole culture of silencing, brushing under the carpet and hiding the past'. For communist functionaries, 'these files were a kind of insurance policy, a method of keeping post-Solidarity politicians in check, a permanent form of blackmail. Their revelation is the first step towards the fall of the Third Republic system.' Similarly, sociologist Mateusz Fałkowski (2016) said that the existence of secret archives containing documents such as those discovered in the Kiszczak files seriously complicated the 'reform of state institutions ... the functioning of the state ... good governance ... the legitimation of the state, transparency and effectiveness'. Bronisław Wildstein (2016b) also argued that '[l]ustration, unveiling the truth would have blown this [possibility of blackmail and behind-the-scenes pressure on public figures] apart. That is why the old-new establishment fought it so bitterly, the more its position was undermined.' The communist security service entanglements of Mr Wałęsa, who became the Third Republic establishment's 'ideal ally ... against the revelation of the truth', proved 'how fatally the lack of a reckoning with the [communist] past, which would have negated all of these [communist security service] entanglements, has burdened our history'.

Some of Mr Wałęsa's critics also argued that the 'Bolek affair' highlighted the weakness in the Polish lustration model more generally. For example, Law and Justice spokesman Arkadiusz Mularczyk (2016) also argued:

> Firstly, Lech Wałęsa was judged to be innocent [of failing to disclose his communist security service links] in a lustration trial.... [Secondly,] the Institute of National Remembrance declared that he was 'persecuted' [by the communist regime] while his collaboration file lay in the home of a Security Services agent ... showing that for several years he was an active collaborator who was rewarded financially for his collaboration.

This, according to Mr Mularczyk, showed 'that the whole [Polish] model of lustration ... while not completely a fiction did not fulfil its role in a proper manner'. It also raised the question of 'how many other people in the country benefited from such verdicts, [and] who said, on the basis of these [false] judgements, that they were innocent but had [actually] collaborated [with the communist security services] for years?'

Conclusions

The 'Bolek' affair, therefore, shows how the question of truth revelation recurred because it was an instance, probably the most controversial and high profile, of how the communist security service archives were used to legitimate and de-legitimate the post-communist state's genesis and foundational myths, specific political actors and formations, and the transitional justice process itself. Allegations that Lech Wałęsa was a paid communist security service informant codenamed 'Bolek' in the early 1970s surfaced and re-surfaced on a number of occasions in post-communist Poland, and they appeared to be confirmed unequivocally following the discovery of the files hidden illegally in the home of former communist interior minister General Kiszczak. Mr Wałęsa's own statements regarding the authenticity of these allegations were confusing and contradictory: at some points coming close to admitting that he had collaborated, on other occasions denying it vehemently and dismissing the incriminating documents as forgeries.

Some of Mr Wałęsa's staunchest supporters also questioned the authenticity of the evidence that he was an informer, but, especially after the release of the Kiszczak files, even most of those commentators who were sympathetic to him accepted that he almost certainly did collaborate between 1971 and 1976. Instead, rather than dismissing the allegations outright, they attempted to relativise Mr Wałęsa's actions and locate them within a broader historical context. They proposed various mitigating circumstances, minimised Mr Wałęsa's involvement, and argued that he had compensated for the weaknesses of his youth by his subsequent actions as a legendary figure of international standing who embodied Poland's struggle for freedom and democracy. Mr Wałęsa's critics, on the other hand, argued that his collaboration was not just an 'episode' but had lasted for several years, during which time he was an ardent informer rewarded financially for betraying his friends and fellow workers. They said that fear of being blackmailed by representatives of the outgoing regime explained his erratic behaviour during the democratic transition and the early years of post-communism, particularly his questionable presidential personnel and policy choices. They also raised questions about whether Mr Wałęsa used his powers as head of state to cover up his communist secret service involvement.

Both sides of the political conflict in post-1989 Poland accused each other of trying to develop an image of Mr Wałęsa that was politically advantageous to them and being instrumental in their attitudes towards his collaboration. A cynical observer might argue that the attitudes of many Polish politicians and commentators towards his security service collaboration depended primarily on whether or not it was in their interests at any given time to use the issue against Mr Wałęsa or to defend him. The 'Bolek' affair was used to legitimate and de-legitimate specific political actors and formations, particularly after the 2005 elections, when party competition became structured around Law and Justice and Civic Platform. This was not surprising, given that attitudes towards Mr Wałęsa's alleged collaboration emerged as an important issue dividing these two post-Solidarity groupings and the main Polish political actors that emerged in the post-2005 period. As we shall see in the next chapter, which discusses public attitudes towards transitional justice and truth revelation, party political orientations were also of key importance in determining public attitudes towards the former Solidarity leader. Similarly, the 'Bolek' affair was used to legitimate and de-legitimate the transitional justice and truth-revelation process itself as either vitally necessary or dangerously politicised.

More broadly, it was used to both legitimate and de-legitimate the post-communist Third Republic state's genesis and foundational myths, highlighting, entrenching and deepening the lines of division among Poles, which manifested themselves in a number of fundamental disputes about the communist past and the post-communist transformation. Supporters of the post-1989 Third Republic status quo argued that Mr Wałęsa's critics were attempting to use the 'Bolek affair' to undermine the idea of the 1989 'round table' negotiations as an honourable compromise that paved the way for the successful transition to democratic rule, and thereby de-legitimise one of the Third Republic's key foundational myths. Critics of the Third Republic status quo, on the other hand, argued that the handling of the 'Bolek' affair explained post-communist elites' lack of willingness to deal with the communist past, reinforcing their belief that the transition was engineered by the representatives of the previous regime. Thus, during the post-communist period, the country's political, economic and cultural establishment were manipulated behind the scenes by former (but still influential) communist-era security service functionaries so that those ex-ruling elites could maintain their wealth and influence in the new Poland. Mr Wałęsa, these critics argued, symbolised the Third Republic, not in the way that his supporters claimed but, rather, through how his past communist security service links explained the betrayal of Solidarity's ideals. For them, the 'Bolek' affair revealed fundamental truths about the nature of the Third Republic and demonstrated the mechanisms through which the outgoing regime was able to transition so smoothly to post-communism, and the communist security services deformed the Polish transformation by keeping a group of individuals who were under their influence in positions of power.

Notes

1 This was one of the tools of what might be termed 'historical policy' (polityka historyczna). In contemporary Polish political debate, this concept developed increasingly ideological overtones. It was linked to the idea of presenting historical events and narratives in ways that strengthened Poland's national unity and cohesion by defending the country's interpretation of history and trying to ensure that it was widely accepted in international circles in order for the country to achieve its wider political goals. See, for example, Gawin et al. (2005).
2 According to some sources, Mr Wałęsa confessed his previous collaboration when he became active in the Free Trade Unions in 1977 and promised not to have any further contacts with the communist security services. See, for example, Chodakiewicz (2009).
3 As discussed in Chapter 2, in 2009 another (controversial) publication by Paweł Zyzak (2009), a former Institute of National Remembrance intern, also connected Mr Wałęsa to the communist security services.
4 The documents contained a note saying that they were not to be made available until five years after Mr Wałęsa's death.
5 Gontarczyk and Cenckiewicz's critics argued that their book was highly circumstantial and, although the authors analysed excerpts from agent 'Bolek''s denunciations stored in police files, they were not in possession of this most vital document, the very file found in Kiszczak's house. For critical reviews of the Cenckiewicz–Gontarczyk book, see, for example, Friszke (2008) and Machcewicz (2008). For the authors' responses, see Cenckiewicz and Gontarczyk (2008c, 2008d).
6 See, for example, Stróżyk (2008).
7 Cf. wPolityce (2016a).
8 Some commentators argue that this was impossible and it was delusional of him to think that he could have manipulated the security services in this way. See, for example, Płociński (2016).
9 'Paths of health' ('ścieżka zdrowia') was an ironic euphemism for a form of torture carried out by the communist security services on opposition activists, which involved beating those arrested with clubs as they ran between two lines of functionaries.
10 The Workers' Defence Committee (Komitet Obrony Robotników: KOR) was one of the first major anti-communist opposition groups in Poland set up to provide aid to persecuted worker leaders and their families after the government crackdown that followed the June 1976 anti-regime protests.
11 For an attempt to present evidence linking Mr Wałęsa's later actions as Solidarity leader to his earlier communist security service collaboration, see, for example, Cenckiewicz (2017). These arguments are set out at greater length in Cenckiewicz (2013). Cf. Friszke (2017).
12 See, for example, Semka (2016a) and Wildstein (2016b).
13 A close friend and aide (and at one time chauffeur) of Mr Wałęsa, who became head of his presidential chancellery and was rumoured to have been a communist security service officer. See, for example, Semka (2014).
14 See, for example, Cenckiewicz and Gontarczyk (2008e).
15 See, for example, Komorowski (2014) and *Economist* (2014).

16 See, for example, Michnik (2014).
17 See, for example, Zybertowicz (1993), Łoś and Zybertowicz (2000) and Zybertowicz (2013).
18 For a good analysis of the different right-wing discourses on the meaning of the events of 1989, including 'rejectionist' ones that viewed the 'round table' and Magdalenka meetings themselves as playing a critical role in determining the future, flawed path of post-communism transformation, see Lipiński (2008, 2013).
19 See, for example, Śpiewak (2008) and Semka (2016d).
20 See, for example, Gmyz (2008, 2009) and Borusewicz (2008).

Bibliography

Adamski, Ł., 2016. *Zmiana tonu w ocenie TW 'Bolka' przez takich ludzi jak Friszke nie jest istotna. Adam Michnik będzie trawł w obronie Wałęsy. To obrona panstwa, które stworzył'*, wPolityce [online], wPolityce, 25 February. Available from: http://wpolityce.pl/polityka/282964-zmiana-tonu-w-ocenie-tw-bolka-przez-takich-ludzi-jak-friszke-nie-jest-istotna-adam-michnik-bedzie-trwal-w-obronie-walesy-to-obrona-panstwa-ktore-stworzyl (accessed 25 February 2016).

Beylin, M., 2016. *Melanż zemsty i spiskowej wyobraźni* [online], wyborcza.pl, 19 February. Available from: http://wyborcza.pl/1,75968,19649304,melanz-zemsty-i-spiskowej-wyobrazni.html (accessed 19 February 2016).

Borusewicz, B., 2008. IPN nie może podsycać złych emocji. *Rzeczpospolita*, 19 September.

Cenckiewicz, S., 2009. Jak Wałęsa dostał status pokrzywdzonego. *Rzeczpospolita*, 15 April.

Cenckiewicz, S., 2013. *Wałęsa: Człowiek z teczki*. Warsaw: Wydawnictwo Zysk i S-ka.

Cenckiewicz, S., 2016a. Ikona system kłamstw. *Do Rzeczy*, 22–28 February.

Cenckiewicz, S., 2016b. Author interview, 6 June.

Cenckiewicz, S., 2017. *Sławomir Cenckiewicz obala 14 mitów Wałęsy* [online], niezalezna.pl, 2 February. Available from: http://niezalezna.pl/93236-tylko-u-nas-slawomir-cenckiewicz-obala-14-mitow-walesy (accessed 3 February 2017).

Cenckiewicz, S. and Gontarczyk, P., 2008a. *SB a Lech Wałęsa. Przyczynek do biografii*. Warsaw: IPN.

Cenckiewicz, S. and Gontarczyk, P., 2008b. Jak lustrowano prezydenta Wałęsę, *Rzeczpospolita*, 18 June.

Cenckiewicz, S. and Gontarczyk, P., 2008c. O recenzji pisanej na raty. W odpowiedzi prof Andrzejowi Friszkemu. *Gazeta Wyborcza*, 26 June.

Cenckiewicz, S. and Gontarczyk, P., 2008d. Książka w krzywym zwierciadle. *Rzeczpospolita*, 8 July.

Cenckiewicz, S. and Gontarczyk, P., 2008e. Gdzie są akta TW 'Bolka'. *Rzeczpospolita*, 17 June.

Chodakiewicz, M.J., 2009. Agent Bolek. *Intelligencer: Journal of US Intelligence Studies*, 17 (2), 108–110.

Czuchnowski, W., 2008. IPN: Wałęsa do weryfikacji. *Gazeta Wyborcza*, 26 August.

Czuchnowski, W., 2016a. *Trzy teczki Kiszczaka o 'Bolku'. Co jest w dokumentach udostępnionych przez IPN* [online], wyborcza.pl, 22 February. Available from: http://wyborcza.pl/1,75398,19664441,trzy-teczki-kiszczaka-o-bolku-co-jest-w-dokumentach-udostepnionych.html (accessed 22 February 2016).

Czuchnowski, W., 2016b. *'Bolek' story, czyli jak władze komunistyczne chciały skompromitować Wałęsę* [online], wyborcza.pl, 18 February. Available from: http://

wyborcza.pl/1,75398,19642883,bolek-story-czyli-jak-wladze-komunistyczne-chcialy-skompromitowac.html (accessed 18 February 2016).

Czuchnowski, W., 2016c. *Ścieżki agenta 'Bolka'. Co zapisali esbecy w latach 70?* [online], wyborcza.pl, 24 February. Available from: http://wyborcza.pl/1,75398,19669361,sciezki-agenta-bolka-co-zapisali-esbecy-w-latach-70.html (accessed 24 February 2016).

Czuchnowski, W., 2017. *Kim jest TW 'Bolek'? Oskarżyciele Wałęsy triumfują* [online], wyborcza.pl, 31 January. Available from: http://wyborcza.pl/7,75398,21315268,kim-jest-tw-bolek-oskarzyciele-walesy-triumfuja-podsumowanie.html (accessed 31 January 2017).

Czuchnowski, W., and Kublik, A., 2016. *Misja IPN: zniszczyć Wałęsę, uratować Kamińskiego* [online], wyborcza.pl, 28 February. Available from: http://wyborcza.pl/1,76842,19692936,misja-ipn-zniszczyc-walese-uratowac-kaminskiego.html (accessed 28 February 2016).

Czuchnowski, W. and Leszczyński, A., 2016. *Wałęsa w cieniu teczek. Pośmiertna zemsta komunistyczne Służby Bezpieczeństwa* [online], wyborcza.pl, 23 February. Available from: http://wyborcza.pl/1,75398,19664435,walesa-w-cieniu-teczek-posmiertna-zemsta-komunistycznej-sluzby.html (accessed 23 February 2016).

Dudek, A., 2016. Author interview, 7 June.

Economist, 2014. Poland's second golden age. *Economist*, 26 June.

Fałkowski, M., 2016. Akta 'Bolka' i dobre rządzenie. *Rzeczpospolita*, 22 February.

Ferfecki, W., 2016. Polityczny spór o 'Bolka'. *Rzeczpospolita*, 18 February.

Fijołek, M., 2016. *Legendzie Lecha Wałęsy najbardziej szkodza nie 'hnwejbini i lustratorzy', ale on sam i front jego obrońców zamykających oczy na rzeczywistość* [online], wPolityce, 24 February. Available from: http://wpolityce.pl/polityka/282841-legendzie-lecha-walesy-najbardziej-szkodza-nie-hunwejbini-i-lustratorzy-ale-on-sam-i-front-jego-obroncow-zamykajacych-oczy-na-rzeczywistosc (accessed 24 February 2016).

Friszke, A., 2008. Zniszczyć Wałęsę. *Gazeta Wyborcza*, 21–22 June.

Friszke, A., 2016. Jak czytać te teczki. *Polityka*, 2–8 March.

Friszke, A., 2017. *Friszke rozbija w OKO.press 14 mitów Cenckiewicza o Wałęsie: to oszczerstwa, insynuacje i manipulacje* [online], wyborcza.pl, 8 February. Available from: http://wyborcza.pl/7,75968,21346393,friszke-rozbija-w-oko-press-14-mitow-cenckiewicza-o-walesie.html (accessed 9 February 2017).

Gajca, A., 2016. Akta uderzają w Wałęsę. *Rzeczpospolita*, 22 February.

Gawin, D., Łubieński, T., Majcherek, J.A., Merta, T. and Jędrysik, M., 2005. *Po co nam polityka historyczna?* [online], wyborcza.pl, 30 September. Available from: http://wyborcza.pl/1,76842,2945729.html (accessed 17 February 2017).

Gmyz, C., 2008. Koalicja: IPN trzeba zmienić. *Rzeczpospolita*, 24 June.

Gmyz, C., 2009. Donald Tusk grozi IPN. *Rzeczpospolita*, 31 March.

Hall, A., 2016. *Aleksander Hall o rewolucji nihilizmu* [online], wyborcza.pl, 22 February. Available from: http://wyborcza.pl/1,75968,19659367,aleksander-hall-o-rewolucji-nihilizmu.html (accessed 22 February 2016).

Harłukowicz, J., 2016a. *Władysław Frasyniuk. Kto rzuca w Lecha Wałęsę kamieniem* [online], wyborcza.pl, 20 February. Available from: http://wyborcza.pl/magazyn/1,124 059,19652285,wladyslaw-frasyniuk-kto-rzuca-w-lecha-walese-kamieniem.html (accessed 20 February 2016).

Harłukowicz, J., 2016b. *Pinior: Chcą zastąpić Wałęsę Lechem Kaczyńskim* [online], wyborcza.pl, 19 February. Available from: http://wroclaw.wyborcza.pl/wroclaw/1,35771,19650606,pinior-chca-zastapic-walese-lechem-kaczynskim.html (accessed 19 February 2016).

138 The 'Bolek' affair

Karnowski, M., 2016. *Szafa Kiszczaka to prawdziwa konstytucja III RP, fundament państwa zbudowanego na krzywdzie ofiar i bogactwie oprawców* [online], wPolityce, 18 February. Available from: http://wpolityce.pl/spoleczenstwo/282121-szafa-kiszczaka-to-prawdziwa-konstytucja-iii-rp-fundament-panstwa-zbudowanego-na-krzywdzie-ofiar-i-bogactwie-oprawcow (accessed 18 February 2016).

Kolodziejski, K., 2016. Gdyby Wałęsa ujawnił współpracy z SB. *Rzeczpospolita*, 26–27 February.

Komorowski, B., 2014. *Pełny tekst przemówienia Bronisława Komorowskiego wygłoszonego w 25. rocznicę wyborów z 4 czerwca 1989* [online], gazeta.prawna.pl, 4 June. Available from: www.gazetaprawna.pl/artykuly/801396,pelny-tekst-przemowienia-bronislawa-komorowskiego-wygloszonego-w-25-rocznice-wyborow-z-4-czerwca-1989.html (accessed 5 June 2014).

Kozubal, M., 2016. Udostępnią akta z domu Kiszczaka. *Rzeczpospolita*, 22 February.

Kozubal, M., 2017. Wałęsa jednak podpisał. *Rzeczpospolita*, 1 February.

Krzemiński, I., 2016. *Obalenie bohatera* [online], wyborcza.pl, 29 February. Available from: http://wyborcza.pl/1,75968,19693207,obalanie-bohatera.html (accessed 29 February 2016).

Kubiak, P., 2008. Lech Wałęsa: gryzą mnie po kostkach. *Rzeczpospolita*, 26 August.

Kublik, A., 2016. *Magdalenka, czyli stare sensacje redaktora Gmyza* [online], wyborcza.pl, 24 February. Available from: http://wyborcza.pl/1,76842,19675153,magdalenka-czyli-stare-sensacje-redaktora-gmyza.html (accessed 24 February 2016).

Kurski, J., 2008. *Tusk: Brońmy Sierpnia* [online], wyborcza.pl, 19 June. Available from: http://wyborcza.pl/1,75248,5326837,Tusk_Bronmy_Sierpnia.html (accessed 19 June 2008).

Kurski, J., 2016. *Operacja 'Bolek': Czego nie było w szufladzie Kiszczaka* [online]. wyborcza.pl, 19 February. Available from: http://wyborcza.pl/1,75968,19648199,operacja-bolek-czego-nie-bylo-w-szufladzie-kiszczaka.html (accessed 19 February 2016).

Leszczyński, A., 2016a. *Prof Friszke: Teczki Wałęsy to nie są śmieci* [online]. wyborcza.pl, 23 February. Available from: http://wyborcza.pl/1,75398,19664506,prof-friszke-teczki-walesy-to-nie-sa-smieci.html (accessed 23 February 2016).

Leszczyński, A., 2016b. *Telewizyny spektakl, który miał pogrzebać Wałęsę. Broniący legendy 'S' znokautował jego tropiciela* [online], wyborcza.pl, 18 February. Available from: http://wyborcza.pl/1,75968,19648109,telewizyjny-spektakl-ktory-mial-pogrzebac-walese-broniacy.html (accessed 18 February 2016).

Leszczyński, A., 2016c. Author interview, 8 June.

Lipiński, A., 2008. Mitologizacja czy dyskursywna reprezentacja? Okrągły stół, Magdalenka i 'gruba kreska' jako kategorie dyskursu prawicy. In B. Szklarski, ed., *Mity, symbole i rytuały we współczesnej polityce. Szkice z antropologii polityki*. Warsaw: Wydawnictwo Naukowe Scholar, 277–291.

Lipiński, A., 2013. Meanings of 1989: Right-Wing Discourses in Post-Communist Poland. In K. McDermott and M. Stibbe, eds, *The 1989 Revolutions in Central and Eastern Europe: From Communism to Pluralism*. Manchester: Manchester University Press, 235–252.

Lisicki, P., 2016. Coup de grace. *Do Rzeczy*, 22–28 February.

Łoś, M.W. and Zybertowicz, A., 2000. *Privatising the Police State: The Case of Poland*. Basingstoke: Macmillan.

Machcewicz, P., 2008. Wałęsa w krzywym zwiercadle. *Rzeczpospolita*, 30 June.

Maziarski, W., 2016. *Przejścia Lecha na jasną strone mocy* [online], wyborzca.pl, 25 February. Available from: http://wyborcza.pl/1,75968,19674969,przejscia-lecha-na-jasna-strone-mocy.html (accessed 25 February 2016).

Michnik, A., 2014. *Wykorzystaliśmy szansę daną przez historię* [online], wyborcza.pl, 6 February. Available from: http://wyborcza.pl/1,75968,15406245,Wykorzystalismy_szanse_dana_przez_historie.html (accessed 6 February 2014).
Mirowski, M., 2016. Męstwo Lecha Wałęsy. *Rzeczpospolita*, 27–28 February.
Moszyński, P., 2016. *Dzięki, Lechu. A co, jeśli sie okaże, że to nie fałszywki?* [online], wyborcza.pl, 22 February. Available from: http://wyborcza.pl/1,75968,19663857,dzieki-lechu-a-co-jesli-okaze-sie-ze-to-nie-falszywki.html (accessed 22 February 2016).
Mularczyk, A., 2016. Author interview, 8 June.
Paczkowski, A., 2016. Author interview, 9 June.
Paradowska, J., 2008. Wymazać Wałęsę. *Polityka*, 28 June.
Paradowska, J., 2016. Author interview, 6 June.
Płociński, M., 2016. Historyk: Wałęsa to nie Piłsusdski. *Rzeczpospolita*, 12–13 March.
Rokita, J., 2016. Nowa pedagogika wstydu. *wSieci*, 14–20 March.
Rzeczpospolita.pl, 2016a. *Waszczykowski o Wałęsie: Mógł być marionetką sterowaną* [online], rzeczpospolita.pl, 19 February. Available from: www.rp.pl/Archiwum-Kiszczaka/160219187-Waszczykowski-o-Walesie-Mogl-byc-marionetka-sterowana.html#ap-1 (accessed 19 February 2016).
Rzeczpospolita.pl, 2016b. *PiS i Kukiz '15: prawda o Wałęsie należy się Polakom. PSL i N krtykują pośpiech IPN* [online], rzeczpospolita.pl, 22 February. Available from: http://rp.pl (accessed 22 February 2016).
Semka, P., 2014. Niewyjaśniona tajemnica Lecha Wałęsy. *Do Rzeczy*, 14–21 April.
Semka, P., 2016a. Czego jeszcze nie wiemy o Lechu. *Do Rzeczy*, 29 February–6 March.
Semka, P., 2016b. 'Hakoteki' esbeków. *Do Rzeczy*, 22–28 February.
Semka, P., 2016c. Author interview, 6 June.
Semka, P., 2016d. Lech Wałęsa, cyli udana transakcja. *Do Rzeczy*, 8–14 February.
Siedlecka, E., 2016. Author interview, 8 June.
Skórzyński, J., 2016. Oskarzony: Lech Wałęsa. *Polityka*, 24 February–1 March.
Stankiewicz, A., 2016a. Lech Wałęsa bliżej 'Bolka'. *Rzeczpospolita*, 3 March.
Stankiewicz, A., 2016b. Lech Wałęsa, niewolnik 'Bolka'. *Rzeczpospolita*, 22 February.
Stankiewicz, A., 2016c. Archiwum Kiszczaka: Upadki i wzloty Lecha Wałęsy. *Rzeczpospolita*, 19 February.
Stasiński, M., 2016. *Bez Wałęsy nie byłoby podziemia* [online], wyborcza.pl, 22 February. Available from: http://wyborcza.pl/1,75398,19659449,bez-walesy-nie-byloby-podziemia.html (accessed 22 February 2016).
Stróżyk, J., 2008. Lech Wałęsa: Kiedyś dokumenty same przemowią. *Rzeczpospolita*, 31 May–1 June.
Szostkiewicz, A., 2016. Nasz Lech, wasz Bolek. *Polityka*, 24 February–1 March.
Szułdrzyński, M., 2016. Ujawnienie archiwum Kiszczaka w sprawie Wałęsy. *Rzeczpospolita*, 19 February.
Śpiewak, P., 2008. Wałęsa – ofiara własnych obrońców. *Rzeczpospolita*, 28 August.
Wachnicki, M., 2016. *Schetyna: Zlikwidujemy IPN, CBA. Powołamy zespół ds. badania manipulacji katastrofą smoleńską* [online], wyborcza.pl, 2 October. Available from: http://wyborcza.pl/7,75398,20777413,schetyna-zlikwidujemy-ipn-cba-powolamy-zespol-ds-badania.html (accessed 2 October 2016).
Wałęsa, L., 1990. *Droga nazdzei*. Kraków: Znak.
Wildstein, B., 2016a. *Wałęsa to typ wiejskiego cwianiaczka* [online], fakt.pl, 26 March. Available from: www.fakt.pl/wydarzenia/polityka/bronislaw-wildstein-dla-faktu/t1lmsg6 (accessed 27 March 2016).
Wildstein, 2016b. 'Solidarność' to nie Wałęsa. *wSieci*, 29 February–6 March.

Wildstein, B., 2016c, Author interview, 9 June.
wPolityce, 2016a. *Wildstein o oświadczeniach Wałęsy: To jest kolejna wersja zdarzeń, kolejny świadek, którego nikt nie widział. On mówi od rzeczy* [online], wPolityce, 19 February. Available from: http://wpolityce.pl/polityka/282318-wildstein-o-oswiadczeniach-walesy-to-jest-kolejna-wersja-zdarzen-kolejny-swiadek-ktorego-nikt-nie-widzial-on-mowi-od-rzeczy (accessed 19 February 2016).
wPolityce, 2016b. *Prof Friszke za, a nawet przeciw ws. TW Bolka? Teczka nie może być traktowana jako klucz do zrozumienia całej historii Lecha Wałęsy* [online], wPolityce. pl, 16 March. Available from: http://wpolityce.pl/polityka/285288-prof-friszke-za-a-nawet-przeciw-ws-tw-bolka-teczka-nie-moze-byc-traktowana-jako-klucz-do-zrozumienia-calej-historii-lecha-walesy (accessed 16 March 2016).
wPolityce, 2016c. *Oświadczenie Sławomira Cenckiewicza, Wałęsa był współpracownikem SB o ps. 'Bolek'* [online], wPolityce, 17 February. Available from: http://wpolityce.pl/polityka/281950-oswiadczenie-slawomira-cenckiewicza-walesa-byl-wspolpracownikiem-sb-o-ps-bolek (accessed 17 February 2016).
wPolityce, 2016d. *Histeria na ulicach Warszawy! KOD broni Wałęsy. Kijowski: 'Chcemy pokazać naszą solidarność z Lechem Wałęsą, symbolem zwycięskiej walki o wolność i demokrację'. A w tle Schetyna, Petru i Nowacka ...* [online], wPolityce, 27 February. Available from: http://wpolityce.pl/polityka/283263-histeria-na-ulicach-warszawy-kod-broni-walesy-kijowski-chcemy-pokazac-nasza-solidarnosc-z-lechem-walesa-symbolem-zwycieskiej-walki-o-wolnosc-i-demokracje-a-w-tle-schetyna-petru-i-nowacka (accessed 27 February 2016).
Zaremba, P., 2016a. *To Wałęsa się uwikał, nie Solidarność. To było uwikłanie częsciowe, ale zabójcze dla jego roli po 1989* [online], wPolityce, 18 February. Available from: http://wpolityce.pl/polityka/282210-to-walesa-sie-uwiklal-nie-solidarnosc-to-bylo-uwiklanie-czesciowe-ale-zabojcze-dla-jego-roli-po-1989-roku (accessed 18 February 2016).
Zaremba, P., 2016b. Pod dyktando teczek SB. *wSieci*, 22–28 February.
Ziemkiewicz, R., 2016. Solidarni z 'Bolkiem'. *Do Rzeczy*, 22–28 February.
Zybertowicz, A., 1993. *W uścisku tajnych służb: Upadek komunizmu i układ postnomenklatury*. Warsaw: Wydawnictwo Antyk Marcin Dybowski.
Zybertowicz, A., 2008. Lustracja w świecie hypokrzyji. *Rzeczpospolita*, 15 May.
Zybertowicz, A., 2013. *III RP: Kulisy systemu*. Warsaw: Wydawnictwo Słowo i Myśli.
Zybertowicz, A., 2016. Author interview, 7 June.
Zyzak, P., 2009. *Lech Wałęsa. Idea i Historia*, Kraków: Arcana.

6 Communist-forgiving or seeking historical justice?

Public attitudes towards truth revelation and dealing with the communist past[1]

This chapter examines polling data on how public attitudes towards transitional justice, truth revelation and dealing with the communist past evolved in post-communist Poland. Specifically, it considers the notion that the issue of lustration and secret service file access may have recurred in Polish politics due to public demand for more radical transitional justice. There is some debate in the academic literature as to whether, and to what extent, the process of 'late lustration' was elite-driven or developed (in part at least) in response to public demand. For example, in co-authored papers with Williams and Fowler, I cited continued public support for lustration as one of the five reasons why the issue recurred and became instrumentalised in post-communist politics (Williams *et al.* 2003, pp. 14–15, 2005, pp. 33–34). On the other hand, some authors, such as Nalepa (2010), have argued that the issue was of low salience to most voters in countries like Poland. Nalepa did not see any relationship between public opinion or popular demand for transitional justice and the renewal of interest in lustration, which she viewed as being almost entirely an elite-driven process. For example, in her explanation of why the truth revelation issue recurred, Nalepa (2010, p. 126) claimed that 'lustration laws are not … a response to popular demand for holding various members of the ancient regime accountable for human rights violations'. Rather, she argued, lustration laws were 'supplied by political elites who stood to gain from having lustration laws in place'. To support her claim, Nalepa (2010, p. 28) presented statistical analysis that, she argued, showed 'little support for the hypothesized correlation between voters' support for lustration and their willingness to elect politicians who adhere to a lustration platform'. Indeed, 'even voters who would like to see former collaborators exposed', she claimed, 'appear unwilling to make their vote depend on this preference.' Moreover, Nalepa (2010, p. 105) also claimed that the harshest lustration laws were introduced when public support for radical transitional justice had actually declined.

This chapter undertakes a detailed examination of Polish public attitudes towards lustration and file access, including those towards Mr Wałęsa's alleged communist security service collaboration, based on an analysis of publicly available polling data. This includes an analysis of the shifts that occurred over time and the caveats that need to be placed on the overall finding of continuing broad public support for lustration and file access. It examines whether truth revelation was salient in determining voting and election outcomes. It considers whether headline polling figures often masked the true salience of these issues by examining how attitudes towards the lustration and file access processes may have interacted with other, more salient ones relating to concerns about the shortcomings of the democratic system in Poland. It also looks at whether and how concerns about truth-revelation procedures may have mapped onto, and structured, post-communist ideological and party alignments more generally.

Continuing broad public support for lustration

Even if, as we shall see, most of them did not necessarily view this issue as a priority, and although there were various waves and patterns of support, Poles were broadly sympathetic towards fairly radical approaches to dealing with the communist past. This applied to both the general principle of transitional justice and truth revelation as well as lustration and communist security service file access as specific, necessary measures. For example, as the time series poll conducted by the CBOS agency in Table 6.1 shows, a clear majority of Poles consistently supported lustration, understood as vetting public officials for their links with the communist-era security services. Support for lustration remained high throughout the 1990s, reaching a peak of 76 per cent in favour (and only 12 per cent against) in 1997. Other polls conducted during this period confirmed this pattern of support. For example, a September 1999 survey by the PBS agency found that 52 per cent of Poles felt that lustration should continue and only 27 per cent felt that it should be halted (*Rzeczpospolita* 1999). Similarly, an August 2000 PBS poll conducted during the process of lustration of the candidates in that year's presidential election found that 52 per cent of voters felt that it was essential, while only 36 per cent said that it was not, and 12 per cent did not know (*Rzeczpospolita* 2000).

As Table 6.1 also shows, there was continued support for lustration during the early 2000s, with an increase in the middle of the decade as the issue moved up the political agenda from 56 per cent in March 2002 to 68 per cent (and 39 per cent strongly in favour) in February 2005. At the same time, the number opposed to lustration fell from 31 per cent to only 20 per cent (with only 13 per cent strongly opposed) over the same period. Again, this was confirmed by other

Table 6.1 Polish attitudes towards vetting key public officials, 1994–2005 (%)

	June 1994	December 1996	December 1997	September 1999	March 2002	February 2005
Yes	57	57	76	56	56	68
No	36	24	12	31	31	20
Don't know	7	19	12	13	13	12

Source: adapted from: CBOS (2005a, p. 2).

polls conducted during this period. For example, a January 2005 TNS OBOP survey found that 77 per cent of respondents agreed (39 per cent strongly) that those in important state positions should undergo lustration (as set out in the 1997 law), while only 12 per cent disagreed; 11 per cent did not know (TNS OBOP 2005, pp. 1–2). Similarly, a June 2005 PBS survey for the *Gazeta Wyborcza* newspaper found that 46 per cent of respondents felt that the information being reported in the media regarding whether or not various public figures were communist security service agents was credible (although only 4 per cent felt it was highly credible), compared with 36 per cent who felt that it was not (8 per cent definitely); 18 per cent did not know (Gazeta.pl 2005). A June 2006 GfK Polonia survey for the *Rzeczpospolita* newspaper also found that 59 per cent of respondents supported extending lustration to all senior officials (Stankiewicz 2006).

A June 2007 GfK Polonia survey for *Rzeczpospolita* found that 56 per cent of respondents agreed that the list of 500 communist security service collaborators occupying senior posts or public authority figures that the Institute of National Remembrance had compiled but could not publish due to the May 2007 constitutional tribunal ruling on the new 2006 lustration law (which contained a requirement for it to publish such lists) should be made publicly available (28 per cent strongly agreed). Only 37 per cent disagreed with publishing this list (17 per cent strongly), while 7 per cent did not know (*Rzeczpospolita* 2007). A November 2007 survey for the Catholic Church Statistical Institute found that 67 per cent of Catholics felt that lustration was necessary and only 2 per cent believed that the process could be harmful (the remainder thought that it was unnecessary) (Wiśniewska 2007). A January 2009 GfK Polonia survey also found that 59 per cent of respondents felt that the Institute of National Remembrance's Lustration Office should declare who had collaborated with the communist security services, while only 37 per cent felt that it should not; 4 per cent did not know (Manys 2009).

Drilling down a bit more to the specific justifications for lustration, a January–February 2005 CBOS survey for *Gazeta Wyborcza* found that, when asked a series of questions, on average around 50 per cent of respondents agreed with pro-lustration arguments, compared with one-third who disagreed. For example, 46 per cent of respondents felt that lustration should be carried out even if the extant communist security service files were incomplete because it was still possible to learn part of the truth, while only 39 per cent felt that one could not learn the truth from incomplete files; 15 per cent did not know. Similarly, 48 per cent felt that justice required that lustration be carried out, while only 32 per cent felt that it did not matter which politicians had collaborated with the communist security services in the past, but only whether they were currently playing a positive or negative role; 20 per cent did not know. Forty-six per cent felt that the dangers of having former communist secret service informers holding public office were greater than the risk that someone innocent could be wrongly accused of having collaborated, while 32 per cent felt that lustration should not be carried out because this risk was too great; 22 per cent did not know (Pacewicz 2005).

Moreover, surveys also found support for casting the net very widely as far as the scope of which groups should be included in the lustration and vetting process was concerned. For example, a different February 2005 CBOS (2005a, pp. 4–6) survey found high – and, over time, increasing – levels of support not only for the lustration of those groups holding executive, legislative and judicial offices in Poland (as defined by the 1997 law), but also for extending its scope to encompass other categories. These could be divided into four broad clusters. First, more than 80 per cent of respondents supported vetting the prime minister and deputy prime ministers (90 per cent), the President (89 per cent), government ministers and deputy ministers (89 per cent), parliamentary deputies and Senators (88 per cent), judges and public prosecutors (88 per cent) and high-ranking officials (87 per cent). These figures represented an increase of around 10 percentage points compared with December 1997 (as noted above, the record year as far as levels of public support for lustration was concerned), from 82 per cent for the prime minister and deputy ministers, 81 per cent for the President, 79 per cent for parliamentary deputies and Senators, 79 per cent for judges and public prosecutors, and 75 per cent for high-ranking officials. Second, the same February 2005 CBOS survey found that more than 70 per cent of respondents supported the vetting of high-level managers of state enterprises (78 per cent), policemen (76 per cent), army officers (76 per cent), senior TV managers (72 per cent), senior bank officials (72 per cent) and senior state officials (71 per cent). Again, these figures represented a 10–15 percentage points increase in each category compared with 1997, from 65 per cent for policemen, 64 per cent for army officers, 60 per cent for senior TV managers, 56 per cent for senior bank officials and 57 per cent for senior state officials (no data was available for high-level state enterprise managers for that year). Third, in February 2005 over 50 per cent of respondents supported the vetting of local councillors (68 per cent), journalists (60 per cent), priests (56 per cent) and University lecturers (53 per cent). Compared with 1997, there was an increase of 12 percentage points in support for the lustration of local councillors (from 56 per cent) and 11 percentage points for journalists (from 49 per cent); no data was available for that year for priests and lecturers. Fourth, respondents were almost evenly divided on whether school teachers should be vetted, with 45 per cent in favour and 42 per cent against; in 1997, the figures were reversed, with 40 per cent in favour and 46 per cent against.

The same February 2005 CBOS (2005a, pp. 6–8) survey also found that a substantial majority of respondents thought that it was important to know whether candidates in elections had collaborated with the communist security services: 65 per cent in the case of parliamentary elections (with 35 per cent saying that it was 'very important'), 66 per cent for presidential elections (33 per cent very important) and 57 per cent for local elections (28 per cent very important). Among those who said that they would definitely vote, these numbers were even higher, increasing to 71 per cent for parliamentary elections, 72 per cent for presidential elections and 63 per cent for local elections.

Certainly, somewhat contradicting the February 2005 CBOS survey cited above, a June 2006 GfK Polonia poll actually found that only 44 per cent of respondents supported extending lustration to priests, 42 per cent to journalists, 32 per cent to teachers and 30 per cent to academics (Stankiewicz 2006). However, in the case of the clergy in particular, a different survey, conducted in January 2007 by the CBOS (2007a, pp. 5–8) agency, found that 65 per cent of respondents felt that vetting priests to check for their links with the communist security services was necessary (27 per cent felt that it was 'definitely' necessary) compared with 24 per cent who were opposed to it; 11 per cent did not know. Moreover, 72 per cent of those who were in favour of the lustration of priests said that it should encompass all Polish clergy regardless of the position that they held, compared with only 16 per cent who felt that it should only include senior clerics; 12 per cent did not know. A March 2007 GfK Polonia survey for *Rzeczpospolita* also found that 78 per cent of respondents supported the lustration of priests, while only 10 per cent were opposed. However, 33 per cent felt that the process should be conducted by a special Church commission and only 25 per cent by a secular institution such as the Institute of National Remembrance; 20 per cent said that it did not matter who conducted the process, and 12 per cent did not know (Czaczkowska 2007a).

It is not surprising that such collaboration with the communist security services was always regarded as a particularly shameful form of engagement with the previous regime, because it involved betraying what most people saw as elementary standards of morality. There are few actions that are almost universally perceived as deserving of such strong and unconditional condemnation as the betrayal of friends and colleagues, particularly when one feels closely linked to them through participation in an important common cause or activity, in this case illegal and clandestine opposition to the communist regime. By being perceived as having betrayed 'their own' in this way, communist security service collaborators were felt to have violated universally recognised moral and ethical norms in a particularly loathsome and reprehensible way. From this perspective, lustration and file access were viewed by many Poles as important steps on the road towards the restoration of the basic moral order.

For example, while a May 2009 CBOS (2009a, pp. 4–8) survey found a 76 per cent to 18 per cent majority of respondents opposed to the idea of seeking a reckoning with the communist past in principle, when asked to consider specific forms of transitional justice, 43 per cent were in favour of revealing communist security service collaborators and only 38 per cent were against; 19 per cent did not know. Even 36 per cent of those who opposed the idea of historical justice in principle supported revealing information about secret service collaborators (47 per cent were against); as, perhaps even more strikingly, did 66 per cent of former communist party members.[2] Not surprisingly, therefore, the same survey also found that only 29 per cent of respondents felt that former communist security service functionaries had served their country well during the communist period, while 49 per cent (including 52 per cent of former communist party members) felt that they had not; 22 per cent did not know. In contrast, 48 per cent of respondents felt that a former communist party member could have served Poland well (30 per cent disagreed), while 48 per cent felt the same way about members of the communist-run state government (30 per cent disagreed) and 54 per cent in relation to middle-ranking communist state officials (24 per cent disagreed); 22 per cent did not know in all three cases (CBOS 2009a, pp. 3–4).

Indeed, perhaps for this reason, Poles appeared to be much more evenly divided in their attitudes towards 'de-communisation' – that is, excluding former communist party officials from public office – although this policy was still supported by a sizeable body of the public, according to surveys conducted during the mid-to-late 1990s. For example, as Table 6.2 shows, OBOP surveys found that between June 1996 and October 1999, 40–50 per cent of respondents supported de-communisation, while 38–53 per cent were opposed; 5–15 per cent did not know. Nonetheless, it was clearly involvement in, and collaboration with, the security services that attracted particular moral opprobrium from a large majority of Poles.

Support for opening up the communist security service files

As with the lustration and vetting issue, although it did not necessarily generate widespread public enthusiasm, most Poles wanted there to be wide access to, and supported the opening up and publication of the information contained in, the communist secret service security archives, especially those held on public figures and officials fulfilling important state functions. For example, a January 1999 CBOS (1999a, pp. 1–3) survey found that 55 per cent of respondents felt that every citizen should have access to their communist security service files, regardless of whether or not they had been invigilated themselves. Just over one-third (35 per cent) wanted some kind of restrictions on this: 22 per cent felt that access should be limited only to those who had been persecuted by the security services as a result of their opposition activities (except for those who had, at the same time, collaborated with those services), while 13 per cent felt that no private individuals should have access to these files; 10 per cent did not know. Even 53 per cent of those who voted for the communist successor Democratic Left Alliance supported full file access for all citizens, while only 24 per cent felt that individuals should not have access to these files at all.[3]

A later January 2005 PBS survey for *Rzeczpospolita* found that 43 per cent of respondents felt that the communist security service files should be accessible to everyone, compared with 36 per cent who felt that they should only be available to historians and those who had been victims of secret service invigilation, and only 12 per cent who felt that the files should not be made available to anyone (Gawryś and Kaczyński 2005). CBOS (2005b, pp. 3–4; 2005c, p. 2) surveys conducted in February and March 2005 also found that 45–47 per cent of respondents supported the publication of the 'Wildstein list', compared with 27–34 per cent who were opposed; 19–28 per cent did not know. Similarly, a July 2005 CBOS (2005d, pp. 6–7) survey found that 57 per cent of respondents felt that everyone who wanted to consult their communist security service files should be able to do so, compared with 29 per cent who felt that only those who

Table 6.2 Polish attitudes towards de-communisation, 1996–1999 (%)

	June 1996	November 1996	February 1997	August 1997	May 1998	June 1998	November 1998	September 1999	October 1999
Yes	43	46	50	50	45	42	45	40	42
No	47	45	40	38	46	53	42	46	46
Don't know	10	9	10	12	9	5	13	14	15

Source: adapted from: OBOP (1999, p. 6).

Note
The October 1999 column adds up to 103; this is presumably due to rounding up by the polling agency. The 'Yes' and 'No' figures were composites of 'definitely for' and 'rather for' and of 'definitely against' and 'rather against'; this may have magnified the rounding effect.

148   Communist-forgiving or seeking justice?

had been invigilated and recognised as victims of persecution by the regime should have such access; 13 per cent did not know (not providing anyone with file access was not given as an option).[4] Asking the question in a slightly different way, a September 2006 CBOS (2006, pp. 7–8) survey found that 43 per cent of Poles felt that anyone who was in any way affected by the communist security service archive materials should have the right to access them, while 26 per cent felt that this should be restricted to only those who were subject to lustration. Fifteen per cent felt that even those who were included in the files should not have access to them, while 16 per cent did not know. A June 2008 GfK Polonia survey for *Rzeczpospolita* also found that 66 per cent of respondents felt that the communist security service archives should be opened up (and 42 per cent agreed with this strongly), while only 35 per cent (19 per cent strongly) said that access should remain limited; 5 per cent did not know (Gmyz and Waszkielewicz 2008).

However, a large number of Poles also felt that these revelations should only be confined to the files held on public officials and that there should be restrictions on what was made available from them. For example, as Table 6.3 shows, the number of Poles who supported opening up communist security service archives in the July 2005–May 2009 period ranged from 53 per cent to 69 per cent (peaking in July 2005). However, throughout this period, only 24–38 per cent of respondents wanted full disclosure of all communist security service archives (again, peaking in July 2005), while 29–35 per cent supported the limited opening up of materials held on state officials only. Those opposed to any disclosure ranged from 20–25 per cent in July 2005 to June 2007 but increased sharply to 40 per cent in May 2009, due largely to a 9 per cent fall in the number of 'don't knows' (from 16 per cent to 7 per cent) and a 6 per cent drop in those who wanted limited archive disclosure on public officials only (from 35 per cent to 29 per cent).

Similarly, a February 2005 CBOS (2005b, pp. 5–6) survey found that although only 18 per cent of respondents were against the publication of the names of, and materials associated with, communist security service informers, and more than two-thirds (67 per cent) wanted the public to have access to these archives, there were major differences of opinion as to what (and how it) should be revealed. Eighteen per cent said that the Institute of National Remembrance

Table 6.3 Polish attitudes towards opening up communist security service archives (%)

	July 2005	Sept 2006	June 2007	May 2009
Open all archives	38	24	24	24
Open state officials' archives only	31	35	35	29
No opening up of archives	20	25	25	40
Don't know	11	16	16	7

Source: adapted from: CBOS (2009a, p. 9).

should only publish lists of the names of former communist security service functionaries and collaborators. At the same time, 19 per cent of respondents wanted all the materials collected by the communist security services to be published, while a further 30 per cent supported publication only after sensitive personal information had been removed; 15 per cent did not know. Moreover, a June 2006 GfK Polonia survey found that 58 per cent of Poles were opposed to employers having access to their workers' communist security service files, while only 35 per cent were in favour; 7 per cent did not know (Stankiewicz 2006). A June 2007 CBOS (2007b, p. 7) poll found that 55 per cent of respondents felt that sensitive materials containing information on the private lives of those who had been invigilated should not be published. Twenty per cent felt that they should be, but only in the case of important public officials, while only 11 per cent supported full disclosure of all of this kind of information.

A January 2009 GfK Polonia survey for *Rzeczpospolita* also found that while only 16 per cent of respondents felt that communist security service archives should not be opened up at all, 19 per cent said that their entire contents should be made available to everyone. Thirty-four per cent felt that they should be made available to everyone but in a redacted form, while 27 per cent said that only academics and journalists should have access to them; 4 per cent did not know. The same survey found that Poles were almost evenly divided on whether these files should be made available via the Internet: 46 per cent were in favour and 49 per cent against (Manys 2009). Certainly, a November 2009 Gemius survey for the *Newsweek Polska* weekly found that 54 per cent of respondents felt that communist security service file information *should* be published on the Internet, while only 27 per cent were opposed; 19 per cent did not know. However, of those who supported Internet publication, only 32 per cent felt that the contents of the archives should be published in their entirety, while a further 22 per cent only supported publication if they were redacted to delete information on sensitive personal matters such as health and sexual preferences (*Newsweek* 2009).

As in the case of lustration, there was also support for making public the contents of the communist security service files held on a very wide range of groups, regardless of whether or not they were informers or had been invigilated themselves. For example, a July 2005 CBOS (2005d, pp. 5–6) survey found that these groups could be divided into four broad clusters. First, more than 80 per cent of respondents supported revealing the files held on judges and public prosecutors (88 per cent), the President (87 per cent), the prime minister and deputy prime ministers (86 per cent), ministers and deputy ministers (86 per cent), parliamentary deputies and Senators (86 per cent) and high-level state and local government officials (86 per cent). Second, more than 70 per cent of respondents supported revealing the files of policemen (74 per cent), army officers (74 per cent), high-level managers of state enterprises (72 per cent) and TV managers (71 per cent). Third, over 50 per cent of respondents supported revealing the files held on senior bank officials (63 per cent), local councillors (60 per cent), priests (59 per cent) and journalists (56 per cent). Fourth, however, respondents were more evenly divided on revealing the secret service files of University lecturers

(49 per cent in favour, 44 per cent against), ordinary state officials (48 per cent in favour, 46 per cent against) and school teachers (46 per cent in favour, 48 per cent against). The same survey also found substantial majorities in favour of making public the communist security service files held on presidential candidates (82 per cent), parliamentary candidates (81 per cent) and candidates standing in local government elections (80 per cent).

Support for removing communist security service informers from office (but with mitigating circumstances)

At the same time, regarding what consequences should flow from the revelation of such links, survey evidence suggested that most Poles were strongly against former communist security service agents and informers holding important public office and, in spite of the fact that this was not stipulated in Poland's lustration laws, in many cases supported their automatic removal from office. For example, a September 1997 PBS survey taken in the run-up to that month's parliamentary election found that 73 per cent of respondents said that they would not vote for a former secret service collaborator, while only 15 per cent said that they would consider doing so (Wróbel 1999). Similarly, an October 1999 CBOS (1999b, p. 7) survey found that a majority of respondents (52 per cent with 33 per cent against) felt that anyone who was even *under suspicion* of having lied in their lustration declaration about their involvement with the communist security services should resign from office while their trial was in progress.

This hostility did not appear to diminish over time. For example, a June 2006 GfK Polonia survey found that 45 per cent of respondents felt that *all* former security service collaborators – and not just 'lustration liars' who failed to reveal their links in their declarations – should be punished, while 42 per cent said that they should not (Stankiewicz 2006). Similarly, a June 2007 CBOS (2007b, pp. 9–10) survey found that 62 per cent of respondents supported the automatic removal from office of those who had admitted to past collaboration with the communist security services, while only 15 per cent were against; 23 per cent did not know. This figure had actually increased steadily over the years from 53 per cent in May 1999 (28 per cent against) to 56 per cent in July 2005 (23 per cent against) and 59 per cent in April 2006 (20 per cent against). A January 2009 GfK Polonia survey also found that 78 per cent of Poles felt that individuals who had collaborated with the communist security services should not hold public office, while only 18 per cent felt that they should be allowed to do so; 4 per cent did not know (Manys 2009).[5]

In terms of attitudes towards collaboration by the clergy specifically, the revelation of whose links with the communist security services helped to revive the lustration and files access issue and kept it at the forefront of media attention in the mid-2000s, a January 2007 CBOS (2007a, pp. 7–8) survey found that 69 per cent of respondents felt that senior clerics who had worked as secret service informers should resign from Church positions (46 per cent felt this strongly). Sixteen per cent felt that they could continue in office if they admitted to, and showed remorse for, having such links, and only 4 per cent that they should continue to fulfil their functions regardless. Similarly, a January 2007 GfK survey for *Rzeczpospolita* found that, following the revelation of Archbishop Stanisław Wielgus' involvement with the communist security services, nearly half (46 per cent) of respondents said that they could not accept someone who had been a secret service collaborator as the new Archbishop of Warsaw and felt that he should have either resigned (23 per cent) or delayed his investiture until the matter had been resolved (23 per cent). Only 29 per cent felt that his investiture should have gone ahead, saying either that they had no objections to him taking on the job if he clarified the circumstances of his collaboration (21 per cent) or that he did not have anything to explain or apologise for (8 per cent). Twenty-two per cent of respondents felt that the decision belonged to the Pope, and 3 per cent did not know (Czaczkowska 2007b). A March 2007 GfK Polonia survey for *Rzeczpospolita* also found that 69 per cent of respondents felt that clergymen who had collaborated with the communist security services should stand down (37 per cent strongly agreed with this), while only 29 per cent felt that this was unnecessary (and only 5 per cent felt this strongly); 12 per cent did not know (Czaczkowska 2007a).

Interestingly, a June 2006 GfK Polonia survey revealed a somewhat different picture. Certainly, 33 per cent of respondents felt that parish priests should be sacked if they were found to have been communist secret service informers, compared with only 21 per cent who thought that they could continue in their positions with no consequences. However, the largest group of respondents (39 per cent) felt that this should depend on the specific circumstances, suggesting a pattern of more nuanced views when particular individual contexts and mitigating circumstances were taken into account (Stankiewicz 2006). Similarly, and again suggesting that opinions might have been less one-dimensional in local cases where the clergyman was well known to respondents, a survey carried out by the Catholic Church Statistical Institute found that 84 per cent of the faithful said that they would not lose trust in *their* priest if they found out that he had been a communist security service collaborator in the past, compared with only 15 per cent who said that they would (Wiśniewska 2007).

There was also other evidence to suggest that, while a majority appeared to be in favour of excluding former communist security service collaborators from office, when drilling down a bit further, some surveys found that many Poles needed strong evidence to justify such exclusion. This was particularly the case when one looked at data on the specific mitigating circumstances in which the person subject to lustration, or otherwise accused of collaboration, might have found themselves. For example, on the basis of a July 2006 TNS OBOP survey for the *Polityka* magazine, Janicki distinguished between two overall clusters of opinion on the lustration and file access issue (Reykowski 2006). First were what he termed the 'lustration hard core', who were not inclined to accept any mitigating circumstances and felt that prima facie evidence of an individual's links with the communist security services contained in the archives could be interpreted as evidence of collaboration. Depending on the question asked, 13–14 per cent of respondents took a very radical stance on this issue, with another 23–29 per cent also broadly located within this cluster, albeit taking a somewhat milder position. Second, there was a group of around 53–57 per cent of respondents who were more inclined to treat those individuals who found themselves entangled with the communist security services in a more sympathetic fashion, including a hard core of 18–28 per cent who were strongly opposed to identifying someone as a collaborator solely on the basis of the extant archive materials.

Turning to respondents' answers to specific questions, the same survey found that 69 per cent agreed that those who had acted as informers for the communist security services under some kind of duress (either direct force or the threat of it) should not be regarded as collaborators (28 per cent felt this strongly), while only 25 per cent felt that they should (7 per cent strongly). Similarly, 57 per cent of respondents felt that those who had passed on information to the communist security services should not be regarded as collaborators if it did not harm others within their circle (21 per cent felt this strongly), while only 39 per cent felt that they should (13 per cent strongly). Sixty per cent felt that those who had signed an obligation to collaborate but never actually undertook any such activity should not be regarded as communist security service informers (28 per cent felt this strongly), while only 36 per cent felt that they should (13 per cent strongly). Fifty-three per cent felt that those who had collaborated initially but then ceased to do so and were later active in the democratic opposition movement should not be regarded as informers (21 per cent agreed with this strongly), compared with 41 per cent who felt that they should (14 per cent strongly). Opinions regarding whether those for whom the only trace of collaboration was an entry in the register of agents or functionaries, and there was no evidence of any field reports, should be regarded as communist security service informers were more divided: 43 per cent of respondents felt that they should not (18 per cent felt this strongly), and 39 per cent felt that they should (10 per cent strongly).

Shifts in Polish public attitudes towards lustration and file access

Although (as discussed above) there was always broad public support for both lustration and opening up access to communist security service files in principle, there were fluctuations in the patterns of support for these over time. First, there was a radicalisation of attitudes in the mid-to-late 1990s, which could be seen in both (as Table 6.1 shows) an increase in 'headline' levels of support for lustration and files access and also, as discussed in more detail below, in perceptions of the salience of the issue. Indeed, as Table 6.4 shows, the CBOS agency found an increase in the number of Poles who saw lustration as a priority from 27 per cent in February 1993 to 44 per cent in February 1996, while the number who did not see it as urgent fell from 50 per cent to 36 per cent over the same period.

Second, as Table 6.1 also shows, there was something of an upsurge in support for lustration and communist security service file access in the early-to-mid-2000s, particularly between 2002 and 2005. This could be seen in both an

Table 6.4 Polish attitudes on the urgency of lustration, 1993–1996 (%)

	February 1993	April 1994	February 1996	December 1996
Urgent	27	34	44	39
Not urgent	50	46	36	42
Don't know	23	20	20	19

Source: adapted from: CBOS (1997, p. 4).

increase in the overall numbers supporting lustration and file access and in support for widening its scope to include new categories. There also appeared to be an increase in the numbers who believed that truth revelation was an important and salient political issue. For example, a February 2005 CBOS (2005a, pp. 6–7) survey found that the number of respondents who said that whether a candidate had collaborated with the communist security services was an important factor in determining their vote nearly trebled to (as noted above) 65 per cent in the case of parliamentary elections (35 per cent saying that it was 'very important'), 66 per cent for presidential elections (33 per cent 'very important') and 57 per cent in local elections (28 per cent 'very important). This compared with only 23 per cent who said that it was an important factor in elections (and only 6 per cent 'very important') in August 2000 (the survey did not ask separate questions about particular kinds of polls). Similarly, only 27–35 per cent of respondents (depending on the type of election) said that this was an issue of little or no significance (with only 10–13 per cent saying it was the latter) compared with 72 per cent of respondents who gave this response in August 2000: 37 per cent saying that it was of little significance and 35 per cent saying that it had no significance.

Third, however, as the decade progressed, at a certain point in the mid-2000s, Poles started to get somewhat lost in and disillusioned with the lustration debate as it appeared to run out of control. The Polish public appeared to feel that, rather than being urgent issues that required immediate resolution, dealing with the communist past and revealing secret service files had increasingly become elements of the political game and had little in common with accurate, solid analysis and historical justice. In particular, the way that the debate on the new 2006 lustration and file access law was conducted seemed to alienate a substantial number of Poles, who started to feel that much of the information that was being revealed was of questionable accuracy. This was also exemplified by the largely negative public reactions to the Institute of National Remembrance's 2008 book on Lech Wałęsa's alleged communist security service links, discussed in greater detail below. All of this started to generate societal opposition to the way that truth-revelation procedures were being carried out. By the mid-to-late 2000s, opinion surveys started to pick up the fact that Poles appeared to be tiring of lustration and file access and showed a decline in public support for them. As we shall see, this fall-off in support was particularly striking among Civic Platform voters.

For example, a September 2006 CBOS (2006, p. 11) survey found that 48 per cent of respondents felt that the new, more radical 2006 lustration law would worsen the political climate in Poland, and only 18 per cent said that it would improve it; 34 per cent did not know. Similarly, a June 2007 CBOS (2007b, pp. 1–2) poll found that, regardless of whether they thought it was desirable in principle, only 19 per cent of respondents felt that lustration and opening up communist secret service files to facilitate a reckoning with the communist past was one of the most important issues that needed to be addressed immediately, while 69 per cent thought it was a distraction. The same survey also found that 48 per cent of Poles supported the May 2007 constitutional tribunal ruling – which, as discussed in Chapter 2, questioned substantial elements of the 2006 lustration law as being unconstitutional – while only 19 per cent disagreed with its judgement, although a substantial number (33 per cent) also said that they did not know (CBOS 2007b, p. 3).

Interestingly, as Table 6.3 shows, a May 2009 CBOS poll found that the number of respondents who supported revealing the contents of the communist security service archives fell by 16 per cent over the course of four years, from 69 per cent in July 2005 (just before Law and Justice came to office) to only 53 per cent. Over the same period, the number who wanted to open up all of the archives had fallen from 38 per cent to only 24 per cent, while the number who wanted a more limited opening up of the files held on state officials also fell, albeit only slightly, from 31 per cent to 29 per cent. However, the numbers opposed to the disclosure of any security service archive material had doubled over the course of four years, from 20 per cent to 40 per cent.[6]

CBOS (2005d, pp. 5–6; 2006, pp. 5–6) survey data also found a substantial 5–10 per cent drop between July 2005 and September 2006 in the numbers in favour of making the communist security service files held on a number of different groups available to the public. This could be seen in the fall in the number of respondents supporting revealing the files of ministers and deputy ministers (from 86 per cent to 77 per cent); the President (from 87 per cent to 76 per cent); the prime minister and deputy prime ministers (from 86 per cent to 76 per cent); parliamentary deputies and Senators (from 86 per cent to 75 per cent); judges and public prosecutors (from 88 per cent to 75 per cent); high-level state and local government officials (from 86 per cent to 72 per cent); policemen (from 74 per cent to 65 per cent); army officers (from 74 per cent to 64 per cent); senior state enterprise managers (from 72 per cent to 63 per cent); senior bank officials (63 per cent to 59 per cent); and journalists and senior press, TV and radio managers (from 71 per cent to 57 per cent, although the 2005 figure was for TV managers only). Somewhat steadier were the levels of support for revealing the files held on priests (unchanged at 59 per cent) and ordinary state officials (down from 51 per cent to 48 per cent).[7]

Public attitudes towards the 'Bolek affair'

Moreover, the publication of Cenckiewicz and Gontarczyk's 2008 Institute of National Remembrance book did not appear to fundamentally change public

Communist-forgiving or seeking justice? 155

attitudes towards Mr Wałęsa's alleged collaboration with the communist security services. For example, a July 2008 CBOS (2008, pp. 3–5) survey found that although 88 per cent of respondents said that they had heard of the allegations against him, only 34 per cent said that they were interested in them (the same number who said that they would consider reading the book), while 54 per cent said that they were not (60 per cent were not interested in reading it). Only 8 per cent said that the book had led them to hold a more negative view of Mr Wałęsa, while 76 per cent said that its publication had had no impact on their opinion of him, and 3 per cent even felt that it led them to evaluate him more positively; 13 per cent did not know (CBOS 2008, pp. 1–2). Thirty-seven per cent of respondents said that they believed Mr Wałęsa's claim that most of the documents cited in the Cenckiewicz–Gontarczyk book had been fabricated by the communist security services while only 20 per cent believed the authors' claim that the documents on which they based their analysis were authentic, although the largest number (43 per cent) did not know (CBOS 2008, p. 5). Similarly, a July 2008 TNS OBOP survey found that 71 per cent of respondents felt that discussions on Mr Wałęsa's alleged communist security service collaboration surrounding the publication of the Cenckiewicz–Gontarczyk book were elements of the day-to-day political struggle, while 66 per cent felt that it was not worth engaging in heated political debates over these issues. Only 44 per cent said that they were interested in the allegations (56 per cent were not), while only 24 per cent felt that Mr Wałęsa's links with the security services were a subject worth discussing at all (Wyborcza.pl 2008a). A 2008 SMG/KRC poll also found that 45 per cent felt that the authors' intentions were, above all, to discredit Mr Wałęsa and gain publicity, with only 22 per cent saying that they were interested in revealing the truth; 31 per cent did not know (*Warsaw Voice* 2008).

The same survey found that only 26 per cent of Poles believed that Mr Wałęsa had collaborated with the security services, compared with 43 per cent who did not; 31 per cent did not know or were unsure (*Warsaw Voice* 2008). Similarly, a July 2008 PBS survey for *Gazeta Wyborcza* found that only 27 per cent of respondents believed that Mr Wałęsa was agent 'Bolek', while 41 per cent felt he was not; 32 per cent did not know (Szacki 2008). A July 2008 CBOS (2008, pp. 9–10) survey found that only 28 per cent of respondents felt that Mr Wałęsa had, at some point, been a communist security service informer, compared with 31 per cent who said he had not, although the largest number (41 per cent) did not know. A plurality of respondents (34 per cent to 27 per cent) felt that even if he had agreed to collaborate with the security services, he did so in order to understand their methods better so that he could defeat communism, although, again, 39 per cent did not know. A July 2008 PBS survey for *Gazeta Wyborcza* found that only 34 per cent of respondents felt that his communist security service contacts in the 1970s had influenced his actions as President, while 42 per cent felt that they had not; 24 per cent did not know. Only 25 per cent believed that Mr Wałęsa had destroyed documents proving his collaboration during his presidency, while 40 per cent did not; 35 per cent did not know (Szacki 2008).[8]

A July 2008 CBOS (2008, p. 10) survey found that even among those respondents who felt that Mr Wałęsa had been a communist security service collaborator in the 1970s, 40 per cent agreed with the proposition that he had compensated for this unfortunate episode through his later actions and services to Poland (49 per cent disagreed), as did 61 per cent of those who felt that he had been acting out of fear in a moment of weakness (26 per cent disagreed). Similarly, a July 2008 PBS survey for *Gazeta Wyborcza* found that 53 per cent of respondents felt that even if Mr Wałęsa had collaborated at the beginning of the 1970s, this did not diminish his services to Poland, compared with only 34 per cent who felt that it did; 13 per cent did not know (Szacki 2008). It also found that respondents had a charitable interpretation of the reasons why Mr Wałęsa was interrogated by the communist security services in the 1970s, with the most common answers being that he was fighting for workers' interests (33 per cent), fear (29 per cent), because people did as the authorities told them in those days (25 per cent), and because he was trying to outsmart them (15 per cent). Only 14 per cent said that he was motivated by wanting money and a flat or to betray, and 6 per cent that he wanted to harm his colleagues. Similarly, most respondents felt that discussions about Mr Wałęsa's communist security services links were unnecessary scraping around in the distant past (34 per cent), a 'shooting party' against a man who was a symbol of the struggle for independence (21 per cent), or a political campaign aimed at helping Law and Justice return to office (18 per cent). Only 17 per cent felt that it was about determining a historical truth that was difficult to accept, and 11 per cent that it was because someone finally had the courage to tell the truth about the Third Republic's authority figures.

The publication of the Cenckiewicz–Gontarczyk book also led to a fall in public support for the Institute of National Remembrance. Since its formation, the Institute had been the object of constant criticism from the liberal-left cultural and media establishment, which had been hostile to lustration and truth revelation from the outset; as noted above, from 2008 onwards it also came under intense criticism from the Civic Platform-led government. Consequently, a July 2008 CBOS (2008, pp. 8–9) survey showed a 15 percentage point drop in those who evaluated it positively, from 49 per cent (11 per cent very positively) in February 2005 to only 34 per cent (6 per cent very positively) three years later, and a 10 percentage point increase in those who evaluated it negatively, from only 10 per cent (3 per cent very negatively) to 20 per cent (7 per cent very negatively) over the same period. The number who held a neutral opinion also increased by 7 percentage points, from 26 per cent to 33 per cent. However, interestingly, in spite of this, other than a brief period at the beginning of 2009 coinciding with the publication of Piotr Zyzak's critical biography of Mr Wałęsa,[9] the Institute's approval rating remained consistently fairly high in the CBOS tracking poll: between June 2006 and September 2016, those who approved of its activities ranged between 38 per cent and 53 per cent, and those who disapproved between 11 per cent and 30 per cent (don't knows, 28–45 per cent), with the exception of April 2009, when only 29 per cent of respondents approved and 44 per cent disapproved (28 per cent did not know) (CBOS 2007c, 2009b, 2014, 2016a; Szacki 2009).

Certainly, the discovery of the Kiszczak files made Poles much less convinced by Mr Wałęsa's declarations of innocence. For example, a March 2016 CBOS (2016b, pp. 3–5) survey found that 34 per cent of respondents now felt that the documents found in Mr Kiszczak's house indicating that Mr Wałęsa was a communist security service informer were authentic, while 26 per cent felt they were not, although most respondents (40 per cent) did not know. Their publication also led to a substantial increase in the numbers who felt that Mr Wałęsa had at some point been a communist security service informer, from only 28 per cent of respondents in July 2008 to 46 per cent in March 2016, while the numbers who rejected the idea fell from 31 per cent to 18 per cent over the same period, although the number of don't knows also remained high at 36 per cent (down from 41 per cent). The same survey found that the number of respondents who believed that Mr Wałęsa had had an episode of collaboration when he succumbed to a moment of weakness and allowed himself to be frightened by the communist security services, but regretted it subsequently, increased from 38 per cent to 51 per cent over the same period, while the number who disagreed with this statement fell from 27 per cent to 19 per cent; 29 per cent did not know (down from 35 per cent). A February 2016 IBRiS survey also found that 38 per cent of respondents agreed that Mr Wałęsa had collaborated with the communist security services, compared with only 28 per cent who felt that he had not; 34 per cent did not know (wPolityce 2016).

Nonetheless, most Poles still appeared to feel that his collaboration was not a very significant or meaningful episode in his life and had been forced upon him by circumstances rather than being a fully conscious long-term entanglement that harmed his colleagues and friends. For example, a March 2016 CBOS (2016b, pp. 4–5) survey found that only 23 per cent of respondents believed that Mr Wałęsa was a long-term communist security service collaborator working consciously to undertake activities that harmed his former colleagues and friends, although this was an increase from only 9 per cent (and just 3 per cent who felt this strongly) in 2008, while 45 per cent rejected this idea (although, again, down from 53 per cent in 2008); 32 per cent did not know (38 per cent in 2008). A February 2016 IBRiS survey also found that only 34 per cent of respondents thought that the publication of the Kiszczak files was an important matter, compared with 59 per cent who did not. Sixty-three per cent said that it did not affect their view of Mr Wałęsa, compared with only 20 per cent who said that it had had a negative impact, while 9 per cent said that it had actually improved their opinion of him (Stankiewicz 2016).

Moreover, even though subsequent revelations made his collaboration appear more credible, most Poles still felt Mr Wałęsa had played a positive role in the country's recent history and that the scale of his subsequent achievements lessened or overshadowed his past mistakes. For example, a March 2016 CBOS (2016b, pp. 6–8) survey found that 66 per cent of respondents still felt that, all things considered, Mr Wałęsa had played an important role in contemporary

Polish history by helping to facilitate the downfall of the communist regime and transition to democracy (albeit down from 73 per cent in 2008), compared with only 21 per cent who felt he had played a negative role (15 per cent in 2008); 13 per cent did not know (12 per cent in 2008). Similarly, by a margin of 49 per cent to 29 per cent (compared with 45 per cent to 22 per cent in 2008), they felt that even if Mr Wałęsa had at one time agreed to collaborate, all of his later activity and services to Poland negated this episode; 22 per cent did not know (33 per cent in 2008). His role as leader of Solidarity was evaluated positively by 78 per cent of respondents and negatively by only 12 per cent (10 per cent did not know), and as co-organiser of the 'round table' and leader of the opposition in 1989 by 65 per cent to 17 per cent; 18 per cent did not know. Even 56 per cent of respondents evaluated his very controversial 1990–95 presidency positively, compared with 28 per cent who viewed it negatively; 28 per cent did not know. A February 2016 IBRiS survey also found that for 64 per cent of respondents (including 49 per cent of Law and Justice voters), the 'Bolek' affair had not changed the fact that Mr Wałęsa remained a national hero and legendary Solidarity leader; only 26 per cent did not regard him as such (Stankiewicz 2016).

Low salience and criticisms of lustration in practice

Overall, then, Poles appeared to be generally receptive to, and supportive of, the arguments for historical justice, lustration and providing access to communist security service files, in principle at least. Notwithstanding changing trends – both among Poles in general and specifically among the supporters of various parties (as we shall see, this was particularly striking among Civic Platform voters) – there was also some evidence that the issue of how to deal with the communist past structured left–right self-placement, a key determinant of voting behaviour in the1990s and early 2000s, and party divisions in Poland during the whole of the post-communist period. However, other survey evidence suggested that any evaluation of public attitudes towards lustration and file access, as part of more general views on transitional justice, had to be accompanied by a series of caveats and qualifications.

When one both looks at the broader context and drills down beneath the headline figures, it becomes clear that attitudes towards how to deal with the communist past were actually rather complex, and Poles often appeared to be somewhat schizophrenic on this issue. On the one hand, as discussed above, they often supported particular transitional justice (and, specifically, truth revelation) measures (and sometimes quite radical ones) as a means of dealing with the communist past. On the other hand, Poles were far from unanimous – indeed, very divided – in their evaluations of the communist period, just as they were about how its legacies should be dealt with, and, when asked, they often responded that this was an issue that was best left to historians. For example, a more recent December 2008 TNS OBOP survey found that only 38 per cent of Poles felt that the former ruling communist Polish United Workers' Party had played a negative historical role, a 5 per cent fall compared with a similar survey conducted 10 years earlier

(Wyborcza.pl 2008b). Similarly, a May 2009 CBOS (2009a, pp. 1–2) survey found that 44 per cent of respondents evaluated the communist period positively (including 9 per cent who definitely felt positively about it), while 43 per cent were negative about it (12 per cent definitely negative); 13 per cent did not know. Interestingly, under-35s were just as likely to evaluate the communist period negatively (45 per cent) as were over-35s (42 per cent), although, at 31 per cent, the number of don't knows among young people was considerably higher than it was among the over-35s (only 4 per cent). It is important to bear in mind here that, except for brief periods, the number of people involved in ongoing, active opposition to the communist regime was relatively small. At the same time, many Poles were linked to the regime through their affiliations with the party-state and so were reluctant to condemn what were, in effect, their own biographies.

Lack of salience

Broadly speaking, there are three important caveats to bear in mind when looking at the headline polling figures that suggested broad popular support for lustration and communist security service file access in post-1989 Poland. The first is the issue of salience, or rather the lack of it. Opinion surveys appeared to suggest that, regardless of the fact that Polish citizens supported the idea of achieving historical justice and introducing truth-revelation procedures in principle, they did not appear to believe that lustration and file access were, on their own, especially important issues of interest to more than a small group of politicians, nor was it felt that they required immediate resolution and should play a central, or even dominant, role in public debates. Indeed, the question of dealing with the communist past and revealing communist security service files and links with these agencies did not appear, at first sight at least, to be particularly important in determining voting patterns and election outcomes in Poland. For example, as Table 6.4 shows, the CBOS agency found that between February 1993 and December 1996 the number of respondents who saw lustration as a priority issue ranged from 27 per cent to 44 per cent, while the number who did not see it as urgent was 36–50 per cent, and only in February 1996 did more see it as urgent (44 per cent) than not (36 per cent); the number of don't knows ranged from 19 per cent to 23 per cent.

Moving into the next decade, an August 2000 CBOS (2000a, pp. 4–5) survey found that only 23 per cent of respondents said that whether or not a presidential candidate had collaborated with the communist security services was an important factor in determining their vote (and only 6 per cent said that it was 'very important'), while 72 per cent said that the issue was of either little (37 per cent) or no (35 per cent) significance.[10] Similarly, a January 2004 OBOP survey for *Gazeta Wyborcza* found that only 37 per cent of respondents wanted to re-open the issue of de-communisation, while 48 per cent were opposed (*Gazeta Wyborcza* 2004). A January–February 2005 CBOS survey for *Gazeta Wyborcza* also found that only 31 per cent of respondents felt that lustration was one of the most important issues facing the country that had to be resolved without delay, while 49 per cent said that it was a subject of interest to only a small group of politicians; 20 per cent did not know (Pacewicz 2005).[11] A June 2005 PBS survey for *Gazeta Wyborcza* found that 43 per cent of respondents felt that there was too much coverage of lustration in the media, compared with only 21 per cent who thought that it was about right and 20 per cent who said there was too little; 16 per cent did not know (Gazeta.pl 2005). Certainly, a November 2006 TNS OBOP survey found that (depending on the area in question) 35–39 per cent of respondents felt that the influence of the former communist secret services in politics, the economy and the media was either as great as (19–22 per cent) or greater than (16–17 per cent) the then Law and Justice-led government said, and only 30–31 per cent felt that they were less influential than claimed; around one-third in each category (32–34 per cent) did not know. However, 47 per cent of respondents also felt that the government was devoting too much time to the issue, while only 19 per cent said that it was doing too little (Gazeta.pl 2006).[12]

As noted above, a June 2007 CBOS (2007b, pp. 1–2) poll found that, regardless of whether or not they thought that lustration and opening up communist secret service files were desirable in themselves, only 19 per cent of respondents felt that this was one of the most important issues that had to be resolved immediately, while 69 per cent thought it was a distraction. As noted above, in July 2008 only a minority of Poles appeared to be interested in the findings of the Cenckiewicz–Gontarczyk book on Lech Wałęsa's alleged communist security service collaboration, and the vast majority felt that they were simply elements of the day-to-day political struggle. A May 2009 CBOS (2009a, p. 4) survey also found that 76 per cent of respondents felt that it was time to end the process of coming to terms with the communist past and leave it solely to historians, while only 18 per cent felt that there had been an insufficient reckoning; 6 per cent did not know.

Moreover, although public attitudes towards Mr Wałęsa's alleged collaboration appeared to crystallise somewhat by the time of the revelation of the Kiszczak files compared with the mid-2000s, there was still a huge amount of public uncertainty, which also pointed to the low salience of the issue. For example, a March 2016 CBOS (2016b) survey found that 41 per cent of respondents did not know whether he had had an 'episode' of collaboration; 40 per cent whether the documents found in Mr Kiszczak's safe were authentic; 36 per cent whether he had ever been a communist security service collaborator (albeit down from 41 per cent in 2008); 29 per cent whether he had been frightened by the security services and had a moment of weakness which he then retracted (down from 35 per cent in 2008); 32 per cent whether or not he was a long-standing and conscious security service collaborator working to harm his friends and colleagues (down from 38 per cent in 2008); and 22 per cent whether he had at one time agreed to collaborate but then negated this episode through his later activity and services to Poland (down from 33 per cent in 2008).

Potentially destructive effects

Second, many Poles had serious concerns that the processes of lustration and revealing communist security service files often became elements of the political game and felt uneasy about their potentially destructive effects. For example, a September 1999 CBOS (1999b, p. 5) survey found that 59 per cent of respondents said that lustration had worsened the political climate in Poland, compared with only 26 per cent who felt that it had improved it; 15 per cent did not know. Similarly, a January–February 2005 CBOS survey for *Gazeta Wyborcza* found that only 24 per cent of respondents felt that lustration would improve the political climate in Poland, while 52 per cent felt that it would worsen it; 24 per cent did not know (Pacewicz 2005). A different February 2005 CBOS (2005b, pp. 7–8) survey also found that 42 per cent of respondents felt that revealing the entire contents of the communist security service files would have negative effects on the political situation in Poland, and only 29 per cent said that it would improve it, while 9 per cent said that it would make no difference; 20 per cent did not know. A June 2005 PBS survey for *Gazeta Wyborcza* found that 56 per cent of respondents felt that revealing communist security service agents had had a negative impact on public life in Poland, while only 27 per cent thought that its impact had been positive; 17 per cent did not know (Gazeta.pl 2005). As noted above, a September 2006 CBOS (2006, p. 11) survey also found that 48 per cent of respondents felt that the proposed new, more radical lustration law, which extended its scope considerably, would worsen the political climate in Poland, and only 18 per cent said that it would improve it; 34 per cent did not know.

Lustration in practice

Third, regardless of whether or not they supported the idea of truth revelation as a means of dealing with the communist past *in theory*, most Poles appeared to have considerable misgivings about, and to be very critical of, the way that the lustration and file access legislation and proposals had been implemented *in practice*. This may have been a result of unrealistic expectations, and it was sometimes difficult to discern whether this dissatisfaction was motivated by concerns that the laws were too mild or too harsh. For example, a May 1999 CBOS (1999c, p. 7) survey discovered that critics of lustration were divided between those who felt that it was being implemented too slowly or ineffectively (40 per cent) and those who opposed it in principle because of its unfairness (60 per cent). A September 1999 CBOS (1999b, pp. 2–3) survey found that 40 per cent of respondents viewed the impact of the 1997 lustration law unfavourably and only 26 per cent favourably (3 per cent very favourably); 12 per cent did not know.[13] Interestingly, the same survey also found that 47 per cent of respondents actually felt that lustration was proceeding too slowly, compared with only 5 per cent who said that it was too fast and 9 per cent at the right pace; 24 per cent were not interested in the issue, and 15 per cent did not know (CBOS 1999b, p. 6). Similarly, an August 2000 CBOS (2000b, p. 8) survey found that 40 per cent of respondents evaluated the activities of the lustration court negatively and only 24 per cent positively, although as many as 36 per cent did not know. Another August 2000 CBOS (2000a, pp. 2–3) survey revealed clear majorities negatively evaluating the lustration processes of Mr Kwaśniewski (57 per cent unfavourably and 23 per cent favourably) and Mr Wałęsa (53 per cent unfavourably and 25 per cent favourably) during the 2000 presidential election campaign. Interestingly, even a majority of right-wing Solidarity Electoral Action voters (43 per cent to 41 per cent) were critical of the way that Mr Kwaśniewski's lustration trial had been conducted. An August 2000 PBS survey also found that 38 per cent of respondents felt that the lustration of the candidates in that year's presidential elections was not conducted properly, compared with only 29 per cent who felt that it was, although, again, as many as 33 per cent did not know (*Rzeczpospolita* 2000).

More recently, and with six years of experience with which to evaluate its record, a January 2005 TNS OBOP (2005) survey found that only 33 per cent of respondents trusted the lustration court (and only 3 per cent a great deal), compared with 52 per cent who did not (16 per cent trusted it very little); 15 per cent did not know.[14] The same survey found respondents evenly divided on whether or not the lustration process had been beneficial: 36 per cent felt that it had done more good than harm, 35 per cent that it had done more harm than good, and 29 per cent were unsure. Similarly, a November 2006 TNS OBOP survey found that only 11 per cent of respondents felt that post-1989 Polish governments had dealt with the problem of the communist security services properly, while 46 per cent felt that they had not, although, again, a substantial number (43 per cent) said that it was difficult to say (Gazeta.pl 2006). As noted above, a June 2007 CBOS (2007b, p. 3) poll also found that 48 per cent of respondents supported the May 2007 constitutional tribunal ruling, which questioned substantial elements of the 2006 lustration law as being unconstitutional, while only 19 per cent disagreed with its judgement, although 33 per cent said that they did not know.

One of the reasons why Poles may have been dissatisfied with the work of the lustration court and uncertain about its impact was that, whatever their views on the necessity for truth-revelation procedures in theory, they had very mixed opinions about whether it was actually possible to prove unambiguously that someone had collaborated with the security services. For example, the same January 2005 TNS OBOP (2005) survey that revealed low levels of trust in the lustration court also found Poles to be evenly divided on whether it was possible to prove this, with 41 per cent saying that it was (8 per cent definitely so) and 41 per cent disagreeing (9 per cent definitely not); 18 per cent did not know. Indeed, asking the question in a more general way that broadened the focus out from communist security service agents and informers, a May 2009 CBOS (2009a, pp. 5–6) survey actually found that 69 per cent of respondents felt that it was not possible to evaluate fairly those who had occupied governing functions during the communist period (21 per cent felt this strongly), compared with only 21 per cent who felt that it was (5 per cent strongly); 10 per cent did not know.

Did headline polling figures mask lustration's true salience?

Entanglement with other issues

However, 'headline' polling data that pointed to the low salience of the truth revelation issue, and apparent lack of public demand for lustration and file access as a priority, may have been misleading. As well as failing to account for the ebb and flow of public opinion (discussed above), they also underestimated and masked the extent to which lustration and file access were, in the public mind, often considered in conjunction, and became entangled, with a package of other, possibly more salient, issues. As we saw in Chapters 4 and 5, these often related to the shortcomings of the political system in post-communist Poland and concomitant measures aimed at deepening democratisation and promoting moral and political renewal. They included, among other things, questions of freedom of information and the public's 'right to know' the backgrounds of their public officials and authority figures; the need to tackle corruption; and the importance of renewing the political system more generally. Specifically, as discussed in Chapter 4, in the run-up to the 2006–2007 legislative changes, the lustration and file access issue became entwined with the so-called 'Fourth Republic' project that encompassed more general demands for the renewal of the Polish state and the need to fight the corruption that was felt to be endemic within it; although it is questionable to what extent the need for more radical lustration was a *major* and *explicit* element of this, rather than an indirect and implicit one. At the same time, the very fact of opening up the communist security service files by the Institute of Public Remembrance also created an appetite for more truth revelation, although it may have ultimately discredited the process, as the evidence cited above on public support for the constitutional tribunal's judgement on the 2006 law and attitudes towards the allegations of collaboration directed against Lech Wałęsa suggest.

This entanglement with other issues, rather than attitudes towards questions of historical justice and retribution per se, could well be the key to understanding the dynamics of Polish public opinion on truth revelation. In particular, the desire for greater lustration and file access was often linked to a more general feeling that the public had the right to know about the past of its political elite and public officials, and at least have the opportunity to hold them to account for their actions. This meshed with the particularly strong feelings of revulsion that Poles felt towards collaboration with the communist-era security services, which, as noted above, was seen as an especially reprehensible form of pro-regime activity. We can see this entanglement clearly when we look at surveys examining *why* people said that they supported lustration, file access and truth revelation, which showed that a particularly powerful driver of public attitudes on this issue was the fact that these processes afforded the possibility of learning the truth. For example, a May 1999 CBOS (1999c, pp. 6–7) survey found that the most popular reason given for backing lustration was a desire to promote openness in public life, cited by 33 per cent of respondents, with a further 5 per cent saying that they wanted to 'test politicians' truthfulness'.[15]

A later March 2005 CBOS (2005b, pp. 3–4) survey found similar motivations among those who supported the publication of the 'Wildstein list': that the files had to be opened so that people knew whether individuals had worked for or collaborated with (or, indeed, been invigilated by) the communist security services. Forty-six per cent of those respondents who supported the list's publication cited the possibility of learning the truth about who had played what role in the past as their main motive. Eighteen per cent said that people had a right to access this kind of information, 13 per cent that they had the right to know the truth about politicians specifically, and a further 13 per cent that publishing the list enabled people to learn the truth about the activities of those exercising power during the communist period. Eleven per cent also mentioned the fact that publishing these kinds of lists enabled people to access their own security service files, thanks to which they could discover the truth about themselves and those who might have been involved in invigilating them, including members of their family, friends and neighbours. However, only 10 per cent of respondents specifically mentioned the possibility of using this information as a basis for coming to terms with the past or punishing individuals by, for example, removing them from office.

Similarly, one of the impacts of the revelation of the Kiszczak files appeared to be to make Poles feel somewhat less protective towards historical 'authority figures' such as Mr Wałęsa. For example, a March 2009 GfK Polonia survey for *Rzeczpospolita* had found that 58 per cent of respondents felt that the biographies of well-known, public authority figures like Mr Wałęsa should be subject to special protection, compared with 40 per cent who felt that they should not; 2 per cent did not know (Olczyk and Stróżyk 2009). This compared with a March 2016 CBOS (2016b, p. 10) poll which found that 59 per cent of respondents felt that it was more important to establish the truth about Mr Wałęsa, even if this meant revising previously held beliefs, while only 39 per cent gave priority to making sure that his legend was not damaged, as this would have harmed Poland's image abroad; 7 per cent did not know.

In other words, although, as noted above, Poles were realistic about the limited scope of the positive effects that lustration might have, and knew that it would not necessarily end disputes over how to deal with the communist past, they nevertheless thought that freedom of information was something worth striving for, even if it came at a price. Indeed, when considering the file access issue, one needs to bear in mind that citizens in any context are invariably very unwilling to agree to limitations on their freedom of information rights. This means that, when presented with a range of alternatives, they often tend to choose the option which involves them being able to secure the widest possible access to information for themselves.

Truth revelation and party and ideological alignments

It is also important to bear in mind that 'headline' polling data about the salience of the lustration and file access issue did not take into account the fact that in

Poland, attitudes towards the communist past and truth revelation became strongly linked with political identities in general, and ideological and party alignments in particular. Indeed, it is striking how views on this issue were, for a long time, one of the key factors in determining left–right ideological self-placement in Polish politics. In fact, they formed one of the main elements of what Grabowska (2004) termed the 'post-communist divide' between the ex-communist and post-Solidarity electoral blocs that dominated – and, at one point, appeared to provide a structural order to – the Polish party system as the key determinant of voting behaviour during the 1990s.

This also encouraged Polish parties to draw on the transitional justice and truth revelation issues as elements of political competition (Pacewicz 2005). For example, at the end of the 1990s, support for de-communisation was particularly strong among right-wing Solidarity Electoral Action voters, while opposition was especially striking among supporters of the left-wing Democratic Left Alliance. An October 1999 OBOP (1999, p. 10) survey found that while 66 per cent of Solidarity Electoral Action voters were in favour of de-communisation, compared with 28 per cent against (6 per cent did not know), only 25 per cent of Democratic Left Alliance voters supported the measure, and 69 per cent were against (6 per cent did not know); the average among all voters was 42 per cent in favour and 46 per cent against (15 per cent did not know). Similarly, an August 2000 CBOS (2000b, p. 9) survey found while 43 per cent of Solidarity Electoral Action voters evaluated the activities of the lustration court favourably and only 22 per cent negatively, 45 per cent of Democratic Left Alliance voters had an unfavourable view, compared with only 14 per cent who were favourable, although as many as 35 per cent and 29 per cent of respondents, respectively, did not know. Moreover, the same survey found that while right-wing voters were evenly divided in their evaluations of the lustration court (35 per cent favourable, 35 per cent unfavourable and 29 per cent uncertain), left-wing ones were clearly hostile (56 per cent unfavourable, 20 per cent favourable and 24 per cent don't knows); the average among all respondents was 40 per cent unfavourable, 24 per cent favourable and 36 per cent don't knows. In other words, attitudes towards lustration and transitional justice appeared to mesh with other political factors, particularly the widespread feeling that there had been insufficient reckoning with the communist period, to maintain the salience of anti-communism as a mobilising issue throughout the 1990s.

Attitudes towards this issue continued to be a major determinant of left–right self-placement, even as the 'post-communist divide' appeared to decline in the mid-to-late 2000s following the collapse in support for first Solidarity Electoral Action and then the Democratic Left Alliance and the emergence of a duopoly of two post-Solidarity parties, Civic Platform and Law and Justice, following the 2005 elections. For example, a January 2005 TNS OBOP (2005) survey found that 85 per cent of centre-right and 87 per cent of right-wing voters felt that those in important state positions should undergo lustration as set out in the 1997 law (9 per cent and 10 per cent, respectively, disagreed), compared with only 67 per cent of left-wing and 69 per cent of centre-left voters who felt this way (23 per cent and 24 per cent, respectively, disagreed); the average among all respondents was 77 per cent in favour and 12 per cent against (11 per cent did not know). Similarly, a January–February 2005 CBOS survey for *Gazeta Wyborcza* found that 65 per cent of right-wing respondents felt that the dangers of having former communist security service informers in office were greater than the risk that someone innocent could be wrongly accused of having been a collaborator, compared with 53 per cent of centrist respondents and only 40 per cent of left-wing respondents who felt this way; the average among all respondents was 46 per cent. At the same time, 53 per cent of left-wing respondents felt that lustration should not be carried out because the risk that someone innocent would be wrongly accused was too great, compared with 37 per cent of centrist respondents and only 19 per cent of right-wing ones; the average was 32 per cent (Pacewicz 2005). A February 2005 CBOS (2005a, p. 3) survey found that 84 per cent of right-wing respondents supported lustration (understood as checking whether those in important state positions had collaborated with the communist security services) compared with 70 per cent of centrists but only 47 per cent of left-wing respondents; the average among all respondents was 68 per cent. A June 2007 CBOS (2007b, p. 2) poll also found that 36 per cent of right-wing respondents thought that lustration and opening up communist secret service files in order to facilitate a reckoning with the communist past was one of the most important issues that needed to be resolved immediately, compared with only 15 per cent of centrist and 9 per cent of left-wing respondents; the average was 19 per cent.

Moreover, even while the 'post-communist divide' declined as the main driver of voting behaviour in Poland, attitudes towards the communist past remained a key determinant of support for the Democratic Left Alliance and, initially at least, distinguished their electoral base from that of the two large post-Solidarity parties. For example, a March 2002 CBOS (2002, p. 3) survey found that 81 per cent of Civic Platform and 78 per cent of Law and Justice voters supported lustration, while only 15 per cent and 13 per cent, respectively, were against. This compared with only 40 per cent of Democratic Left Alliance supporters who were in favour of lustration, while 52 per cent were opposed; the average among all respondents was 56 per cent in favour and 31 per cent against. Similarly, a January 2004 OBOP survey found that 40 per cent of Law and Justice and 53 per cent of Civic Platform voters supported re-opening the issue of de-communisation, while 53 per cent and 40 per cent, respectively, were against, compared with only 21 per cent of Democratic Left Alliance voters who wanted to return to this question and 68 per cent who were against; the average among all voters was 37 per cent in favour of re-opening the debate and 48 per cent against (*Gazeta Wyborcza* 2004). A January 2005 TNS OBOP (2005, p. 5) survey also found that (as noted above) 92 per cent of Civic Platform and 85 per cent of Law and Justice voters agreed that those officials who occupied important state positions should undergo lustration (as set out in the 1997 law), while 5 per cent and 15 per cent, respectively, disagreed. This compared with only 59 per cent of Democratic Left Alliance voters who supported lustration, while 31 per cent were against; the average among all respondents was 77 per cent in favour and 12 per cent against.

Certainly, a February 2005 CBOS (2005a, p. 9) survey found that 87 per cent of Civic Platform and 85 per cent of Law and Justice voters supported lustration, defined as checking whether those who held important state positions had collaborated with the communist security services (and only 8 per cent and 10 per cent, respectively, were opposed), although 70 per cent of Democratic Left Alliance voters did so too (only 13 per cent were opposed). While lower than the level for lustration among the post-Solidarity parties, this was still above the average of 68 per cent support in favour (and 20 per cent against) recorded among all respondents. However, the same survey also found that an overwhelming majority (and significantly above the average) of Civic Platform and Law and Justice voters thought that it was important to check whether candidates in the parliamentary (86 per cent and 84 per cent, respectively), presidential (86 per cent and 84 per cent) and local elections (74 per cent and 75 per cent) had collaborated with the communist security services; the average among all respondents was 65 per cent, 66 per cent and 57 per cent, respectively. At the same time, only 38 per cent of Democratic Left Alliance voters felt that it was important to know this for presidential and local election candidates (in both cases, 62 per cent felt that it was not) and 45 per cent for parliamentary candidates (55 per cent felt it was unimportant).

Interestingly, a June 2005 PBS survey for *Gazeta Wyborcza* found, by a margin of 42 per cent to 38 per cent, that only Law and Justice voters felt that revealing communist security service agents had had a positive impact on public life. Supporters of *all* other parties felt that the impact of these revelations had been negative, and an average of 56 per cent among all respondents felt this way, with only 27 per cent saying that the impact was positive. These included, not surprisingly, Democratic Left Alliance voters, by a margin of 79 per cent to 19 per cent, but also Civic Platform supporters, by 66 per cent to 25 per cent (Gazeta.pl 2005). However, other subsequent polling conducted in the run-up to the 2006 lustration law debates suggested that this PBS survey may have been something of an outlier in terms of the attitudes of Civic Platform voters at this time. For example, a July 2005 CBOS (2005d, p. 2) poll found that only 6 per cent of Democratic Left Alliance voters thought that revealing the contents of the communist security service files was an important issue (79 per cent did not), compared with 34 per cent of Civic Platform and 31 per cent of Law and Justice voters (63 per cent and 62 per cent, respectively, did not think that it was important); the average among all voters was 20 per cent (65 per cent did not think that it was important). It also found that 77 per cent of Law and Justice and 72 per cent of Civic Platform voters were in favour of removing former communist security service informers from office (13 per cent and 17 per cent, respectively, were against) compared with only 39 per cent of Democratic Left Alliance voters who agreed with this (although this was still a plurality, with only 33 per cent against and 28 per cent undecided); the average among all respondents was 56 per cent in favour and 21 per cent against (CBOS 2005d, p. 9).

The same survey found that 92 per cent of Civic Platform and 84 per cent of Law and Justice voters wanted to open up the communist security service archives, compared with only 46 per cent of Democratic Left Alliance supporters and an average of 69 per cent among all voters. This included 51 per cent of Civic Platform voters and 43 per cent of Law and Justice voters who wanted 'full' disclosure of all archives, compared with only 21 per cent of Democratic Left Alliance supporters and an average of 38 per cent among all voters. Only 5 per cent of Civic Platform voters and 8 per cent of Law and Justice voters opposed any opening up of the files, compared with 39 per cent of Democratic Left Alliance supporters and an average of 20 per cent among all respondents (CBOS 2005d, p. 5). A later September 2006 CBOS (2006, p. 4) survey found that, although the number of Law and Justice and Civic Platform voters who wanted to open up the archives had fallen to 73 per cent and 70 per cent, respectively, it was still substantially higher than the 36 per cent of Democratic Left Alliance supporters and the average of 58 per cent among all voters who felt this way. Similarly, while the number who wanted 'full disclosure' of all archives fell to 35 per cent among Law and Justice and 26 per cent among Civic Platform voters, again this was higher than the 20 per cent among Democratic Left Alliance voters; the average among all voters was 26 per cent. While the numbers who were opposed to any opening up of the files had increased to 18 per cent among Law and Justice voters and 24 per cent among Civic Platform voters, it was still much higher, at 54 per cent, among Democratic Left Alliance supporters; 26 per cent among all respondents. The same survey also found that 55 per cent of Civic Platform and 52 per cent of Law and Justice voters felt that anyone who had been affected in any way by the communist security service archive materials should have the right to access them, while 26 per cent and 31 per cent, respectively, felt that this right should be restricted only to those who were subject to lustration, and 11 per cent and 8 per cent, respectively, that even those who were included in the files should not have access to them. In contrast, only 31 per cent of Democratic Left Alliance voters wanted full access to all who felt affected by the files, 23 per cent access only to those who were undergoing lustration, and 38 per cent did not want any disclosure. As noted above, the averages among all respondents were 43 per cent for full access, 26 per cent for access to those undergoing lustration only and 15 per cent against any disclosure (CBOS 2006, p. 8).

Differences emerge between Law and Justice and Civic Platform voters

However, while they had previously been largely indistinguishable in terms of their attitudes towards lustration and file access (CBOS 2002, 2005a, 2005d),[16] later polls (coinciding with the debates surrounding the passage of the 2006 lustration law) showed a significant difference emerging between Civic Platform and Law and Justice voters. This involved an apparent sharp decline in support for truth revelation among the former, and somewhat greater convergence between the views of its voters and those supporting the Democratic Left Alliance on this issue. Indeed, the change in attitudes towards, and decline in support for, lustration and file access as the 2000s progressed, particularly after the 2006 lustration law debates and controversy surrounding the publication of the Cenckiewicz–Gontarczyk book, was particularly striking among Civic Platform supporters. For example, the same September 2006 CBOS (2006, pp. 11–12) survey cited above found that, not surprisingly, 76 per cent of Democratic Left Alliance voters felt that the new, more radical 2006 law, which considerably extended the scope of lustration, would worsen the political climate in Poland, compared with only 33 per cent of Law and Justice voters who said that it would do so. However, 59 per cent of Civic Platform voters also felt this way, considerably more than the average among all respondents (48 per cent). At the same time, only 6 per cent of Democratic Left Alliance voters felt that the new law would improve the political climate, compared with 37 per cent of Law and Justice supporters. However, only 18 per cent of Civic Platform voters felt this way, the same proportion as the average among all respondents.

Similarly, a June 2007 CBOS (2007b, p. 3) poll found that while 52 per cent of Law and Justice voters thought that lustration and opening up communist secret service files in order to facilitate a reckoning with the communist past was one of the most important issues that needed to be resolved immediately, only 7 per cent of Civic Platform voters and 5 per cent of those who supported the Democratic Left Alliance-led 'Left and Democrats' electoral coalition[17] felt this way; the average among all respondents was 19 per cent. Ninety-three per cent of 'Left and Democrats' and 87 per cent of Civic Platform voters thought that it was a distraction, compared with only 39 per cent of Law and Justice voters who felt this way; the average was 69 per cent. The same survey found that while 83 per cent of Law and Justice voters supported automatically removing those who had admitted to past collaboration with the communist security services from public office (3 per cent were against), only 34 per cent of 'Left and Democrats' voters supported this (44 per cent against), with Civic Platform voters somewhere between the two poles at 62 per cent in favour of removal (17 per cent against); the average among all respondents was 62 per cent in favour (15 per cent against) (CBOS 2007b, p. 10). It also found that 78 per cent of Civic Platform and 73 per cent of 'Left and Democrats' voters (well above the average of 48 per cent among all respondents) supported the constitutional tribunal's May 2007 decision to strike down substantial elements of the 2006 lustration law as unconstitutional. On the other hand, only 18 per cent of 'Left and Democrats' and 8 per cent(!) of Civic Platform voters disagreed with the tribunal's judgement. In contrast, 31 per cent of Law and Justice voters agreed with the tribunal, while 39 per cent disagreed; 30 per cent did not know. The average among all respondents was 48 per cent in favour and 19 per cent against; 33 per cent did not know (CBOS 2007b, p. 4).

The same June 2007 CBOS (2007b, p. 6) poll also found that the number of Civic Platform voters who supported opening up the communist security service archives had fallen from 92 per cent in July 2005 and 81 per cent in September 2006 to only 68 per cent. This was still above the 55 per cent recorded for 'Left and Democrats' voters and 59 per cent average for all respondents, but much lower than the 81 per cent for Law and Justice voters. The number of Civic

Platform voters who wanted to open up all communist security service archives had fallen from 51 per cent in July 2005 and 26 per cent in September 2006 to only 20 per cent, the same as for 'Left and Democrats' voters, below the average among all respondents (24 per cent) and much lower than the 48 per cent recorded among Law and Justice voters. Twenty-four per cent of Civic Platform voters were opposed to any opening up of the files, the same number as in September 2006 but a large increase compared with only 5 per cent in July 2005. This was below the 36 per cent of 'Left and Democrats' voters who opposed any disclosure and roughly the same as the average among all respondents (25 per cent), but substantially above the 10 per cent of Law and Justice voters who felt this way.

Not surprisingly, given that Mr Wałęsa's alleged communist security service collaboration emerged as an important line of division between Law and Justice and Civic Platform after 2005, party political orientations were also of key importance in determining public attitudes towards this issue from the late 2000s. For example, a July 2008 CBOS (2008, p. 3) survey found that 94 per cent of Civic Platform voters felt that Mr Wałęsa had played a positive role in Polish contemporary history by helping to facilitate the collapse of communism and the introduction of a democratic regime, compared with 70 per cent of Law and Justice voters who felt this way; the average among all respondents was 73 per cent. Only 2 per cent of Civic Platform voters evaluated Mr Wałęsa negatively, compared with 25 per cent of Law and Justice voters; the average was 15 per cent. Similarly, only 2 per cent of Civic Platform voters said that the publication of the Cenckiewicz–Gontarczyk book had led them to hold a more negative view of Mr Wałęsa, compared with 21 per cent of Law and Justice voters; the average was 8 per cent. Eighty-eight per cent of Civic Platform voters said that the book had had no impact on their view of the former Solidarity leader, compared with 65 per cent of Law and Justice voters who felt this way; the average was 76 per cent (CBOS 2008, p. 8). Fifty-eight per cent of Civic Platform voters also said that they believed Mr Wałęsa's claim that most of the documents cited in the Cenckiewicz–Gontarczyk book had been fabricated by the communist security services, compared with only 21 per cent of Law and Justice voters who agreed with this statement; the average was 37 per cent. Only 8 per cent of Civic Platform voters believed that the documents were authentic, compared with 46 per cent of Law and Justice voters who said that they were; the average was 20 per cent (CBOS 2008, p. 6).

Similarly, a March 2016 CBOS (2016b, p. 2) survey found that 71 per cent of Law and Justice voters supported the Institute of National Remembrance's decision to release the contents of the Kiszczak files to journalists and historians (18 per cent were opposed), compared with only 20 per cent of Civic Platform voters (72 per cent were opposed) and an average of 45 per cent among all voters (43 per cent were opposed). Fifty-nine per cent of Law and Justice voters agreed that these materials were credible and authentic (7 per cent disagreed, 34 per cent did not know) compared with only 8 per cent of Civic Platform voters (55 per cent disagreed, 37 per cent did not know) and an average of 34 per cent among all respondents (28 per cent disagreed, 40 per cent did not know) (CBOS 2016b, p. 4). Forty-seven per cent of Law and Justice voters agreed that Mr Wałęsa had been a long-standing and conscious communist security service collaborator working to harm his friends and colleagues (28 per cent disagreed, 25 per cent did not know), compared with only 7 per cent of Civic Platform voters (78 per cent disagreed, 7 per cent did not know) and an average of 23 per cent among all respondents (45 per cent disagreed, 32 per cent did not know) (CBOS 2016b, p. 6).

Only 42 per cent of Law and Justice voters agreed that even if Mr Wałęsa had at one time collaborated, then his later activity and services to Poland negated this episode in his life (40 per cent disagreed, 18 per cent did not know), compared with 76 per cent of Civic Platform voters (20 per cent disagreed) and an average of 49 per cent among all respondents (29 per cent disagreed, 22 per cent did not know) (CBOS 2016b, p. 7). Only 51 per cent of Law and Justice voters also agreed that, all things considered, he had played a positive role in Polish history (40 per cent disagreed), compared with 89 per cent of Civic Platform supporters; the average among all respondents was 66 per cent (21 per cent disagreed) (CBOS 2016b, p. 9). By a margin of 76 per cent to 18 per cent, Law and Justice supporters also felt that it was more important to establish the truth than to avoid damaging Mr Wałęsa's legend, while Civic Platform voters felt the opposite by a margin of 72 per cent to 24 per cent; the average among all respondents was 59 per cent for establishing the truth and 39 per cent for keeping his legend intact (CBOS 2016b, p. 11).

Conclusions

Poles generally supported radical approaches towards transitional justice. This applied to both the general principle of truth revelation as well as lustration and communist security service file access as specific, necessary means of dealing with the communist past. Most Poles wanted there to be wide access to, and supported the opening up and publication of the information contained in, the communist secret service security archives files, especially those held on public figures and officials fulfilling important state functions. They were also in favour of radical lustration based on vetting those holding a wide range of public offices and strongly against former communist security service agents and informers holding important public offices. In spite of the fact that this was not stipulated in Poland's lustration laws, in many cases they supported their automatic exclusion and removal from these posts. As we saw with political elites in Chapter 4, the very fact of opening up the communist security service files by the Institute of National Remembrance appeared to create a greater public appetite for more truth revelation.

However, many Poles also felt that strong evidence was needed to justify such exclusion and were prepared to countenance mitigating circumstances. For example, while the discovery of the Kiszczak files appeared to convince most Poles that Mr Wałęsa had indeed been a communist security service collaborator, they also seemed prepared to interpret his actions charitably and did not change their broadly positive view of his contribution to the country's recent history. Moreover, although there was always broad public support for both lustration and opening up access to communist security service files in principle, there were fluctuations in levels of support for these policies over time. There was a radicalisation of attitudes in the mid-to-late 1990s, which could be seen in both an increase in 'headline' levels of support for lustration and files access and perceptions of the salience of the issue. There was also something of an upsurge in support in the early to mid-2000s, particularly between 2002 and 2005. However, as the decade progressed, Poles started to tire of lustration and file access as the debate appeared to spiral out of control; a fall-off in support was particularly striking among Civic Platform voters.

Indeed, public attitudes towards how to deal with the communist past, and lustration and file access specifically, were actually, in many ways, rather complex, and Poles often appeared to be somewhat schizophrenic and driven by conflicting impulses on this issue. On the one hand, there was a desire to move on from debates about the communist past, together with a feeling that transitional justice was not a priority and that the process of achieving it was potentially a destructive one. On the other hand, Poles felt that they had a right to know about the past of their political elites and public authority figures. This was allied with a particularly strong feeling that collaboration with the communist security services was an especially reprehensible form of pro-regime activity, together with a sense that individuals should be held to account for their actions, or at least that people should know what they were, so that they had the opportunity to do this.

Broadly speaking, there are three important caveats to bear in mind when looking at the headline polling figures that suggest broad popular support for lustration and communist security service file access in post-1989 Poland. First, regardless of the fact that Polish citizens supported the idea of achieving historical justice and truth-revelation procedures in principle, they did not appear to believe that lustration and file access were, on their own, especially important issues. For example, although public attitudes towards Mr Wałęsa's alleged collaboration appeared to crystallise somewhat following the release of these documents, they were still characterised by high levels of uncertainty. Lustration and file access, and the question of how to deal with the communist past more generally, did not, on their own, appear to have been especially salient in determining election outcomes, and there was no clear evidence of a linear relationship between voter demand and transitional justice supply in Poland. Second, many Poles had serious concerns that the processes of lustration and revealing communist security service files often became elements of the political game and felt uneasy about their potentially destructive effects. Third, regardless of whether or not they supported the idea of truth revelation as a means of dealing with the communist past *in theory*, most Poles appeared to have considerable misgivings about the way that the lustration and file access legislation and proposals had been implemented *in practice*.

However, it is also important to bear in mind that 'headline' polling data pointing to the low salience of the truth revelation issue, and apparent lack of public demand for lustration and file access as a priority, may have been misleading. Apart from failing to account for the ebb and flow of public opinion, it underestimated the extent to which calls for greater truth revelation were, in the public mind, often felt to be of much greater importance when considered in conjunction with other, more salient issues and policy packages aimed at securing freedom of information, tackling corruption and renewing the political system more generally. Attitudes towards the communist past and truth revelation also became strongly linked with political identities and ideological alignments. Party political orientations were, for example, of key importance in determining public attitudes towards Mr Wałęsa's alleged communist security service collaboration and emerged as an important issue dividing the supporters of the two post-Solidarity groupings. Moreover, even if voters did not see these issues as a priority, politicians may have *perceived* that there was greater support for and interest in lustration and file access than there actually was. In other words, the relationship between political supply and voter demand for truth-revelation procedures was more complex and interactive than commentators like Nalepa gave credit for. Voter demand, or perceived voter demand, for more radical lustration and file access may have been one, even if not necessarily the most important, contributory factor in explaining the recurrence of truth-revelation debates.

Notes

1 An earlier version of this chapter was published as Szczerbiak (2017). I am grateful to Taylor and Francis publishers (www.tandfonline.com) for their permission to reproduce material from this article in this book.
2 There were also majorities in favour of evaluating and condemning what was felt to be morally wrong during the communist period (56 per cent in favour, 26 per cent against), and putting on trial and (presumably if found guilty) punishing those who broke the law at the time (50 per cent in favour, 33 per cent against). The dissonance between a general opposition to transitional justice and support for specific measures might be explained by the fact that the issue was not a priority for those being surveyed, and it was only when they started to consider it in more detail, through being asked their opinion about particular methods of dealing with the communist past, that their deeper preferences were revealed.
3 See also Krzemiński (2005).
4 The analogous figures for August 2004 were very similar, with 60 per cent supporting access for everyone, 30 per cent for victims of persecution only and 10 per cent uncertain (CBOS 2004, pp. 1–2).
5 A February 2007 GfK Polonia survey for *Rzeczpospolita* also found that 60 per cent of respondents felt that former communist security service functionaries should receive the lowest possible level of pensions, compared with 25 per cent who felt that they should continue to benefit from a higher rate (Zieliński 2007).
6 These are interesting findings, as the same survey also found, as discussed below, that most respondents felt that the communist past should be dealt with primarily by historians but wanted to limit access to the archives that would have allowed such research to occur (CBOS 2009a, pp. 8–9)!

7 On the other hand, support for revealing the files of University lecturers and teachers actually increased slightly, from 49 per cent and 46 per cent to 51 per cent and 48 per cent, respectively.
8 However, a 2008 SMG/KRC agency poll found opinions on whether or not Mr Wałęsa had erased traces of his past when he was President to be more evenly divided: 38 per cent of respondents felt he had, and the same number that he had not; 24 per cent did not know or were unsure (*Warsaw Voice* 2008).
9 A later November 2009 Gemius survey for the *Newsweek Polska* magazine also found that 48 per cent of respondents felt that the Institute's leadership was partisan and that its activities supported one political grouping (17 per cent agreed strongly with this), while only 20 per cent felt that it was not (5 per cent felt this strongly); 32 per cent did not know (*Newsweek* 2009).
10 However, as noted above, by 2005, when the question was asked in relation to particular kinds of elections (presidential, parliamentary and local), the number who said that it was an important factor had increased substantially to between 57 per cent and 65 per cent, with only 27–35 per cent saying that it was of little or no significance (CBOS 2005a, pp. 6–7).
11 Interestingly, and perhaps not surprisingly, the same survey found that young people (those under 34) considered lustration to be less important than those who were adults during the communist period, but, more counter-intuitively, they were also more receptive to pro-lustration arguments.
12 Indeed, when asked, without prompting, to say what should be the most important topic for the government to tackle, only two respondents mentioned lustration or access to former security service files!
13 This compared with 21 per cent who viewed the conduct of the process favourably in May 1999 and only 23 per cent who viewed it unfavourably; 35 per cent had no opinion, and 12 per cent were undecided (CBOS 1999c, p. 5).
14 The figures for September 2003 were very similar, with 28 per cent trusting the court and 49 per cent not trusting it.
15 Interestingly, only 17 per cent of Poles saw lustration as a means of explicitly securing historical justice for past wrongs. Certainly, the second most popular reason for supporting the process (cited by 22 per cent of respondents) was a wish to remove security service collaborators from office. However, this could, in turn, have been rooted in both moral considerations, such as a desire to settle scores with the communist past, and more pragmatic objectives, such as protecting the state from the threat of key officials being blackmailed.
16 Indeed, some of the polls discussed above even found Civic Platform supporters to be more radical on this issue, although it has been suggested that this may have been because, first, Law and Justice voters might have thought at the time that they were responding that it was not worth re-opening the issue as little could be done (with the Democratic Left Alliance in government), or, second, because the issue was not necessarily seen as the most important in its own right but more as one element of the fight against corruption and the renewal of the Polish state, which was the most significant question for them (*Gazeta Wyborcza* 2004; TNS OBOP 2005).
17 The 'Left and Democrats' (Lewica i Demokraci: LiD) was an electoral alliance formed to contest the September 2007 parliamentary election led by the Democratic Left Alliance and encompassing a number of smaller left-wing political groupings but also including the liberal-centrist post-Solidarity 'Democrats' party.

Bibliography

CBOS, 1997. *Lustracja – Problem Społeczny czy Gra Polityczna*. Warsaw: CBOS.
CBOS, 1999a. *Polacy o lustracji*. Warsaw: CBOS.

CBOS, 1999b. *Ocena procesu lustracyjnego*. Warsaw: CBOS.
CBOS, 1999c. *Polacy o lustracji i ustawie lustracyjnej*. Warsaw: CBOS.
CBOS, 2000a. *Sprawa lustracji kandydatów na Prezydenta*. Warsaw: CBOS.
CBOS, 2000b. *Opinie o działalności rządu, parlamentu, urzędu prezydenta i sądu lustracyjnego*. Warsaw: CBOS.
CBOS, 2002. *Polacy o lustracji i zminach w ustawie lustracyjney*. Warsaw: CBOS.
CBOS, 2004. *Opinie o dostępie do archiwów służb specjalnych w czasów PRL*. Warsaw: CBOS.
CBOS, 2005a. *Powracające dylematy lustracji i dekomunizacji w Polsce*. Warsaw: CBOS.
CBOS, 2005b. *Polacy o IPN, 'liście Wildsteina' i teczkach SB*. Warsaw: CBOS.
CBOS, 2005c. *Zainteresowanie 'listą Wildsteina' i ocena skutków jej publikacji*. Warsaw: CBOS.
CBOS, 2005d. *Opinia społeczna o sposobie i zakresie ujawniania materiałów zgromadznonych w IPN*. Warsaw: CBOS.
CBOS, 2006. *Polacy o lustracji i ujawnianiu materiałów zgromadzonych w IPN*. Warsaw: CBOS.
CBOS, 2007a. *Kościół wobec lustracji*. Warsaw: CBOS.
CBOS, 2007b. *O lustracji i sposobie ujawniania materiałów zgromadzonych w IPN*. Warsaw: CBOS.
CBOS, 2007c. *Opinie o działalności instytucji publicznych*. Warsaw: CBOS.
CBOS, 2008. *Polacy o Lechu Wałęsie i jego przeszłości*. Warsaw: CBOS.
CBOS, 2009a. *Oceny i rozliczenia okresu PRL w opinii publicznej*. Warsaw: CBOS.
CBOS, 2009b. *Oceny instytucji publicznych*. Warsaw: CBOS.
CBOS, 2014. *Oceny instytucji publicznych*. Warsaw: CBOS.
CBOS, 2016a. *Oceny instytucji publicznych*. Warsaw: CBOS.
CBOS, 2016b. *Opinie o Lechu Wałęsie, jego przeszłości i historycznej roli*. Warsaw: CBOS.
Czaczkowska, E.K., 2007a. Wierni nie chcą agentów w sutannach. *Rzeczpospolita*, 14 March.
Czaczkowska, E.K., 2007b. Arcybiskup Stanisław Wielgus prosi wiernych o wybaczenie. *Rzeczpospolita*, 6–7 January.
Gawryś, F. and Kaczyński, A., 2005. Zajrzeć do esbeckich teczek. *Rzeczpospolita*, 14 January.
Gazeta Wyborcza, 2004 .Zapomnieć? Pamiętać? *Gazeta Wyborcza*, 4 February.
Gazeta.pl, 2005. Sondaż 'Gazety': za duzo lustracji w mediach [online]. gazeta.pl, 27 June. Available from: www.gazeta.pl (accessed 27 June 2005).
Gazeta.pl, 2006. TNS OBOP: *Specsłużby mało obchodzą Polaków* [online]. www.gazeta.pl, 6 December. Available from: www.gazeta.pl (accessed 8 December 2006).
Gmyz, C. and Waszkielewicz, B., 2008. Gowin: nie zmieniać ustawy o IPN. *Rzeczpospolita*, 25 June.
Grabowska, M., 2004. *Podział postkomunistyczny: Społeczne podstawy polityki w Polsce po 1989 roku*. Warsaw: Wydawnictwo Naukowe Scholar.
Krzemiński, I., 2005. Pamięć, lustracja, media. *Rzeczpospolita*, 14 February 2005.
Manys, K., 2009. Jaka przyszłość lustracji. *Rzeczpospolita*, 19 January.
Nalepa, M., 2010. *Skeletons in the Closet: Transitional Justice in Post-Communist Europe*. New York: Cambridge University Press.
Newsweek, 2009. E-lustracja. *Newsweek*, 22 November.
OBOP, 1999. *Polacy o Lustracji i Dekomunizacji*. Warsaw: OBOP.
Olczyk, E. and Stróżyk, J., 2009. Dlaczego PO walczy o Wałęsę. *Rzeczpospolita*, 1 April.

Pacewicz, P., 2005. *Polak o lustracji: nie chcę, ale muszę* [online], gazeta.pl, 8 February. Available from: www.gazeta.pl (accessed 8 February 2005).
Reykowski, J., 2006. Zapraszamy na lincz. *Polityka*, 8 July.
Rzeczpospolita, 1999. Zeznawali pierwsi świadkowie. *Rzeczpospolita*, 5 October.
Rzeczpospolita, 2000. Lustracja konieczna. *Rzeczpospolita*, 11 August.
Rzeczpospolita, 2007. Ponad połowa Polaków chce poznać spis agentów SB. *Rzeczpospolita*, 20 June.
Stankiewicz, A., 2006. Księży i media lustrujmy ostrożnie. *Rzeczpospolita*, 17–18 June.
Stankiewicz, A., 2016. Wałęsa wciąż bohaterem. *Rzeczpospolita*, 29 February.
Szacki, W., 2008. *Lech wielki, nawet jeśli..* [online], wyborcza.pl, 10 July. Available from: wyborcza.pl, http://wyborcza.pl/gazetawyborcza/2029020,75478,5441225.html (accessed 12 July 2008).
Szacki, W., 2009. *Oceny prezydenta w dół. IPN-u też w dół* [online], wyborcza.pl, 16 April 2009. Available from: www.wyborcza.pl/2029020,75478,6503130.html (accessed 16 April 2009).
Szczerbiak, A., 2017. Communist-forgiving or Communist-purging? Public Attitudes towards Transitional Justice and Truth Revelation in Post-1989 Poland. *Europe-Asia Studies*, 69 (2), 325–347.
TNS OBOP, 2005. *Lustracja w lustrze TNS OBOP*. Warsaw: TNS OBOP.
Warsaw Voice, 2008. Row over Wałęsa's Past [online], *Warsaw Voice*, 9 July. Available from: www.warsawvoice.pl/WVpage/pages/article.php/18283/article (accessed 10 July 2008).
Williams, K., Fowler, B. and Szczerbiak, A., 2003. *Explaining Lustration in Eastern Europe: 'A Post-Communist Politics Approach'*. Sussex European Institute Working Paper 62. Brighton: Sussex European Institute.
Williams, K., Fowler, B. and Szczerbiak, A., 2005. Explaining Lustration in Central Europe: A 'Post-Communist Politics' Approach. *Democratization*, 12 (1), 22–43.
Wiśniewska, K., 2007. *Lustracja jest potrzebna* [online], gazeta.pl, 14 November. Available from: www.gazeta.pl (accessed 14 November 2007).
wPolityce, 2016. *Sondaż IBRiS: Polacy wierzą w agenturalną przeszłość Wałęsa* [online], wPolityce, 19 February. Available from: http://wpolityce.pl/polityka/282331-sondaz-ibris-polacy-wierza-w-agenturalna-przeszlosc-walesy (accessed 19 February 2016).
Wróbel, R., 1997. Wyborca nie chce głosować na agenta. *Rzeczpospolita*, 27 June.
Wyborcza.pl, 2008a. *Kogo obchodzi Bolek?* [online], wyborcza.pl, 22 July. Available from: http://wyborcza.pl/2029020,75478,5478,5477928.html (accessed 24 July 2008).
Wyborcza.pl, 2008b. *Polacy o PZPR* [online], wyborcza.pl, 12 December. Available from: www.wyborcza.pl (accessed December 12 2008).
Zieliński, M.A., 2007. Zmnieszyć emerytury esbekom. *Rzeczpospolita*, 2 February.

7 Conclusions
The unfinished business of a contested transition?

This chapter summarises and synthesises the main findings of the book and attempts to draw some broader theoretical conclusions that go beyond the Polish case. It returns to the three key questions that were posed in Chapter 1 and have been tackled in this book: why do truth-revelation debates recur in post-communist Poland; to what extent was such recurrence explained by instrumental-strategic or programmatic-ideological factors; and was recurrence popular demand- or political elite supply-driven? In doing so, it considers whether the existing comparative literature and theoretical frameworks examined in Chapter 3 that attempt to explain the trajectories of lustration and transitional justice in post-communist states help us to understand the Polish case of late implementation of truth-revelation laws. It also reflects on the wider lessons and broader theoretical conclusions that can be drawn about the politics of lustration and transitional justice in post-communist Central Europe beyond the Polish case. It thereby examines the implications of, and insights from, the Polish case of late truth revelation for understanding politics in Poland, the region and other democratising states more generally.

As discussed in Chapter 1, although lustration is one of the most (if not the most) controversial means of dealing with the authoritarian past, post-communist Eastern Europe was the first region that embraced lustration as an important transitional justice method, so much so that many commentators have used it as a yardstick to measure progress in this area in these countries more generally. There is some debate in the academic literature as to whether the term 'lustration' should include just those who worked for or collaborated with the communist secret police or those who held senior positions within the party-state bureaucracy more generally. There is also disagreement as to whether it encompasses exclusion from, or limiting of access to, certain offices, or simply vetting individuals for these links without any such consequences flowing automatically. Here, I have defined lustration as vetting or screening individuals – generally occupants of, or candidates for, particular posts, such as public officials and other prominent individuals – for their past associations and links with the communist regime that were kept secret from the public, such as functionaries of or collaborators with the communist-era state security services, without any sanctions (such as banning them from public office or positions of influence in society) necessarily following.

However, as lustration greatly depends on access to the secret archives compiled by the communist-era security services, here I have adopted a distinctive and relatively novel approach and studied it as not just, as David and Horne, respectively, call it, a 'personnel system' or 'employment vetting policy' but also, more broadly, as a 'truth-revelation procedure' in conjunction with the issue of security service file access. Truth-revelation procedures are a particular kind of transitional justice measure that, in other contexts, have also involved establishing historical or 'truth' commissions, temporary bodies of formal inquiry appointed to re-examine the past and document the repressive activities of the previous regime (sometimes with the objective of achieving societal reconciliation). However, in Poland and post-communist Central and Eastern Europe generally, where they have been the most commonly used transitional measure, truth-revelation procedures have involved lustration *and* de-classifying and providing access to the former communist security services' extant secret archives and files for public inspection. My argument here is that because these two questions are so inter-linked, it is extremely difficult to understand and get to grips properly with one procedure without looking at the other. This clearly has implications for attempts to understand the recurrence of debates about (late) lustration in other post-communist states.

In this book I have attempted to tackle three broad questions. First, why do truth-revelation debates recur in post-communist Polish politics? As we saw in Chapter 2, one of the key characteristics of the Polish case was the way that the question of how to deal with the communist past recurred. Poland was characterised by a relatively mild approach to truth revelation when measured by various cross-country comparative indices. However, the really interesting and distinctive thing about Poland is that it is an archetypal case of the phenomena of late and recurring lustration and communist security service file access debates. The country began with an initial avoidance of these issues, exemplified by the Mazowiecki government's so-called 'thick line' policy that ruled out radical transitional justice measures in the early 1990s. Nonetheless, they retained a remarkable ability to endure and remain on the political agenda, and the early to mid-1990s were punctuated by various unsuccessful attempts aimed at passing lustration laws and securing file access. This culminated in the passage of a belated mild, court-based lustration law in 1997 and legislation to open up access to the communist security service files in 1998, with the two finally becoming operational and taking effect in 1999 and 2000, respectively, after several amendments and delays.

However, even then the debate continued to rumble on, and attempts were made to extend these truth-revelation processes in the mid-2000s. This led to the passage of a more radical lustration and file access law in 2006, which expanded their scope significantly; although many of its provisions were not fully enacted and were struck down subsequently by the constitutional tribunal. While the issue of communist security service collaboration declined in political salience, it retained the capacity to re-surface and flare up very dramatically in Polish public and political debates even two decades after the collapse of the communist regime. One of the best examples of this was the publication of a 2008 book by two Institute of National Remembrance historians claiming to show compelling circumstantial evidence that proved long-standing allegations that Lech Wałęsa had been a communist security service collaborator codenamed 'Bolek' in the early 1970s. This was followed in 2016 by the release of original documents recovered from the home of the deceased former communist minister of the interior, General Kiszczak, which apparently proved unequivocally that the former Solidarity leader had indeed been a paid informer. As we saw in Chapter 2, it is this significant delay in introducing truth-revelation procedures – and, more broadly, the recurrence of the issue in political debates – that is one of the most striking features of lustration and file access debates in Poland, and one that needs analysis and explanation. The Polish case thus provided us with an excellent basis for examining and developing frameworks to explain the phenomenon of 'late' and recurring truth revelation.

Second, to what extent could recurrence be explained by instrumental-strategic factors or more normative programmatic-ideological motivations? The key problem with frameworks that try to account for varying patterns of transitional justice through historical and structural factors – such as those developed by Moran and Huntington focusing, respectively, on the nature of the previous communist regime and the process of transition to democracy – is that they are too static. Certainly, such approaches successfully predicted the lack of early interest in lustration and transitional justice in countries such as Poland. However, they have problems in accounting for the re-emergence of the issue and the often quite radical changes of trajectory. In particular, they struggle to explain the phenomenon of 'late' lustration and file access – specifically why, in cases such as Poland, the issue recurred strongly, with calls for progressively more radical legislation to be introduced. Explanatory models that try to blend and synthesise communist, post-communist and sometimes pre-communist factors to explain variations in transitional justice – such as those developed by Welsh, Nedelsky, Moran and Jaskovska, and Stan – are ambitious but vague in explaining the precise mechanisms involved in the ebb and flow of the debate in cases such as post-communist Poland. They have difficulty in accounting for exactly how and why particular historical legacies caused the issue to recur and led to particular outcomes at particular points in time, together with the influence of political elites and actors that, for whatever reason, changed their stance on the issue.

Attempts in the academic literature to explain such changes of lustration trajectory and the recurrence of the issue, specifically the phenomenon of 'late' lustration and truth revelation, can be divided broadly into two main schools of thought. There are those, such as Walsh and my own earlier collaborative work with Fowler and Williams, who adopted the so-called 'politics of the present' approach, and Nalepa, in what I have termed 'political elite strategy' explanations, who focus on whether the protagonists were driven by instrumental-strategic motives, often as an element of broader post-communist party competition and power struggles. Then, there are those authors – such as

180 Conclusions

Calhoun, Appel and Horne – who ascribe more ideological-programmatic motivations to the key actors involved, particularly in the way that calls for lustration and file access map on to debates about the quality of post-communist democracy.

Third, what was the role of public opinion in the recurrence of lustration and file access, and to what extent was it a demand-driven or elite-led process? As we saw in Chapter 6, there are different views in the academic literature as to whether, and to what extent, lustration and transitional justice trajectories were (solely or mainly) elite-driven or whether they were (in part at least) a response to, and prompted by, popular demand. In my own earlier co-authored work, I cited continued public support for lustration as one of the factors explaining why the issue recurred and became instrumentalised in post-communist Polish (and, more generally, Central European) politics. On the other hand, authors such as Nalepa argued that the issue was of low salience to most voters in countries like Poland. They did not see any relationship between public opinion or popular demand for transitional justice and the renewal of interest in lustration and file access, which they viewed as being almost entirely an elite-driven process.

Why do truth-revelation debates recur as an issue in post-communist Polish politics?

Specific incidents at specific times make pro-lustration narratives more credible

Lustration and communist security service file access recurred as issues in Poland partly because they were linked to specific incidents at particular points in time that raised their profile. These developments made pro-lustration narratives more credible and shifted the balance of political forces towards this camp, so that those calling for greater truth revelation were, however briefly, in the ascendant, and made it more difficult for opponents, or those who were less enthusiastic about the process, to criticise it. Such events included the election of the Olszewski government in 1991 and the subsequent (almost accidental) passage of the parliamentary resolution that led to the release of the 'Macierewicz list' in 1992; the 'Oleksy affair' in 1996–1997; and some of the corruption scandals of the early to mid-2000s, such as the 'Orlen affair'. Sometimes these were linked directly to the revelations from, and publications generated by the formation of, the Institute of National Remembrance, such as the release of the 'Wildstein list' in 2005; publicity in the mid-2000s surrounding the links between senior Catholic clergymen and the communist security services; and the publication of Cenckiewicz and Gontarczyk's 2008 book about Lech Wałęsa's alleged secret service collaboration. In this sense, the very fact of opening up the communist security service files to journalists, historians and other individuals by the Institute created a greater appetite for more truth revelation and led ultimately to a more radical lustration and file access regime. On the other hand, some incidents that led to a revival of debate around lustration and truth revelation can be put down to pure chance, such as the events surrounding the release of the 'Kiszczak files' in 2016 following an attempt by the former communist interior minister's widow to sell the documents that she held on agent 'Bolek' to the Institute. All of these events increased the salience of lustration and file access in the context of a public opinion that was always sympathetic to radical approaches towards truth revelation.

The 'unfinished business' of a contested and problematic democratic transition

However, it is also possible to identify a number of ongoing, longer-term drivers of recurrence. First and foremost, truth revelation kept returning as a political issue because it was considered part of the 'unfinished business' of a contested and problematic democratic transition. The transition was felt to be flawed in the sense that either the process of extraction from the previous regime itself was distorted, or the model of democracy that emerged subsequently was unsatisfactory (or both). The notion of 'unfinished business' was also partly the result of dissatisfaction with the judicial, court-based model of lustration that Poland adopted at the end of the 1990s, which, according to its critics, did not deal adequately with the issue and was simply a form of phoney or pseudo-lustration. As we saw in Chapter 4, much of the impetus for revising the Polish lustration law in the mid-2000s came from the fact that the truth-revelation procedures that were established at the end of the 1990s, and became operational at the start of the 2000s, were not felt to be fit for purpose or functioning properly, and, in many ways, simply created an appetite for more radical measures.

Underpinning all of this, the notion of lustration and communist security service file access as 'unfinished business' was rooted in larger debates about the nature of the post-communist transition and democratisation process, particularly concerns about the unsatisfactory nature of the elite bargain that led to the collapse of the Polish communist regime. This was felt by many of the Third Republic's critics to have been petrified as a result of the Mazowiecki government's 'thick line' policy, which ensured that more radical truth-revelation measures were delayed. For the supporters of the Third Republic, Poland's pacted transition process was one of the new democratic state's most important 'foundational myths'. However, for its critics, the round table process, together with the early post-communist government's apparently 'communist-forgiving' policies, meant that, by delaying truth revelation, post-1989 Poland did not deal adequately with the legacy of the country's communist past. This, they argued, produced pathologies that led to the emergence and development of a distorted, flawed form of post-communist democracy.

There was a broad acceptance even among many of the Third Republic's critics that there might have been no alternative to the 'round table' process as a short-term tactical ruse if a peaceful, negotiated transfer of power was to be achieved, although there was a 'harder' version of this critique that rejected the process wholesale, even as a tactical manoeuvre. However, many of these critics felt that the elite pacting process, and the later 'thick line' policy which was rooted in the spirit of compromise that it was felt to embody, became rapidly obsolete with the change in the domestic political and international situation. Indeed, the way that the debate on how to deal with the communist past, which transitional justice measures to adopt, and, specifically, whether this should include truth-revelation processes (and, if so, of what kind) played out showed that there was strong contestation of the broader underlying logic or 'spirit' of the round table processes that the 'thick line' policy exemplified.

A good example of the way that debates about truth revelation were entwined with the notion of a 'flawed' transition was the 'Bolek affair'. As we saw in Chapter 5, this was one of the most controversial and high-profile instances of how debates over the communist security service archives were used more broadly to both legitimate and de-legitimate the post-communist Third Republic state's genesis and foundational myths. Supporters of the Third Republic status quo argued that Mr Wałęsa's critics were, given his key role in this process, attempting to use the 'Bolek affair' to de-legitimise one of its key foundational myths: the idea of the 1989 'round table' negotiations as an honourable compromise that paved the way for the successful transition to democratic rule. Critics of the Third Republic status quo, on the other hand, argued that Mr Wałęsa was, as they put it, the 'icon of a system of lies' and that the handling of the 'Bolek affair' explained the post-1989 elites' lack of willingness to deal with the communist past, reinforcing their belief that the transition was engineered by representatives of the previous regime.

A means of revealing hidden mechanisms and informal networks

This notion of truth revelation as 'unfinished business' was also often linked to the idea of lustration and communist security service file access as a means of revealing the hidden mechanisms and informal networks underpinning the Third Republic state. Specifically, it was tied in with the notion that political, cultural and economic life in post-1989 Poland was manipulated behind the scenes by elites and officials linked to the former regime. These, it was felt, had taken advantage of their connections with powerful and influential networks, including those rooted in the former security services, to retain much of their wealth and influence by turning their old political power and social capital into economic, political and cultural influence in the new Polish state. All of this, it was felt, led to high levels of corruption and penetration of state structures and the economy by the former communist secret services, who retained powerful and influential networks rooted in the pre-1989 period, as well as contributing to the reproduction of a privileged status for the communists (and their allies), specifically through the process of what might be termed the 'propertisation' of the nomenklatura. All of this prompted many Poles, both ordinary citizens and political elites, to question the virtues of the 'thick line' approach towards truth revelation adopted by the first post-communist governments.

We could see this in Chapter 5 in the way that the 'Bolek' affair was used to legitimate and de-legitimate the transitional justice and truth-revelation processes as either vitally necessary or dangerously politicised. According to Mr Wałęsa's critics, the 'Bolek' affair revealed fundamental truths about the nature of the Third Republic and demonstrated the mechanisms through which the outgoing regime was able to transition so smoothly to post-communism. It also showed how the communist security services deformed the Polish transformation by keeping a group of individuals who were under their influence in positions of power. Fear of being blackmailed by representatives of the outgoing regime, they argued, explained Mr Wałęsa's erratic behaviour during the democratic transition and early years of post-communism, particularly his questionable presidential personnel and policy choices, and raised questions about whether he had used his powers as head of state to cover up his communist secret service involvement.

Problems with elite pacting as the most desirable form of regime change

The lustration, file access and truth-revelation issue was, therefore, linked to the questioning of the legitimacy of the Third Republic post-communist state, and specifically the elite-led negotiated transition and 'thick line' communist-forgiving policies of the first post-1989 governments. This key finding highlights the importance of paying attention to the nature of the transition from non-democratic to democratic rule when examining the progress of lustration and communist security service file access. But this was not necessarily in the sense argued by Huntington and other analysts who tried to explain patterns of transitional justice through such historical-structural models. Rather, the findings here question, and draw our attention to the problems associated with, the idea posited in much of the comparative democratisation literature: of elite pacting as the most normatively desirable form of regime change. In many ways, Poland's democratic transition could be cited as a model of such a peaceful, consensual process of 'transition by pacting'. The Mazowiecki government's 'thick line' policy also exemplified and appeared to conform to the idea of trying to ensure that old elites felt comfortable with the new democratic settlement. Indeed, to supporters of the Third Republic status quo, it was precisely the way that the country extracted itself from communist rule through an elite pacting process which ensured that democracy was embedded with no significant actors, including representatives of the former ruling elite, opposing the new liberal democratic order and wanting a return to the *status quo ante*. This tied in with their narrative of the post-1989 period as one of unbridled success, with Poland – apparently boasting a consolidated liberal democracy, a dynamic and successful market economy, and close integration into Euro-Atlantic international structures – portrayed as a leader in terms of the post-communist transformation process.

However, the fact that the nature and meaning of Poland's transition were highly contested – indeed, as we saw, a key dividing line in post-communist Polish politics – made it a problematic model. Indeed, the way that concerns about how to deal with the legacy of the country's communist past have recurred as issues – and, in doing so, questioned the philosophy underlying the 'thick line' policy and, more broadly, the nature of the post-1989 elite compromise – illustrates that we need to be careful about viewing the Polish process of regime change as a model of a successful democratic transition. It suggests that there may be problems both with the specifics of the Polish democratic transition and, more generally, with 'forgiving' the old regime elites as a model for new democracies in terms of dealing effectively with the legacies of their non-democratic past. For their supporters, the elite pacting processes may be seen as a model of successful transition. To their critics, however, the unsatisfactory nature of the Polish elite bargain, which meant that truth revelation was delayed and there was a lack of (in the eyes of some, a deliberate attempt to avoid) a reckoning with the communist past, blurred the distinction between victims and their oppressors. It also, they claimed, created pathologies in the post-communist political and economic system. Rather than leading to societal reconciliation, this, critics argued, contributed to a demoralising and debilitating effect on society by leaving many Poles with a feeling that nothing had really changed.

Can the recurrence of truth revelation be explained by instrumental-strategic or programmatic-ideological factors (or both)?

Instrumental-strategic motives were evident on both sides

There were clearly instrumental-strategic motives evident on both sides of the political divide over lustration and file access, with a feeling that truth revelation could (fairly or unfairly) disproportionately affect individuals linked to particular political options. However, this was not, as suggested by writers such as Nalepa, based on specific or detailed knowledge of the contents of the communist security service files. Rather, there was a general assumption as to which milieu would be affected most by their revelation, given the balance of probability. As we saw in Chapter 4, supporters of lustration and file access sensed that it would damage the post-1989 Third Republic establishment and those aligned with the liberal-left, and clearly saw it as a mechanism for promoting turnover of the political, cultural and business elites. Supporters of more radical truth revelation in the debates around the 2006 lustration law posited elite turnover as one of their motivations, and the law's strongest parliamentary proponents included younger deputies from all parties who potentially stood to benefit from this. At the same time, opponents of lustration and file access, and especially its more radical variants, also felt that truth revelation could put them on the back foot and threaten their interests. As we saw in Chapter 2, the most bitter resistance to the 2006 law came from specific interest groups who felt that they had the most to lose from such turnover, namely, journalists and academics. As we also saw in Chapter 4, criticisms of (radical) lustration focused on its proponents' alleged instrumental-strategic motivations, accusing them, and supporters of the 'Fourth Republic' project more generally, of using the process as a means of achieving elite turnover and social and political advancement, and weaponising the truth-revelation issue in a socially divisive and politically destructive way.

As we saw in Chapter 5, instrumental-strategic motivations could also be seen in the way that different political actors approached the 'Bolek' affair, which showed how the communist security service archives were used to legitimate and de-legitimate specific political actors and formations. All sides of the political conflict in post-1989 Poland accused each other of trying to develop an image of Mr Wałęsa that was politically advantageous to them, and of being instrumental in their attitudes towards his security service collaboration. This was particularly evident after the 2005 elections, when party competition became structured around two post-Solidarity groupings, Law and Justice and Civic Platform, and attitudes towards Mr Wałęsa's alleged collaboration emerged as an important issue dividing them. From the late 2000s onwards, Civic Platform appeared to use Mr Wałęsa instrumentally as a way of legitimating themselves, which gave them a clear stake in defending his 'legend'. However, arguably, the political right clustered around the Kaczyński brothers acted in a similar fashion at the beginning of the 1990s when it saw Mr Wałęsa as a battering ram against the liberal-left milieu which dominated the Mazowiecki government. A cynical observer might argue that the attitudes of many Polish politicians and commentators towards the former Solidarity leader's security service collaboration depended primarily on whether or not it was in their interests at any given time to use the issue against Mr Wałęsa or to defend him.

Bringing 'programme-ness' back into the equation

However, those pushing for (and opposing) lustration and file access did not appear to be motivated purely and simply by partisan interests and instrumental imperatives to gain a strategic advantage over political competitors. Rather, they seemed, in part at least, programmatically and ideologically driven, certainly on the basis of the arguments examined in this book advanced by supporters and opponents of truth revelation. As we saw in Chapter 4, the idea of pushing forward with more radical lustration and communist security service file access in the mid-2000s was often rooted in wider unease about the perceived failures of the post-communist democratisation process in Poland. Such calls were felt to be a key element of projects designed to deepen and improve the quality of democracy and implement the far-reaching moral and political renewal that many felt was required in post-communist Poland. In particular, questions of truth revelation were often entwined with other post-communist democratisation discourses and linked to issues such as a perceived need to tackle corruption as an endemic feature of post-1989 Polish politics and society, and the importance of freedom of information and satisfying the public's 'right to know' about the backgrounds of its public representatives, officials and authority figures. As we saw in Chapter 5, the latter was a key feature of the arguments used by the critics of Lech Wałęsa when discussing the importance of revealing the nature of his communist security service collaboration.

In other words, continued calls for expanding the scope of truth revelation resonated with a symbolic and institutional sense that something about the country's democratic transition was incomplete. The fact that Poland embarked upon late lustration and communist security file access programmes could, therefore, be seen as an expression of this perceived need to deepen the democratisation process by expanding the scope of transparency measures. In some cases, such critiques of post-communist democratisation and calls for greater transparency were linked to the so-called 'Fourth Republic' project aimed at tackling the apparent pathologies of the post-1989 Republic. Although this was part of a broader, radical (but also somewhat amorphous) critique of post-1989 Poland as corrupt and requiring far-reaching moral and political renewal, the 'Fourth Republic' project came to be most associated with the policies pursued by the 2005–2007 Law and Justice-led governments. The proposal to radically expand the scope of, and change the philosophy underpinning, lustration and file access became one important, flagship element of this government's legislative programme.

At the same time, from the outset, critics of lustration and file access both used liberal democratic arguments to oppose truth revelation in principle – as we saw in Chapter 2, this was one of the justifications for Mr Mazowiecki's 'thick line' policy – and continued to do so when criticising the more radical versions of truth revelation proposed in the mid-2000s. The 2006 law, in its original form at least, shifted the emphasis from lustration declarations verified by a judicial process to one based primarily on certificates outlining the nature of security service collaboration issued by Institute of National Remembrance historians and archivists. Even in its amended version, before large elements of it were struck down by the constitutional tribunal, it involved the publication of lists of apparent communist security service agents and collaborators compiled by the Institute. As we saw in Chapter 4, when criticising the shortcomings of the 2006 law, opponents of radical lustration focused many of their arguments on defending the existing court-based, judicial model adopted in 1997 as being better able to offer protections to those accused of lying in their lustration declarations and, therefore, safeguard the provisions of the rule of law.

One of the key findings of this book is, therefore, the need to bring 'programme-ness' back into discussions of why lustration and security service file access recurred as issues in post-1989 Poland and elsewhere. It suggests that some ideological motivations may have been significant in at least the declared motives of lustration supporters. Thus, the analysis presented here supports the notion that the so-called 'politics of the present' and 'political elite strategy' approaches to explaining the recurrence of lustration – positing the notion that it was often motivated by partisan interests and became instrumentalised as a political tool in post-communist power struggles to gain a strategic advantage over political competitors – need to be modified. They often fail to grasp fully the extent to which the motives of those pushing for lustration and transitional justice were, in part at least, programmatically and ideologically driven. In this sense, the findings here support the arguments of authors such as Horne, Calhoun and Appel, who draw our attention to the fact that one cannot assume a priori that lustration was used simply for political manipulation, which the 'politics of the present' and 'elite political strategy' approaches have a tendency to imply, and, in the case of Horne, saw the emergence of 'late lustration' as being tied specifically to efforts to improve the quality of post-communist democracy.

Both ideology and strategy matter – but are difficult to separate out

However, the findings of this book also suggest that the idea that lustration and truth revelation was driven *solely* by 'legitimate' concerns about the progress of democratisation, rather than being politically manipulated, is also highly contestable. Certainly, the fact that there were opponents of lustration who appeared to change their mind about the issue does provide prima facie evidence that proponents of late truth revelation may have been genuinely motivated by programmatic-ideological concerns. However, in rejecting 'power politics'-type explanations, authors such as Horne may have gone too far to the other extreme by accepting some of the arguments of lustration advocates at face value. While the proponents of late lustration and file access may have presented and *justified* their proposals as being driven by legitimate concerns about the progress of democratisation and correcting problems associated with post-communist transition, this did not, of course, necessarily mean that these were the *actual* reasons why they were proposing them, and certainly not the only ones. The contrasting case of Civic Platform's apparently radical pro-lustration stance and calls for greater file transparency in the run-up to the passage of the 2006 lustration and file access law, and then its apparent change of heart and opposition to further truth revelation, exemplified by its responses to the 2008 and 2016 allegations of Lech Wałęsa's alleged communist security service collaboration, suggest that the party's position on this issue was motivated as much by instrumental-strategic political manoeuvring as it was by ideological-programmatic concerns.

In other words, in practice, it appears to be difficult to separate out instrumental-strategic and ideological-programmatic motives completely for analytical purposes, and the division between the two that writers such as Horne posit may simply be too Manichean. In the case of the recurrence of late truth revelation in post-1989 Poland and the opposition to it, as in the case of virtually every political action more generally, the evidence presented here suggests that both interests and ideas were evident, and the protagonists on both sides were driven by a complex interplay of ideational and interest-based impulses and concerns. While commentators such as Horne cite the fact that some members of the party introducing late truth-revelation programmes may have suffered from them as evidence of ideological-programmatic motives, the overall effect for the party might have been beneficial, or other parties might have suffered more. Moreover, even a 'genuinely' motivated political move, such as a lustration and file access law, could have been bundled together with other concerns in a broader package for purely instrumental reasons as part of a political positioning exercise, with ideological-programmatic considerations used simply as a justificatory narrative. In other words, it is simply impossible to know unambiguously whether the motivation for a particular statement was solely (or even mainly) instrumental or programmatic; or, indeed, whether both sets of concerns might have been (equally) important in law-makers' considerations. This implies that the questions that researchers ask when examining (late) lustration and file access debates may need to be reframed away from the 'ideology versus strategy' dichotomy to how we identify the range and balance of motives driving the recurrence of these debates in any particular national context.

What was the role of public opinion in the recurrence of truth revelation?

Strong support for the public's 'right to know'

As we saw in Chapter 6, the question of whether the recurrence of truth revelation as an issue was driven by party political elite supply or public and voter demand was a complex one. Although there were ebbs and flows, in terms of the trajectory of public opinion Poles were consistently supportive, in some ways very radically, both of the general principle of truth revelation and of lustration and communist security service file access as specific, necessary means of dealing with the communist past. Most Poles favoured a radical approach towards lustration based on vetting those holding a wide range of public offices for their links with the former communist security services. They also supported wide access to, and the opening up and publication of, the information contained in, the communist secret service security archives, especially that held on public figures and officials holding important state functions. This was rooted in both a strong belief in the public's 'right to know' the backgrounds of its public authority figures and revulsion at the activities of the communist security services. Indeed, although this was not stipulated in Poland's lustration law, in many cases they even supported the *automatic* exclusion of former communist security service agents and informers from important public posts.

Lustration and file access are not salient issues on their own

However, attitudes towards lustration and file access were also often driven by conflicting impulses about how to deal with the communist past: a desire to secure historical justice, on the one hand, and a wish to move on from historical debates and look ahead to future challenges, on the other. Regardless of the fact that Polish citizens supported the idea of achieving historical justice and truth-revelation procedures in principle, they did not appear to believe that lustration and file access were, on their own, especially important or salient issues to more than a small group of politicians, or that they required immediate resolution and should play a dominant, or even central, role in public debates. There was no evidence of a clear and unambiguous linear relationship between voter demand and transitional justice supply, and lustration and file access did not seem to determine election outcomes.

Public attitudes towards Lech Wałęsa's alleged security service collaboration were also characterised by high levels of uncertainty. Moreover, even if they were supportive of the idea of truth revelation as a means of dealing with the communist past *in theory*, many Poles appeared to have considerable misgivings about the way that the lustration and file access legislation had worked out *in practice*. In particular, they had serious concerns that truth-revelation processes often became elements of the political 'game' and felt uneasy about their potentially destructive effects.

Moreover, many Poles also felt that strong evidence was needed to determine security service collaboration, especially if this was to be the basis for exclusion from public office. In some cases, there was also a willingness to accept mitigating circumstances that made Poles more sympathetic to those accused of being informers. One of the best examples of this was the case of Lech Wałęsa. While the revelation of the 'Kiszczak files' made Poles much less convinced of Mr Wałęsa's innocence, even most of those who did not entirely believe his claims were prepared to interpret his actions in a very charitable way. As we saw in Chapter 5, his critics argued that Mr Wałęsa's collaboration was not just an 'episode' but lasted several years, when he was an ardent informer rewarded financially for betraying his friends and fellow workers. On the other hand, rather than dismissing the allegations outright (particularly after the release of the 'Kiszczak files'), most of Mr Wałęsa's supporters accepted that he almost certainly did collaborate in the early to mid-1970s but attempted to relativise his actions and locate them within a broader historical context. They posed various mitigating circumstances, minimised his involvement, and argued that Mr Wałęsa had compensated for the weaknesses of his youth by his subsequent actions as a legendary figure of international standing who embodied Poland's struggle for freedom and democracy. As we saw in Chapter 6, most Poles also appeared to evaluate Mr Wałęsa through the prism of his whole life's activities and not just his security service collaboration, and the discovery of the 'Kiszczak files' did not change their broadly positive view of his contribution to the country's contemporary history.

But public demand is a (if not necessarily the main) contributory factor

Nonetheless, 'headline' polling data that pointed to the low salience of the truth-revelation issue, and apparent lack of public demand for lustration and file access as a priority, may have been misleading. For a start, public attitudes towards lustration and communist security service file access appeared to become strongly linked to political identities in general, and party political orientations and ideological alignments in particular. For example, as we saw in Chapter 6, having previously been largely indistinguishable in terms of their attitudes towards lustration and file access, later polls (coinciding with the debates surrounding the passage of the 2006 lustration law) showed the emergence of a significant bifurcation between Civic Platform and Law and Justice voters. There was a sharp decline in support for truth revelation among the former and somewhat greater convergence between the views of its voters on this issue and those supporting the communist successor Democratic Left Alliance. Similarly, party political orientations were of key importance in determining public attitudes towards Mr Wałęsa's alleged communist security service collaboration and emerged as an important issue dividing supporters of the two post-Solidarity groupings.

Moreover, even when the issue itself was not particularly significant in its own right, questions of lustration and file access became more important in the public mind when linked to, and considered in conjunction with, other, more salient questions and policy packages, such as public concerns about corruption or their 'right to know' the backgrounds of senior public officials and political authority figures. These interacted with a public opinion that was always sympathetic to radical lustration and file access in principle. Finally, even if voters did not see these issues as a priority, politicians may have *perceived* that there was greater support for and interest in lustration and file access than there actually was. This was particularly likely to be the case given that, as we saw in Chapter 6, increases in support for truth revelation tended to map on to particular events that highlighted the issue and moved it up the political agenda, such as the 'Oleksy affair' in 1996–1997 or the publication of the 'Wildstein list' in 2005. All of this suggested that voter demand for lustration and file access may, in fact, have been one of the most important – even if not necessarily the most important – contributory factors in explaining the recurrence of truth-revelation debates.

* * *

Truth-revelation debates, therefore, recurred in Poland because they were linked to specific developments at particular points in time that raised the profile of the issue, shifted the balance of political forces towards the pro-lustration camp, and made its narratives more credible and convincing. More fundamentally, truth revelation kept recurring because it was considered part of the 'unfinished business' of a contested and apparently flawed democratic transition. This was rooted in both concerns about the unsatisfactory nature of the elite bargain that led to the collapse of the Polish communist regime, and the idea of lustration and communist security service file access as a means of revealing the hidden mechanisms and informal networks underpinning the post-communist Third Republic state. This questioning of the Third Republic's legitimacy, and specifically the elite-led negotiated transition and 'thick line' communist-forgiving policies of the first post-1989 governments, draws our attention to the problems of elite pacting as the most normatively desirable form of regime change. While, for supporters of the Third Republic status quo, the Polish elite pacting process was seen as a model of successful transition, to its critics it produced a problematic democratisation based on contested foundational myths.

There were clearly 'pragmatic' instrumental-strategic motives evident on both sides of the debate, with a feeling that truth revelation could disproportionately affect individuals linked to particular political options. However, both those pushing for and those opposing lustration and file access were also motivated, in part at least, by 'legitimate' programmatic and ideological concerns. Indeed, the Polish case suggests that examining discussions about lustration and transitional justice separately from other political developments can lead one to underestimate the extent to which these issues often became bundled up with other, broader discourses about the apparent shortcomings of post-communist democratisation. Calls for broadening the scope of lustration and communist security service file access were often rooted in such critiques and indicative of wider concerns about the perceived failures of this project. However, in practice, it was difficult to separate instrumental-strategic and ideological-programmatic motives out completely. Moreover, although Poles were consistently supportive of lustration and communist security service file access, they did not appear to believe that these were especially salient issues that determined election outcomes, had considerable misgivings about how the legislation worked out in practice, and felt that strong evidence was needed to determine security service collaboration. Nonetheless, because public attitudes were strongly linked with political identities and party orientations, and truth revelation became more important when linked to other, more salient questions, the recurrence of the issue was clearly not solely elite-driven, and voter demand was at least a contributory factor.

Appendix

List of interviewees

6 June 2016

Sławomir Cenckiewicz – a former historian with the Institute of National Remembrance and author of several books alleging that Lech Wałęsa was a communist security service informer, including the seminal Cenckiewicz and Gontarczyk (2008) and Cenckiewicz (2008, 2013). At the time that the interview took place, Dr Cenckiewicz was director of the Military Historical Bureau, and shortly afterwards he was elected a member of the Institute of National Remembrance College.

Janina Paradowska – a journalist and political commentator for the liberal-left and anti-lustration *Polityka* weekly, who covered all of the main lustration and file access debates in parliament from the beginning of the democratic transition.

Piotr Semka – a journalist and political commentator for the centre-right *Do Rzeczy* weekly. Co-author of Kurski and Semka (1992), an account of the downfall of the Olszewski government following the release of the 'Macierewicz list', and of Semka (2013), a critical biography of Lech Wałęsa.

7 June 2016

Antoni Dudek – a historian who was connected with the Institute of National Remembrance from its formation, including (from 2006 to 2010) as adviser to the Institute's chairman Janusz Kurtyka and (from 2010 to 2016) as a member of the Institute's Council, and the Council's chairman from 2015 to 2016. He is also author of Dudek (2011), a personal history of the Institute. At the time of the interview he was Professor of Humanities at the Cardinal Stefan Wyszyński University in Warsaw.

Andrzej Zybertowicz – a sociologist at the Mikołaj Kopernik University in Toruń specialising in the links between the former communist security services and post-communist elites, including as author of Zybertowicz (1993, 2013) and

Łoś and Zybertowicz (2000). He was national security adviser to Law and Justice prime minister Jarosław Kaczyński (2007); President Lecha Kaczyński (2008–2010); and, from 2015 and at the time of the interview, to President Andrzej Duda.

8 June 2016

Adam Leszczyński – a commentator for the liberal-left anti-lustration *Gazeta Wyborcza* daily, specialising in contemporary history, particularly the communist period.

Arkadiusz Mularczyk – a Law and Justice parliamentary deputy elected in 2005 who was the party's main spokesman in the debates on 2006 lustration law, which he helped to pilot through parliament. He was a member of the breakaway Solidaristic Poland (Solidarna Polska: SP) party in 2012–2016 but re-joined Law and Justice in 2017.

Ewa Siedlecka – a journalist and commentator for the liberal-left anti-lustration *Gazeta Wyborcza* daily (and subsequently *Polityka* weekly), specialising in human rights issues, who wrote extensively on the 2006 lustration law.

9 June 2016

Andrzej Paczkowski – a historian who was involved with the Institute of National Remembrance from its formation, serving as a member of its College from 1999 to 2011 and Council from 2011 to 2015, including a period as the Council chairman.

Bronisław Wildstein – a journalist and political commentator for the right-wing *WSieci* weekly journal. In 2005, while working for the centre-right *Rzeczpospolita* daily newspaper, he released the famous 'Wildstein list', an Institute of Public Remembrance archival catalogue, which contributed to the revival of lustration and file access in the mid-2000s.

Bibliography

Cenckiewicz, S., 2008. *Sprawa Lecha Wałęsy*. Poznań: Zysk i S-ka.
Cenckiewicz, S., 2013. *Wałęsa. Człowiek z teczki*. Poznań: Zysk i S-ka.
Cenckiewicz, S. and Gontarczyk, P., 2008. *SB a Lech Wałęsa. Przyczynek do biografii*. Warsaw: IPN.
Dudek, A., 2011. *Instytut. Osobista historia IPN*. Warsaw: Wydawnictwo Czerwona i Czarna.
Kurski, J. and Semka, P., 1992. *Lewy czerwcowy*. Warsaw: Editions Spotkania.
Łoś, M. and Zybertowicz, A., 2000. *Privatizing the Police-State: The Case of Poland*. New York: St. Martin's Press.

Semka, P., 2013. *Za, a nawet przeciw. Zagadka Lecha Wałęsy: Pierwsza krytyczna biografia Lecha Wałęsy 1980–2013*. Krakow: Wydawnictwo M.

Zybertowicz, A., 1993. *W uścisku tajnych służb: Upadek komunizmu i układ postnomenklatury*. Warsaw: Wydawnictwo Antyk Marcin Dybowski.

Zybertowicz, A., 2013. *III RP: kulisy systemu*. Warsaw: Wydawnictwo Słowa i Myśl.

Index

Page numbers in *italics* denote tables.

Ackerman, B. 66n17
Adamski, Ł. 127
Agora 86, 91
Albania 11, 12, 37n14
Alganov, V. 87, 88
Appel, H. 45, 62–3, 65, 66n6, 180, 186–7

Baczyński, J. 97, 102
Balcerowicz, L. 14
Baltic states 11, 53, 54
Bentkowski, A. 25
Belka, M. 88
Bertschi, C. 9n5, 45, 48, 49
Beylin, M. 123
Bielecki, J.K. 14, 37n2
Bolek affair *see* Wałęsa, L.: alleged communist security service collaboration
Bulgaria 11, 12, 24, 37n14, 44, 49
Burnetko, K. 97, 101–2
Buzek, J. 25, 88

Calhoun, N. 19, 46, 58, 61–2, 65, 67n18, 180, 186–7
Catholic Church security service collaboration 29, 34, 144–5, 150–1, 180
Cenckiewicz, S. 8, 36, 72, 75, 86, 94, 110, 111, 113, 117, 119, 121, 125, 126–7, 128, 129, 130, 135n5, 135n11, 135n14, 154–5, 156, 160, 169, 170, 180, 192
Central anti-corruption bureau (CBA) 99, 100
Centre Agreement (PC) 15, 17, 59, 66n15
Chodakiewicz, M. 135n2
Christian-National Union (ZChN) 15
Chrzanowski, W. 16, 25
Cimoszewicz, W. 25
Civic Platform (PO) 26, 30, 34, 35, 58–9, 81, 82, 83, 84, 85, 86, 95, 99, 100, 105n10, 125, 127, 128–9, 130, 134, 153, 156, 158, 165, 166, 167, 168, 169, 170, 171, 172, 174n16, 185, 187, 189–90
Confederation for an Independent Poland (KPN) 16, 18
Confederation for an Independent Poland-Patriotic Camp (KPN-OP) 25
constitutional tribunal 23–4, 28, 32, 33, 34, 7, 75, 76–7, 143, 154, 162, 163, 169, 178, 186
corruption 64, 86–93, 98–100, 103, 163, 180, 185, 190
Czarzasty, W. 87
Czech, Mirosław 79
Czechoslovakia 3, 37n14, 44, 51
Czech Republic 11, 12, 24, 37n14, 49, 51, 53, 54, 55, 64, 65n2
Czempiński, G. 121
Czuchnowski, W. 113–14, 116, 130

David, R. 3, 12, 24, 37n12, 37n13, 37n14, 38n15, 45, 66n3, 178; *see also* lustration systems
decommunisation: definition 4–5, 9n5; public attitudes towards 146, *147*
Democratic Left Alliance (SLD) 17, 18, 19, 20, 21, 22, 23, 25, 27, 28, 30, 34, 37n5, 51, 53, 55–6, 57–8, 59, 74, 79, 86, 87, 96, 97, 102, 105n4, 105n7, 146, 165, 166, 167, 168, 169, 174n16, 174n17, 190
Democratic Union (UD) 59, 61
Democrats (Demokraci) 33, 79, 174n17
departmental children 35–6
Do Rzeczy 192
Duda, A. 8, 35, 93, 193
Dudek, A. 27, 57, 74, 94, 117, 122, 124, 126, 130, 192

Index

Elster, J. 43
Estonia 12, 24

Fałkowski, M. 120, 124, 132
Fedyszak-Radziejewska, B. 81, 89
Fijołek, M. 119
file access law 1998 26–7
Fourth Republic project 30, 98–102, 102, 104, 105n10, 163, 184, 186
Fowler, B. 4, 49, 50, 54–5, 85, 141, 179
Frasyniuk, W. 115–16
Freedom Union (UW) 18, 19, 20, 26, 33, 59, 61, 72, 79
Free Trade Unions of the Coast (WZZ) 110, 113, 135n2
Friszke, A. 114, 115, 116, 135n5, 135n11

Gazeta Polska 35, 86
Gazeta Wyborcza 8, 38n16, 86, 87, 193
Geremek, B. 33
German Democratic Republic (GDR) 8n2, 11, 37n14, 44, 45, 53, 54, 62
Giertych, R. 91
Gilowska, Z. 34, 35
Girzyński, Z. 38n17, 71, 78–9, 81, 83, 85
Gontarczyk, P. 36, 110, 111, 113, 117, 126, 128, 129, 130, 135n5, 135n14, 154–5, 156, 160, 169, 170, 180, 192
Gorbachev, M. 120
Grabowska, M. 18, 165
Gwiazda, A. 110, 111
Gwiazda, J. 110, 111, 125

Hall, A. 118
Hejmo, K. 29
historical policy 130, 135n1
Holmes, S. 18
Horne, C. 2, 4, 5, 12, 63–4, 65, 70, 103, 178, 180, 186–7
Hungary 11, 12, 24, 37n13, 44, 49, 54, 55
Huntington, S. 44–7, 49–50, 179

Institute of National Remembrance (IPN) 26–7, 28–9, 30–2, 33–4, 35, 36, 72, 75, 76, 77, 78, 79, 80, 82, 85, 88, 89, 99, 103, 104, 110, 111, 114, 117, 129, 130, 133, 135n3, 143, 145, 148–9, 153, 154–5, 156, 163, 170, 171, 174n9, 179, 180, 186, 192, 193
Iwiński, T. 79, 80, 102

Jagiełło, A. 104n7
Jakubowska, A. 87
Janicki, M. 151–2

Jaruzelski, W. 48, 111, 124
Jaskierna, J. 25
Jaskovska, E. 52–3, 66n11, 179
John Paul II, Pope 29, 130
Jurczyk, M. 24, 25, 28, 73, 74, 76

Kaczmarek, W. 87
Kaczyński, J. 15, 30, 35, 56–7, 59, 66n15, 90, 123, 127–8, 131, 185, 193
Kaczyński, L. 30, 32, 35, 56–7, 59, 66n15, 100, 127–8, 185, 193
Kalisz, R. 79, 80, 96–7
Kamela-Sowińska, A. 105n6
Kamiński, L. 35
Kaminski, M.N. 9n5
Karnowski, M. 120, 126
Karpiniuk, S. 83, 84, 85, 86
Kieres, L. 27, 29
Kiszczak, C. 36, 57, 111, 112, 118, 120, 124, 125, 132, 133, 179; *see also* Kiszczak files
Kiszczak files 36, 57, 111–12, 113, 114, 116, 118–19, 121, 123, 124, 125, 126, 128, 129, 130, 131–2, 133, 157, 160, 164, 170–1, 171–2, 179, 181, 189
Kiszczak, M. 112, 114; *see also* Kiszczak files
Kitschelt, H. 44
Kołodziejski, K. 125, 131
Komorowski, B. 35, 135n15
Konieczny, J. 121
Korwin-Mikke, J. 16
Krzemiński, I. 118, 123–4, 173n3
Kublik, A. 113, 116, 130
Kulczyk, J. 87–8
Kurtyka, J. 35, 75, 76, 110, 192
Kurski, J. 114, 117, 118, 123
Kwaśniewski, A. 18, 19, 20, 22, 23, 26, 27, 28, 58, 88, 162
Kwiatkowski, R. 87

Labour Union (UP) 18, 19, 20
Latvia 12, 64
Law and Justice (PiS) 29–30, 32, 34, 35, 56, 58, 59, 66n15, 71, 72–3, 74, 75–6, 76, 77, 78, 81, 82, 83, 84, 85, 86, 90, 91, 92, 94, 95, 96, 98, 99, 100, 123, 125–6, 127–8, 129, 134, 154, 156, 158, 160, 165, 166, 167, 168, 169, 170, 171, 185, 186, 190, 193
League of Polish Families (LPR) 30, 74, 81, 83, 84, 85, 91, 92
Left and Democrats (LiD) 169, 170, 174n17

Lepper, A. 84–5, 91
Leszczyński, A. 8, 82, 116, 124–5, 193
Liberal-Democratic Congress (KLD) 14, 18, 61
Linz, J. 3, 44
Lipiński, A. 98, 136n18
Lipiński, D. 95–6
Lis, B. 115, 117, 123
Lisicki, P 132
Lithuania 12, 24
Lityński, J. 79–80
Łoś 67n19, 136n17, 193
Luks, K. 25
lustration: court 21, 22, 23, 31, 34, 78, 111, 162; definition 3–5, 176–7; and file access law 2006 29–33, 58–9, 79–80, 169, 178, 186; law 1997 19–24, 55–6, 58, 61–2, 178; systems 24, 45

Macedonia 64
Machcewicz, P. 135n5
Macierewicz, A. 16–17, 49, 88, 128; *see also* Macierewicz list
Macierewicz list 15–17, 25, 26, 110, 111, 127, 180, 192
Magdalenka negotiations 124, 125, 136n18
Markowski, T. 74, 96
Matyja, R. 105n10
Maziarski, W. 116, 118
Mazowiecki, T. 12–15, 18, 20, 31n1, 46, 98, 118, 131, 178, 181, 183, 186; *see also* thick line policy
Michnik, A. 86, 91, 118, 131, 136n16
Milczanowski, A. 18–19, 121
Military Information Service (WSI) 26, 99, 101
Miller, L. 25, 28, 86, 87
Mirowski, M. 121
Misztal, B. 19, 20
Moczulski, L. 16, 25
Modrzejewski, A. 87
Modzelewski, K. 115, 117
Moran, J. 43–4, 47, 49–50, 52–3, 66n11, 179
Moszyński, P. 115, 116
Movement for Poland's Reconstruction (ROP) 59
Movement for the Republic (RdR) 17
Mrozewicz, R. 25
Mularczyk, A. 8, 71, 72, 74–5, 77, 81, 83, 86, 91–2, 95, 100, 132, 133, 193

Nalepa, M. 2, 8n4, 9n5, 24, 33, 47, 55–60, 61, 65, 66n13, 141, 179, 180, 184

Nedelsky, N. 50–2, 66n10, 179
Niesiołowski, S. 81
Niezabitowska, M. 29
Nikolski, L. 87
Nino, C. 43
Nizieński, B. 24–5, 105n3
nomenklatura capitalism 18
Non-Party Bloc to Support Reforms (BBWR) 59

Offe, C. 66n2
Olechowski, A. 26
Oleksy affair 17–20, 180, 190
Oleksy, J. 19, 25, 74; *see also* Oleksy affair
Olszewski, J. 15–16, 17, 18, 20, 37n4, 49, 59, 113, 120, 131, 180, 192
Orlen affair 87–8, 89, 90, 91–2, 93, 102, 180
Osiatyński, W. 66n16, 97–8

pacting, transition by 46, 182, 183–4
Paczkowski, A. 8, 98–9, 122, 126, 193
Paradowska, J. 8, 97, 100, 101, 116, 124, 192
parliamentary denunciation provisions 23, 25, 27
Pawłowiec, D. 81–2, 83
Piekarska, K. 97, 102
Pięta, S. 81, 96, 100
Pinior, J. 118, 123
Piskorski, M. 71, 83, 85
Piwnik, B. 87
Płociński, M. 135n8
Polish Peasant Party (PSL) 17, 19, 20, 25, 27, 28, 53, 58, 71
Polish United Workers' Party (PZPR) 37, 158–9
political elite strategy explanation 54–5, 179, 186–7
politics of the present explanations 47–50, 54, 60, 64, 103, 179, 186–7
Polityka 192, 193
Public Interest Spokesman (RIP) 21, 23, 24–6, 30–1, 32, 74, 76, 77, 78, 105n3
PZU affair 89, 90, 102, 105n6

Raciborski, J. 97, 102
Rokita, J. 30, 34–5, 58–9, 82, 83, 84, 95, 125–6
Romania 11, 12, 24, 37n13, 45, 51
round table negotiations, February–April 1989 14, 45–6, 55, 57, 59, 98–9, 122, 124, 125, 132, 134, 136n18, 158, 181–2

Index

Russia 12, 19, 87–8, 120
Rywin affair 86–7, 89, 90, 93, 105n4, 105n10

Sasin, J. 128
Schetyna, G. 129
Security Service (SB) 13
Self-Defence (Samoobrona) 28, 30, 71, 83, 84, 85, 91
semi-free elections, May–June 1989 45–6, 48, 122, 125
Semka, P. 8, 72, 93, 124, 127, 131, 135n12, 135n13, 136n19, 192
Senyszyn, J. 97
Serbia 37n13, 37n14
Siedlecka, E. 8, 98, 122, 193
Siemiątkowski, Z. 87, 88
Skórzyński, J. 117
Skwieciński, P. 89
Sławecki, T. 71
Slovakia 11, 12, 51, 64
Slovenia 11, 38n15
Sobotka, Z. 105n7
Social Democracy of the Polish Republic (SdRP) 37n5
Sojak, R. 90
Solidaristic Poland (SP) 193
Solidarity Electoral Action (AWS) 23, 25, 26, 30, 52, 56, 59, 162
Solidarity movement 12, 15, 23, 37n11, 45, 72, 100, 110, 111, 117–18, 119–20, 121, 123, 124, 125, 126, 127, 129, 131, 134, 158, 165, 179, 185
South African Truth and Reconciliation Commission 24, 37n12
Śpiewak, P. 105n10, 136n19
Stan, L. 2–3, 11, 53–4, 60, 179
Stankiewicz, A. 114
Starachowice affair 90, 105n7
State Security Office (UOP) 13, 26, 87, 111, 121
Stepan, A. 3, 44
Suchocka, H. 38n15
Suski, M. 81, 83, 91, 100
Szarek, J. 35
Szlachta, A. 96
Szostkiewicz, A. 116, 123

Terlecki, R. 128
thick line policy 12–15, 20, 46, 98, 103, 124, 131, 178, 181, 182, 183, 184, 186, 190; *see also* Mazowiecki, T.

Tomaszewski, J. 25
transitional justice, definition 2–3
truth revelation procedures, definition 2–3, 4, 178
Tusk, D. 30, 34, 129

układ 98, 105n9
Ukraine 12
Union of Real Politics (UPR) 16
United Peasant Party (ZSL)

Wachowski, M. 120
Wagner, M. 25
Walentynowicz, A. 110, 111, 125
Wałęsa, L. 15, 16, 18, 38n23, 57, 59, 109–40, 154–8, 160, 162, 163, 164, 170, 171–2, 173, 179, 180, 182, 183, 185, 187, 188, 189, 192; alleged communist security service collaboration 19, 26, 36, 57, 109–40, 154–8, 160, 163, 164, 170, 171–2, 173, 179, 180, 182–3, 185, 187, 188, 189, 192
Wąsacz, E. 105n6
Waszczykowski, W. 128
Welsh, H. 47–50, 55, 66n8, 179
Wiechecki, R. 74, 84, 85, 92
Wielgus, S. 29, 151
wild lustration 84, 85
Wildstein, B. 8, 29, 38n16, 73, 77, 80, 81, 82, 84, 86, 89, 93, 94, 118–19, 121, 126, 129, 130, 131, 132, 135n12, 193; *see also* Wildstein list
Wildstein list 29, 78, 79, 81, 85, 97, 101, 102, 146, 164, 180, 190, 193
Williams, K. 4, 49, 50, 54–5, 65, 141, 179
Wiścicki, T. 78, 90, 94
Workers' Defence Committee (KOR) 116, 135n10
Wróblewski, T. 94
WSieci 193
Wyszkowski, K. 72, 100–1, 110, 113

Yanayev, G. 120
Yugoslavia: former 52

Żakowski, J. 97, 101, 102
Zaremba, P. 120, 129, 132
Ziemkiewicz, R. 119
Zolkos, M. 18
Zybertowicz, A. 8, 90, 93, 94, 99–100, 126, 136n17, 192–3
Zyzak, P. 36, 129, 135n3, 156